# GOLD AT
# WOLF'S CRAG?

Fast Castle: *above*, the ruins seen from the landward side; *below*, the rugged coast immediately north of the ruins (arrowed).

# GOLD AT WOLF'S CRAG?

*An Inquiry into the treasure of Fast Castle*

FRED DOUGLAS

OLIVER & BOYD · EDINBURGH

First published 1971 by
OLIVER & BOYD
Tweeddale Court
14 High Street
Edinburgh EH1 1YL
A Division of Longman Group Limited

ISBN 0 05 002244 x

Printed in Great Britain by
Western Printing Services Ltd,
Bristol

# Contents

# List of illustrations

# Acknowledgements

GRATEFUL ACKNOWLEDGEMENTS are made to the following for permission to reproduce illustrations: His Grace The Duke of Rutland, C.B.E., Belvoir Castle, Grantham for the plan of Fast Castle, 1549; Edinburgh Public Libraries for 'The Contract of Magic', 1594; National Portrait Gallery of Scotland for the portraits of John Napier, James VI and the illustration of the turret room at Gowrie House; Royal Commission on Ancient Monuments, Scotland for the engraving of Falkland Palace by Slezer; Mr M. I. Berrill for the photographs of the Fast Castle ruins.

PUBLISHERS' NOTE

Fred Douglas died suddenly on 14th May 1971, having completed all preliminary work on the book which was then with the printer. Having enjoyed their collaboration with Mr Douglas in the planning and illustration of this work, the publishers greatly regret that he did not live to see it in its final form.

# Prologue: 1969
# On a wild North Sea shore

AN ANCIENT treasure cave on a wild North Sea shore—facing out towards the modern miracle of rigs drilling for gas and oil beneath the waves. This is the starting point of our search for concealed riches, albeit of a different kind, with their story from the past. In a sense we have set up our rig on a distinctive crag about twenty miles north of the once-debated frontier town of Berwick. The water was still icy there on an early summer day in 1969 when half a dozen skin-divers strapped on their cylinder harness and slipped over the side of an Eyemouth fishing boat. They went down about forty feet to the sea bed below the ruin of Fast Castle. The general nod from the past is towards this ruin.

Down on the ocean floor they looked up at the boat. The skipper was trying to bring the bow round closer to the entrance of the great cave under the castle. They saw a sharp rock pinnacle graze the underside and held their breath, or their compressed air. By good luck no damage was done. The floor, when they turned to examine it, looked fairly featureless. The last time the English held the castle, which was with a Scottish regent's consent, six pieces of Scots ordnance disappeared. These were either dragged up the steep path above the crag, then on to the moors, or they were pitched spitefully over the ramparts into the sea. But there was no hint of any cannon on the sea bed, not much hint either of the castle walls that had tumbled down into the sea during the succeeding centuries.

One feature the divers did notice was a large rock basin scooped out by the action of swirling stones rotated by countless tides. They poked beneath the thick seaweed at the bottom of the basin without reward. It was a marker if nothing else. Its position was directly under the castle's back court, the corner of it indeed where an ancient crane had once protruded and a bucket had swung up and down. Clues concerning the men and goods that had long ago come into this secret harbour might have dropped into the sea just here during the loading and hoisting. Around the rock basin would be a place for a future probe.

When they surfaced about half an hour later the skin divers briefly explored the castle hole or great cave into which the waves were pounding. Looking backwards at sea and sky and looking inwards made a contrast of two worlds, the world of life and the underworld. Once they were two-thirds of the way in the floor of the cave was well beyond the

I

tide but was exceedingly slimy and slippery. A flurry of sea pigeons escaped from the darkness and advertised dry ledges in the tunnel ahead. The direction of the tunnel suggested that it linked up with the bottom of the well which had its upper rim in a grassy hollow on the far side of the cliff top site where the old drawbridge and portcullis had been. This would explain the mystery of how the castle defenders maintained their fresh water supply when the drawbridge was up and they were under siege. At the junction of tunnel and well there might be something interesting, a further passage or another shaft. But the way was choked with rotting driftwood and flotsam, so another heavy task was marked for the future.

The divers from Eyemouth Sub-Aqua Club make their way along the coast and arrive at Fast Castle by boat. The potholers come by the land route over the moors and drop snaking ladders from the crag top down to the cave mouth. David and Jonathan and Eric with other members of the Grampians Speleological Groups have been up and down this perpendicular route almost often enough to make it their own right of way. A rift about a third of the way in to the cave was a feature that intrigued them early on, at least it was the current of fresh air coming through the rift that was intriguing. The rift was too narrow to enter at floor level, but Jonathan figured he could squeeze in nearer the roof if he improvised a ladder. He went down to the castle early one evening to try this along with Eric. Jonathan was on night shift in the Bank of Scotland computer department. The two promised they would be back at Head Chesters Cottage,* a couple of miles from the castle, by ten, but it was near midnight when their Jeep returned.

Jonathan had got through into the rift with his improvised ladder and dropped down on the other side. He proceeded until he came to a dead end, although there was still that draught coming through some crack in the rock and hinting at a chamber beyond. The treasure chamber perhaps! On returning he lacked the aid he had used to reach the roof on the other side and the faces were too slippery for climbing. This had delayed him. Fortunately Eric was there and the receding tide did not threaten to drown him in his trap. His torch was not of much use in deciding whether there was anything beyond the dead-end. He reported in favour of an explosive charge. At the surveying stage however the kind and indulgent landowner had not yet extended permission to the searchers to blow up the crag or themselves—after a while he may be sorely tempted to give permission for the last-named purpose. Along with the tunnel and the rock basin the rift was recorded for closer future scrutiny.

Our pot-holer friends skirted danger on other occasions, once when overwhelmed by a swelling tide while entering the big cave and once when swimming round the crag to find the entrance to a smaller cave

* Used by the author as his search headquarters.

2

on the other side. The funnelling of the tide by the two rock stacks which are nearby sentinels of the crag creates an exceptional swell. It was a group effort and a life-line that saved weaker swimmers on both these occasions. Probably this was a warning that the treasure-guarding gremlins do not intend to make the task easy or uneventful.

Curiosity about the subsidiary caves was aroused by the diviner Freda Stoddart from near Hexham. On her first visit she traced the water course of caves within the crag while walking among the ruins on the summit. Since then she has made a cave map which has been verified in part. Going by this map, entrance has still to be found to a number of subterranean places. There is a tradition of a stairway leading down below which has not been confirmed so far by examination of the great cave's walls and roof. But then it may not have been a stairway to the great cave as is commonly supposed, but a link with one of these lesser and hidden chambers indicated by our diviner. The old sixteenth-century plan indicates spiral stairs within the walls that have since tumbled down. One of these stairways may have continued down through the rock. When we have at length carefully removed the knoll of castle debris and soil we may uncover the opening to the nether stairway, leading to an unrevealed cave.

The diggers, however, apart from some sample probes elsewhere, have concentrated first on clearing the back court overlooking the sea, in the corner of which the crane and bucket once operated. The diggers incidentally are volunteers like the divers, pot-holers and diviners. Among them are young people who find that an excursion into the soil and the past expands their consciousness and imagination more healthily than hashish. Indeed the whole search is a revelation that there are plenty of such healthy young people. Their labour in the back court has not been unfruitful. It has brought them slap alongside the searchers of the last Fast Castle treasure hunt at the end of the sixteenth century.

The few Elizabethan and James VI coins they uncovered in the soil of the court floor provided a material link with their shadowy collaborators of the past. But there was more in it than that. As well as the coins and the interesting pottery fragments and a thirty-eight pound cannon ball there was a curious collection of small animal bones, not edible chickens or rabbits and not anything like complete skeletons. These occurred alongside a charcoal deposit and near to some larger bones— human leg bones and a human skull. The skull has since been placed by an Edinburgh University anatomy department expert within a time bracket of three to five hundred years.

What did these things signify—the skull and cross bones, the charcoal deposit and the mixed grill of small animal bones? Bear in mind the castle back court where they were found is a lonely, lofty platform raised above a yawning black underworld in the shape of the castle hole and that it faces the sea and the East. Freda Stoddart, the diviner, felt

3

that they spelled witch rites. Her answer was not so far-fetched, considering that the former searchers were all described by their contemporaries as sorcerers. It made it seem a question of whether our magic in the search, if we had any, would make a better showing than theirs. After this thought concerning witchcraft cropped up, another somewhat kindred thought replaced it, one also inspired by the presence of the skull and cross bones on this eerie site. It will be referred to later rather than immediately because it belongs to the ultimate stage of the Fast Castle treasure inquiry.

For a spell the digging, which was led by Eric, James and Keith, an Edinburgh numismatic trio, was transferred to the shore below the castle. Here all worked near the shadow of a long, high-galleried rock which screens about half the beach from the sea. It is called the Black Mask and prompts a question as to what it has masked in times past. We had some reason to believe it was helping now to mask a camouflaged concealment in the cliff face. For that reason we made a two hundred feet descent down an awkward gully and the more perspiring climb back Sunday after Sunday, and many weekdays as well.

Perhaps we had no 'reason' for belief in the shore concealment in the strict sense of the term, since it was based on the guidance of Frederick Ritchie, a psychic consultant who had carried out for us an exercise in 'map dowsing', or divining from a distance, in the front room of his home at Farnworthy, Lancashire. We duly received back our large-scale ordnance survey map with an X marking the spot. The remarkable thing was that, without ever having been there, Mr Ritchie described the outstanding physical features of the place where he advised us to work, features certainly not indicated in the map. His description tallied with reality. In addition his cross was supported by rational considerations which would have induced a probe at some time even if no extra-sensory perception had been involved.

One rational consideration was that the spot was adjacent to a series of small caves at the further end of the bay. Frederick, who had been a civil engineer, expounded the matter thus: The gold had been brought in from the sea and had to be hidden hurriedly. There had at that time been another cave visible at the end of the row. The men had entered it and enlarged it by carrying it back. This had enabled them to convey their cargo quickly into the depth of the hillside. Then they had packed the fore-end of the cave with soil and stones and brought down the cave entrance. Finally they had enticed the scree and soil down from the slopes above and covered every trace. We looked up at the scree-covered slopes and rock-faces and realised that a deep concealment could indeed be efficiently manufactured in this way. In no time at all, let alone after four centuries, it would take on the blank look of the rest of the hillside, and never exchange a wink. The other rational consideration was that the chosen spot could be kept under observation from the castle above—a

4

few yards to the one side or the other and the vision from the castle was obstructed.

At the end of the summer of 1969, which came all too soon, this effort on the shore remained inconclusive. We had to split our forces to tidy up among the castle ruins, to ensure that neither man nor sheep would fall into a deep hole and join the Fast Castle ghosts. So the digging below tapered off. When we gathered for the second summer's digging we reappraised the work on the shore. It seemed we would end up by quarrying a fair area of the hill face and to a fair depth before we could be absolutely sure. The damage we would not be able to restore. We therefore decided to bracket the spot with other intriguing places along the bays and defer work on them all until we acquired the sort of drilling or electronic equipment that would make the probing painless and avoid a shambles. Eric's unambitious mine detector and the stolid, standard bed-pans that a squad of Royal Engineers' sappers brought on to the site for a day, were not quite up to it.

The length of our list of intriguing places was surprising, and also daunting. Tunnel openings seemed to lie wedged between great boulders everywhere and rock crevices beckoned from behind many waterfalls. Dark shelves under the water and suspicious hollows in the ground all tried to whisper their secrets to us if we paused only to glance at them. This was apart from the low, importuning siren calls that issued from every cave whose entrance we darkened with our shadows. Self-hypnotism is the treasure hunter's occupational hazard and we had to fight it fiercely to keep our list of future probes within reasonable limits.

Our eventual selection was helped by further diviners' reports. Mr Whetton, a retired civil servant, came up from Worksop and left his findings on half a dozen twenty-five inch ordnance maps. It was against his own credulity to find pointers to the score of concealments which he marked on the maps instead of a single one. He reasoned it must have been the policy of those who concealed the gold not to hide all their golden eggs in one basket. Well, that might have been their policy. On the other hand history has fouled the scent. For more than a century the Berwickshire cliffs were a smugglers' warren, after the drouthy Scots were assimilated into the English customs system. In order to store and hide their contraband the smugglers built, dug or improvised hundreds of concealments. Consequently the Fast Castle treasure trail, so far as the unfortunate diviner is concerned, is confused. The consolation is that if we are led astray and into the wrong store-house, we may come unsteadily home, laden with bales of Holland cloth, after broaching some long-forgotten cask of wine.

Some of the place names of our search areas have frankly the smell of gin—Tod's Rock, for instance, and Tod's Loup. We can almost picture Tod emerging from the concealment of his rock and making his way along the rough shore past the Midden's Craig. A little further on he climbs the giant boulder that stands offshore and just apart from the cliffs. There is a lugger out at sea impatient to discharge its gin and from his perch Tod begins to signal it to come in. Then suddenly the gaugers rise from among the rocks. Instead of sliding down the boulder into their arms Tod makes his historic 'loup' across space on to the hill face and is away like the wind. Let us hope it ended that way instead of in captivity with a broken leg. Meg Watson's Craig, Rob's Rock, Muckle Pitts and Scruffy Hole doubtless all enshrine forgotten sagas of a like kind. Black Mask is not so colloquial. There is something of the air of a natural temple about its solemn mass. Perhaps it was anciently named because it masked the rising sun or moon and the eye of the one or the other shone through the cleft of it. Anything it has masked since is probably of subordinate significance.

In letters from Mr Lumsdaine of Wales we received advice to desert the castle ruins and the lonely smugglers' bays and carry the search inland. Mr Lumsdaine's interest is natural because these are the lands of Lumsdaine that surrounded Fast Castle, the homelands of his forefathers. He is convinced that the gold was brought in at Brander Cove, a mile or two south east of the castle, and carried by donkeys up the course of the Dowlaw Burn, past two waterfalls and on to the cart track leading to where the farm and homestead of the Lumsdaines once stood. The old cart track, sunk among the weeds and wild grasses, is still there. According to Lumsdaine tradition and intuition this is the true path leading to the Fast Castle treasure.

Then again a similar sunken and winding track leads from the sea braes above Fast Castle almost to the door of Head Chesters cottage which is the headquarters of the search. There is besides a local tradition of a tunnel leading up to the Head Chesters from Redheugh Shore. There were smugglers' concealments at Redheugh Shore and at Head Chesters, which was both an inn and a depot of the contraband traffic. One person with childhood memories of the neighbourhood when the smuggling was still rife has left some pictures of it—embroidered pictures it is true. This person was Alexander Somerville the Scots Grey recruit who received a famous hundred lashes at Birmingham cavalry barracks for dabbling in mutiny and Reform politics in the year 1832. Somerville's story also supplies a hint that Head Chesters or its site was linked with an earlier mystery and there are hints elsewhere that the same applies to Redheugh Shore. So the treasure hunters who regularly set out for Fast Castle from Head Chesters may many times have been sitting on the very thing they go out to look for.

All such beguiling thoughts have been disciplined and restrained in favour of an impartial plan to explore the whole Fast Castle area. The task of organising a large scale operation is being put in hand. The castle itself, however, retains its central interest; and its ruined site absorbed most of the time and labour devoted to the second summer of the search. It seems sure and certain to the treasure-hunters that if the gold is not locked within the castle grounds or within the heart of the crag, the key to its secret, or clues towards its discovery, lie slumbering there. Already the skull and cross bones taken from the soil have supplied a significant pointer, as will be explained according to promise already made. Dumb signs stand around.

Naturally it needed signs more overt to bring the searchers to the crag in the first place. If the prospecting for North Sea gas and oil implied some geological insight and knowledge then similarly some historical insight and knowledge lies behind the search for the North Sea treasure. It was in fact a document drafted at the end of the sixteenth century that prompted our first curiosity. Two men of that Elizabethan and Jacobean age signed an agreement to search for treasure at Fast Castle. Our first curiosity was roused by this document. Curiosity gave way to a compulsive interest when we saw by a kind of sudden light that this was not merely a private affair concerning those two men. It involved also the King and the Court, drama and death and the fate of the nation. A glimpse of the nearly incredible story surrounding this early Fast Castle treasure hunt made a new search irresistible—not because of the gold alone but for the sake also of the historical truth that has remained buried along with it for centuries.

The search and research have consequently gone forward together, the digging at Fast Castle and the digging into the records and references, widely scattered, that build up the background story. The record so far of the physical exploration is confined within this prologue. The fruits of the other kind of digging are presented in the Fast Castle inquiry that follows. Following the advice of the mystical and poetical William Blake we have taken the end of a golden string and wound it into a ball. Surprisingly it seems to lead, as he predicted, through Heaven's gate that is built in Jerusalem's wall. This all depends on interpretation of Blake's symbolic and obscure language. To let this thought simmer through the next two hundred or so pages we had better set down the verse from Blake in all its purity:

> I give you the end of a golden string,
> Only wind it into a ball.
> It will lead you in at Heaven's gate
> Built in Jerusalem's wall.

# 1　The contract of magic

THE END of a golden string was left for us to pick up, or left for someone, by two men of another age—Robert Logan and John Napier. They met in Edinburgh on a July day in 1594 to discuss a pois, or hidden treasure, and their talk centred on a search. It was all in earnest because it led to a formally worded contract. Napier laboured at drafting the document which was completed in his hand. He stepped aside to let Logan put his signature to the paper and then added his own. There were no witnesses to the signatures and doubtless none to the discussion. Napier signed as fiar, that is heir, of Merchiston and Logan described himself as the Laird of Restalrig.

Logan's lands of Restalrig lay between the Palace of Holyrood House and the Port of Leith, but also took in the great park of Holyrood with its crags and lochs and extinct volcano. His larger inheritance reached as far as the fishing town of Eyemouth near the English border, where he held the manor house of Gunsgreen and the land of Flemington. The lands of Lumsdaine, which formed a wild coastal strip of the Lammermoors were also part of his patrimony, and here his territory terminated at the cliff edge, except for the grim crag that thrust its mass beyond the line of the cliffs into the North Sea.

A cathedral-like cave opened into this crag and a stark tower with an appendage of domestic buildings rose from its summit. There was a deep-water harbour in front of the cave partially screened by a large sea-stack, the Wheat Stack, and another large pinnacle of rock. It was probably this harbour that caused a castle to be built on the crag in the first place. Now it is known as Fast Castle, but in Logan's time and earlier it was Faux or Faus Castle, implying that its true business had once been shrouded by a pretence or that it had at one time been associated with some signal treachery. It was within or around this castle that Napier and Logan hoped to discover their 'pois'.

Napier's tower stood a little to the south of Edinburgh on a more civilised site. From its battlement walk he could admire the signature in the sky inscribed by the town's roofs at sunset, and salute its bold castle rock and ramparts in the morning. The Burgh Moor and the family's farmlands lay in between. The girdle of Lowland hills was so close it seemed that a hand reaching out from the battlement might touch their tops. All Lothian towards the North Sea was visible at a glance, and only by raising his eye he could take in the coast of Fife backed by green hill, wood and pasture; on the same line of vision westward was the blue mountain barrier of the Highlands. Indeed, from Napier's tower-top almost the whole jewelled country was compressed into a single image; it was a place to commune with the Geist of the land. At night the stairway up to the turret room and the open battlement became the route to a conference with the stars. The tower was, in a way, a place of worship and of mystery as well as a fortress and a home. The commonality then and later regarded it as such; they were liable to skirt it with some dread and they called it the Astrologer's Tower.

Napier himself was held in some awe. He was believed to be a master of magic of many sorts, and altogether the greatest wizard since the time of that mighty wizard of the Border, Michael Scott. Much of this colourful reputation must surely have accumulated after his death, for during his life he was a respected member of the Kirk General Assembly and the author of a theological work dedicated to the King—with some sharp instruction on kingship in the dedication, it is true. Although the Brethren were brave and storming in those days, if Napier had really been the character he was later represented to be they could hardly have sat down beside him without blanching.

He was undoubtedly master of the magic numbers, as he proved by publishing his celebrated *Descriptio* on logarithms. In the matter we are discussing—the matter of the pois which brought Logan and Napier together—he claimed special powers. These were described in the contract to seek out the hidden treasure as his 'craft' and 'ingyne'. Logan believed in Napier's powers to the extent of promising him a third share of the treasure if they were successfully employed at Fast Castle, and Napier himself was so certain and self-confident about them that he undertook either to find the hidden hoard or to ascertain that there was no such thing. He made little allowance for the hiders of the treasure possessing a cunning that was beyond him.

What then were his powers? In the Napier family papers there is an abstract of the Fast Castle treasure contract and in the margin it bears the description, 'contract of magic'. This is a generalised answer to the question by Napier's descendants. His nineteenth century biographer, Mark Napier, was a little more specific; he considered that divining was likely to have been at the heart of them. To make his point he recounted the famous treasure hunt in the cloister of Westminster Abbey conducted, after Napier's day, by the astrologer Lilly, with the aid of a diviner. According to Lilly, it nearly brought disaster, in the shape of the western wall, down on the searchers because no attempt had been made to exorcise the demons who are traditionally the guardians of hidden gold.

Although divining probably was at the heart of the 'craft' and 'ingyne' which Napier undertook to employ, he may also have agreed to supply Logan with some exorcism to lift any curse lying like an evil mist on the gold, and may have undertaken astrological calculation to decide the best hour of attack. In short, there may have been other imponderables, as well as divining. For so much of the miraculous a return of less than a third share would have seemed too little.

On the other hand Napier's 'craft' and 'ingyne' could have had important and practical ingredients too. Napier's father was keeper of the Mint of Scotland and this involved not so much coining precious metals as finding the precious metals to coin. The inquiring son would surely glean from his father knowledge of the methods used to find veins of gold in the Scottish hills, including the Hills of Home, the Pentlands and the Lammermoors. This knowledge could have been part of Napier's equipment for the Fast Castle search.

His 'craft' and 'ingyne' become more meaningful, too, when related to the designs and experiments he was involved in at the time at Merchiston Castle. He was fired with the idea of producing the secret weapons that would ensure Protestant ascendancy in the still undecided wars of the period. A design for a moving armoured field tank, bristling with weapons, was one of his ploys along with an optical fromula that would produce a sun glass capable of burning the enemy to a cinder. Underwater craft and flying machines were intended to take shape on his drawing board too. However far he fell short of solutions, he was setting himself all the main technological problems and ambitions of the war game three centuries or so early.

It is unlikely that his bias towards technology failed to show in his plans for the treasure hunt which, no doubt, he and Logan discussed at length. If it had been a simple spade and mattock job, or a matter of removing suspiciously loose pieces of masonry, Logan would not have needed to call in the specialist. Instead, a search on the sea-bed below the crag probably had to be considered, and penetration of difficult rock fissures, awkward caves and the like. In face of such problems the practical philosopher Napier would tend automatically to think of some underwater contraption and of explosives or even super-explosives. Whatever aid he sought from the occult and invisable world, he was the kind of man who would expect it to be no more than a bonus added to his own inspired effort.

His biographer, Mark Napier, permitted himself a flight of fancy about the opening of the Fast Castle treasure hunt. He pictured a conference of the gold hunters at the castle. Those present were Napier and Logan, of course, and also Francis, Earl of Bothwell, the nephew of Mary Stewart's Bothwell and notorious rebel, who around this time had been using Fast Castle as a refuge—by a sound instinct Mark Napier included him in the picture of the Fast Castle conference: Napier in his cowl and dark philosopher's robes grasping his wine glass with uncertain hand while wedged between the two ruffians, both in their field garb and armed to the teeth. It was an invitation to some romantic painter to put the trio on canvas complete with thick castle walls and thin shafts of light in all their contrasts of costume and character.

But the picture of fancy must make way for reality. It is not certain that Napier ever set foot on Fast Castle drawbridge, although it is certain he never brought back from the place a third share of the hoard. In terms of their agreement Logan was to give him safe convoy home with his share. Then, when the two were back at Merchiston Castle, the document was to be brought out and torn up, as a sign that their bargain was fulfilled.

Of course it was never torn up—or we would not be discussing it. Instead it made a bid for immortality and is extant still, nearly four hundred years after the ink dried on the paper—the sign of an ancient bargain that was somehow frustrated. What form the frustration took it is impossible to say, but there is evidence that it was accompanied by bitterness and anger. Two years later Napier drew up another document, this time a missive for a tenant. In it he inserted a singular condition which prohibited the tenant at any time from sub-renting any part of Napier land to any person bearing the name of Logan. It seems that the gremlins guarding the treasure had been successful in transmuting the amity of the Napier-Logan contract into a powerful hate.

With the evidence of the missive the Fast Castle treasure story appears to expire on the threshold. There is more discouragement, also, if we continue turning the pages of Napier's life story. His biographer deserts the mood of fancy in which he pictured scenes of the treasure hunt at Fast Castle, and works his way round to the idea that the whole thing was probably a blind.

His theory is that Robert Logan and the Earl of Bothwell coveted the fertile brain of John Napier for purposes of their plots. They contrived, therefore, to lure Napier to Fast Castle with the bait of hidden gold, hoping to possess themselves of the plans of his war machines so that they might eventually rout the King in the field. According to this theory, it was Napier's military magic they were after.

This is rather hard on Bothwell. During his life he was locked up in Edinburgh Castle accused of conspiring with a Border wizard to kill the King by witchcraft, after his death posterity gratuitously accuses him of plotting the King's defeat in battle by a species of military magic. But there is nothing to support the idea that Bothwell had any hint of the secrets of Napier's drawing board which were published several years afterwards. In any case, it was a most unpromising procedure for winning the philosopher's collaboration: first to rouse his cupidity with prospect of gold, then let it dawn on him that he had been hoaxed, then to invite him to take part in a dangerous conspiracy.

The biographer's discouragement is not so great on close acquaintance; his idea of the treasure story being a blind is unconvincing speculation. On the other hand, he adds a new character to the story—the Earl of Bothwell, a declared rebel. He also brings in the adjudged traitor, the Earl of Gowrie, when surveying Robert Logan's conspiratorial connections. In general, he adds the extra element of conspiracy along with new characters to the story, whereas we began with the bare 'contract of magic'. A story of hidden gold is not likely to lose anything or become credible because of being mixed up with conspiracy.

These links of Bothwell and Gowrie with Robert Logan and Fast Castle are, moreover, confirmed in the records of the Privy Council and the High Court. Here there is no biographer's flight of fancy, only the degree of fancy that may be imported into the indictments and evidence that form the basis of State trials—which certainly can be considerable.

In all the Fast Castle conspiratorial revelations which emerge from the official records the most curious for us, and the most arresting, is the rendezvous arranged between Logan and the Earl of Gowrie. Gowrie was to have come secretly to the castle, setting out in a little boat just as if he were taking a sail on a pleasant summer day; when half a mile away from the crag he was to give a signal and arrangements would be made to bring him in and receive him. This rendezvous was arranged on the eve of the historic quarrel and affray at Gowrie House which resulted in the Earl of Gowrie and his brother being killed by the King and his hunting party, and led to the Gowrie brothers being posthumously tried as traitors and several of their dependants being hanged. The strange element in this so-called Gowrie conspiracy is that it arose out of a story about hidden treasure, which the King had gone to Gowrie House to investigate on the eve of Earl Gowrie's intended secret visit to Fast Castle, the locus of the Logan and Napier treasure hunt. Clearly we should press on.

We have no cause to lose heart either because of the apparent impasse in the relations between Napier and Logan. The evidence of this lies in the survival of their contract, when it should have been torn up, and in Napier's peculiar hate clause in the missive. When we look at these two papers and ponder them they do not appear to be negative intimations that the story is closed. The more we look and ponder, the more do they appear to be Napier's attempt to keep the story open. Are they not overt signs, even gesticulations? Napier's discriminatory missive was not necessary to keep Logans off his lands; for this he needed only to reserve to himself the right to veto any sub-tenant whom he disliked. On the other hand, as a hate manifesto against the Logans, it had a very limited circulation, not worth the gesture. In our hands to-day the missive supplies a natural sequel to the 'contract of magic' and it informs us that the contract went sour. Might it not be that this is what Napier intended?

And as with the singular missive so with the singular treasure contract; was not its preservation also Napier's intention, a deliberate communication from him? There is communication anyway from the two papers; it is simply a question of whether it was intentional or accidental. It is hard to conceive of the peculiar missive being framed without a deeper motive than the mere expression of spleen. And the treasure contract, which had aroused so much emotion, was unlikely to lie forgotten and be spared through indifference. It was a thing best got rid of, after it had become a dead letter. It had served mainly as a form of life insurance for Napier; if he had been pushed over the cliff at Fast Castle it would have been there to accuse Logan whenever anyone raised the lid of the Napier charter chest. It was something to make Logan pause. But it was a dangerous document, because of the nature of the pois, as we shall discover. It became more dangerous when the Gowries and Logan were being forfeited and hangings were going on—it was not a healthy time to harbour a document showing one's secret dealings with Logan and Fast Castle.

Perhaps it was because the document had an important bearing on these events and on the secret history of the time that Napier continued to preserve it; perhaps he preserved it because innocent men had been wronged. In the wistful hope of ultimate truth and justice he may have resolved to pass it on as a communication to posterity, to be read along with his strange missive as a postscript. The contract and missive together, script and postscript, would affirm that there was gold at Fast Castle, or a belief in it, that there was a beckoning mystery behind it, that his own projected search for it with Logan had been aborted. It would indicate that the gold hunt had gone on without him, leading to the appearence of others on the scene, and leading those others into disaster. For his soul's sake, to make this limited communication was the least he could do; for the sake of his estate it was the most. Of course the message was fragmentary and cryptic, but it was an age of cypher and cryptic communication. Napier had himself indulged in the study of the secret meanings and prognostications contained in the cryptic inner word of the evangel St. John, and on this erected his important work on theology which he had been in such haste to publish that he had deserted his scholarly Latin and put it forth in the vulgar tongue.

In addition the Napier genealogical tree yields a harvest of characters all given to esoteric studies and cryptic records—it ran in the family. Napier's father, for instance, according to the secretary of Mary Queen of Scots, was also a great wizard and predicted the Queen's escape from Loch Leven Castle, and laid wagers on his prediction. There was also the Napier who passed through many veils as a Rosicrucian and kept under numerous seals a notebook in which he jotted down all the secrets of the universe, and then tantalisingly destroyed the whole record before he comfortably settled down to die.

Nothing so maddening, luckily, happened to John Napier's manuscript. Its purport is startling. To begin with, it calls in question the proceedings and verdicts of a whole row of State trials—the trials of the Gowries and their dependants, the trial of Robert Logan and the trial of the poor Eyemouth notary, Sprott.

The Crown's case against Robert Logan was that he arranged with the Earl of Gowrie to come secretly to Fast Castle; the business in hand was the kidnapping or killing of the King. Napier's manuscript points to the only kind of business that could make them choose that God-forsaken place for their conference, the unfinished business of the gold hunt, the business that was to have taken Napier there himself.

The Crown, to give Gowrie an evil character, depicted him as a sorcerer who had spent his student days at Padua studying magic. Napier's manuscript dealing with the 'craft' and 'ingyne' of a treasure hunter showed that this magic confirmed Gowrie's innocent, if secret, purpose at Fast Castle.

The Crown related that the King had gone to Gowrie House to investigate the story of a pois, which turned out to be a bogus story invented by the Gowries to facilitate their plot to kill the King. The Napier manuscript shows that there was a genuine pois associated with Fast Castle which was preoccupying the Gowries on the occasion. In other words, the pois story was not an elaboration the Gowries added to their plot; the plot to kill the King was a fiction and embellishment added by the Crown to the story of a genuine pois.

To begin with the Napier manuscript calls in question this row of State trials. It goes on to disturb the veils of cobwebs and the dark silences behind the treasure story. This, too, is probably what Napier intended when he kept the document for the record. What could Napier know of these secrets? If he was dependent upon the owner of Fast Castle for background knowledge of the treasure he probably did not learn very much, for there was mistrust between them from the start and they soon fell out.

Did Napier, however, necessarily depend on the owner of Fast Castle for knowledge of Fast Castle's treasure? The castle was often in strange hands and Napier may have known the background story as well as Logan. The contract itself suggests the project may have originated from Napier's knowledge as much as from Logan's, since all the initiative in drafting the agreement came from Napier and; it is in his hand and was to remain at his house. The conference of two at the signing of the contract must have been more revealing than the conference at Fast Castle imagined by the biographer. Since the contract was drafted by Napier and was to be kept at his house we may assume that the signing took place there, in his den at Merchiston.

If the biographer had set his fancy to work again he might have pictured the rough baron in black cloak bending over to sign the sheet, his high crowned hat set on the desk beside him and the robed philosopher alongside regarding him warily. In the low room at the top of the turret stair there would be a window on the stars and a wealth of books and papers, globes terrestial and celestial, drawing board, compasses, calculators, instruments and maps. Also, going by tradition, a silent witness would be there in the shadows, the astrologer's pet black cock, and if all stories were true concerning this creature's real identity, it probably had a gleam in its eye while it watched, and there was probably a slight smell of sulphur about the place.

Certainly the search project was hell-born, for already at that date when the 'contract of magic' was signed the pois—with the headsman—had taken toll of a life. Ultimately the search was hell-bent.

## 2 What prize for treasure hunters?

THAT CEREMONY of signing the 'contract of magic' in the Astrologer's Tower has never been treated very respectfully. Generally the document has been dismissed as a piece of antique whimsy. It was printed in facsimile in the already mentioned memoirs of John Napier by his descendant Mark Napier, about the same period the surgeon Carr published the text in his history of Coldinghamshire and previous attention had been drawn to it by Walter Scott in his *Provincial Antiquities*. This is as high as it has rated—a provincial antiquity or curiosity. But when two other 'contracts of magic' appear alongside it, it grows curiouser and curiouser.

The projected business between the Earl of Gowrie and Robert Logan at Fast Castle was more of the same kind. The same ingredients were present: Fast Castle and its secret, the proposed visit of a sorcerer or searcher, and a bargain with the castle owner. In the Gowrie case the bargain was of a different sort, for Logan was not to have the lion's share of the pois but a gift from Gowrie of the family's magnificent coastal castle at Dirleton round the corner, within the Firth.

In the case of Logan and the Earl of Bothwell the evidence of things contractual is more implicit than explicit. It prompted Napier's biographer, nevertheless, to picture Bothwell feverishly ransacking the castle on the crag in search of the treasure. The fact is that the year before he signed the contract with Napier, Logan was denounced by the King's Privy Council for having secret dealings with the rebel Bothwell and is on record as admitting that he sheltered Bothwell under his roof. Moreover, Bothwell is believed to have met Gowrie clandestinely at Brussels not long before the latter planned his rendezvous with Logan at the castle. To round it off Bothwell was also in the class of sorcerers with the other two searchers, Napier and Gowrie.

Instead of one 'contract of magic' then, we have three. If one provokes a smile perhaps three should make us laugh out loud. Or perhaps the three should wipe away the smile and plant the conviction that something sober and serious lay behind apparent mummery. Two leading Scottish noblemen of the age and a leading thinker of the ages are caught up in a hunt for gold and are drawn towards a lonely North Sea fortress in their search. Their prize apparently borders on the fabulous, or such men would not allow themselves to be involved; it must be nearly fabulous or the castle owner's share alone would not equate with Dirleton Castle. Could such persons be victims of their own credulity or duped by an empty tale of pirate gold invented or resurrected by the castle owner, Logan?

A modern answer is that they must have been fools or they would not have been making a show of wizard powers. With three sorcerers chasing a pois it may be said that we are on no firmer ground than with three alchemists preparing to blow up the coals to convert a simmering pot of lead into a pot of gold. There is, how-ever, the difference that while the philosopher's stone never worked in producing gold, the diviner's rod frequently did work in locating the stuff—and still does. Our searchers, moreover, do not appear to have been limited to divining: Napier, as we have noticed—as the world has noticed—possessed some scientific aptitudes and accomplishments, Gowrie had studied chemistry at Padua and the correspondence between Logan and Gowrie had some hint of the use of high explosives at Fast Castle, 'the dangerous toys of Padua'.

Besides this practical aspect of their sorcery, the three men were magicians in their sense of the word, not ours. The occultism in which they were interested or versed was an aspect of Renaissance culture and all three were, in varying degree, ornaments of that culture. At an early age Napier exchanged St. Andrews for the University of Paris where he was surrounded by the main stream of European learning. Gowrie went from Edinburgh University to a five years' residence in Padua and emerged with the reputation of an outstanding scholar and a leading intellect. As token of his intellectual as well as his social rank, he was received at Geneva on his way home by Calvin's successor, Beza, and remained a guest for three months.

As to Bothwell, his cultural attainments were sufficiently manifest to be remarked on by Dr Toby Matthews, the Dean of Durham. The Dean enjoyed, or survived, a night of Bothwell's company when the Earl was even more than his exuberant self, after he had successfully cornered King James. The cleric sat down when the door closed on his guest and wrote to Lord Burghley in London on the dreams and schemes of the man, adding a kind of school-master's report: 'This nobleman hath a wonderful wit and wonderful volubility of tongue; completely learned in the Latin; well languaged in the French and Italian; much delighted in poetry.'

It was their enemies who hung round the necks of Bothwell and Gowrie the placards with the word *Sorcerer* writ large and who sought their discredit by associating them with diabolic magic. Their chief accuser was that author and authority on demonology, Scotland's James VI, who accused Bothwell of an attempt to murder him by black magic and alleged that Gowrie had planned an attempt on his life while sustained by charms and inspired by satanic beliefs. But these charges merely underlined that the two men were involved in a deep political conflict with the Crown which could take no other form than conspiracy. We have already said that hidden gold is no less credible when the men who are looking for it are conspirators. Every plot has its subversive gold which must be hidden and, sometimes, may be concealed too well; or if a gift from the past has been providentially revealed, no conspiracy will sneeze at it.

We promise that the treasure sought by the noble searchers will grow more credible as the politics and plots in the background take clearer shape. What is credible instantly is the choice of Fast Castle as a place for treasure concealment. Its isolated site and private harbour made it a natural venue for secret arrivals and departures and commended it as a screened repository. In that tale of gloom and madness *The Bride of Lammermoor*, the site was introduced by Scott to create a pattern of doom; he called it the Wolf's Crag, a name which fits it like a shroud. When the rising storm and lowering clouds have passed, however, this same Wolf's Crag can shine out like a fairy knoll in a picture book, presiding over the sparkling sea. In either its black or its sunny mood it supplies complete corroboration for any buried treasure story.

There is a buried treasure precedent on the same line of coast. About twenty miles up the Firth of Forth the Traprain treasure was discovered this century, on a hilltop crowning the panoramic landscape of the Lammermoors. The ancient pirates or raiders who hid their battered hoard of Roman silver on such a blatant site knew their own business best, at least they could not have mistaken the place if they had lived to return for it. There were, however, other pirates who remained judiciously just outside the Firth and clung to our cliff-girt corner of the North Sea. In the Wolf Crag environs they found a safe lair to lurk in and a secluded bank for their loot. They had the further advantage that when business was quiet on the main Scottish sea-lane which passed their back door, they might pick up a bit of cash or plate on the Great North Road which meandered by their drawbridge after crossing two leagues of barren moor.

An English freebooter named Thomas Holden held the crag and its castle in the infant years of the fifteenth century, and he seems to have played the plunder game both these ways, by land and by sea. But a Scots patriot, Patrick Dunbar, attacked under cover of night, seized the castle and made Holden a prisoner. Perhaps Holden hid his loot so well that Dunbar never found it or perhaps, like the Traprain pirates, Thomas Holden never lived to return and recover it—an encouraging thought.

William Haliburton was in possession soon after this. During his lordship, in 1419, the Prior of Coldingham and an accomplice held up James Colston who was on his way south with 2,000 marks for the English King. The Prior took the money in bags to Fast Castle for concealment. Could that have been another gift for posterity?

As well as piracy and highway robbery, wrecking was common in the district. Ships were lured on to the merciless rocks which lurked like sabre-toothed tigers under the green waters. Their crews and masters were extremely lucky if they escaped death by drowning or murder, but the cargoes and ships' gear never escaped. The danger was once greatest in front of the empty bays between Redheugh and Wolf's Crag, and the cause of this was made plain in the year 1188 when the Lord of the Manor of Auldcambus was put on trial. He was found guilty of the villainy of wrecking and was sentenced to death under William the Lyon, but his life was spared for a money ransom which he raised by conveying the lands of Auldcambus to Bertram, the Prior of Coldingham. In return for the amount to purchase his life, he also received the less fruitful and less extensive acres of Lumsdaine just along the cliffs, and was also promised small change in the shape of eighty merks in silver. Thereafter the family name became de Lumsdaine instead of de Auldcambus.

One of the Lumsdaine heirs did not like the change of name and liked the change of fortune less. Accordingly, forty years later, he petitioned Pope Gregory to change everything back. The Pope, who referred the matter to the Bishop of Glasgow, summarised the complaint, explaining that de Lumsdaine was unhappy with 'the small particles of land' he had received and held that he had been cheated out of more than half the promised eighty merks. In his adjudication the Bishop ruled that the monks must pay Lumsdaine the balance of his money but that he could not have Auldcambus back. Perhaps the Lumsdaines gave vent to their disappointment by reverting to their wrecking activities, if they had ever given them up; perhaps, also, the pois or treasure that Logan and Napier sought was some of the hidden sea-plunder of those early wreckers.

In Logan's own century, however, the illicit harvest of the sea greatly excelled the proceeds of such early wrecking or piracy. Not all the sixteenth-century glory was monopolised by the English sea captains; there were some famous Scottish names and among them and, heading the list, were the Bartons and Logans whose respective baronies of Duddingston and Restalrig were next door to each other on the south shore of the Forth. These famous Scots mariners were as ruthless as the rest and seized every shadow of a pretext for bloodily claiming their share of the world's floating wealth. The overall arrangement was that the New World and the ancient East supplied the wealth, Spain and Portugal extracted it and the Protestant powers, English, Scots and rebellious Dutch, participated en route. The rules of the game did not, of course, prevent any one of the powers from plundering any other and it was not necessary even to be a Christian to be a pirate.

The Scots, however, were latterly under a heavy handicap, for while the English captains had a queen who encouraged them, the later Bartons and Logans were sternly discouraged by their sovereign. Mary Queen of Scots was busy fostering friendly relations with Portugal and Spain. Unlike Elizabeth, when she received certain complaints about her seamen from the Portugese, the kind that never once whitened a hair of Elizabeth's wig, she acted promtly. The Barton and Logan brothers were brought before the Privy Council, the complaint was read out to them and the penalty they had incurred intimated. Their letters of marque were withdrawn and their licence to arm ships and execute so-called reprisals on behalf of the Queen—their officially sanctioned piracy—was gone. These Logan sea captains were, of course, kinsmen of the Lord of Fast Castle, for they shared with Robert Logan an ancestor who had been Lord Admiral of Scotland. The family until recently had owned the land of Scotland's premier port, the Port of Leith. Old habits die hard. Perhaps the piratical Logans, when they could no longer sail their prizes into open port, brought them into the quiet deep water under Fast Castle at dawn during the night. Could there have been any hidden gift for posterity from this source?

The official blow at the Bartons and Logans occurred early in Robert Logan's life. More recent yet was another glittering possibi-

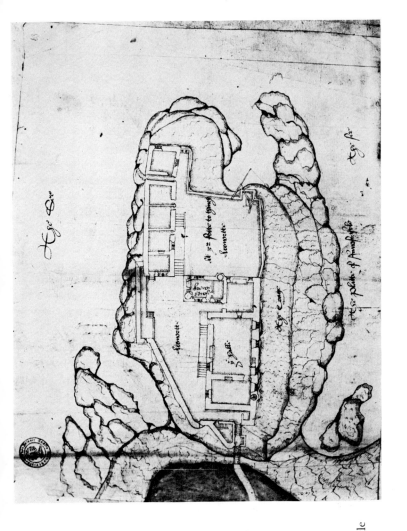

The plan of Fast Castle
made in 1549 (p. 45).

'The Contract of Magic', 1594.

lity—Queen Mary's jewels or her dowry funds. Not our Francis Bothwell but Mary Stewart's Bothwell was believed to have taken certain important items of the Queen's bridal jewels with him when he fled from Dunbar Castle. There might have been gold too. He and the Queen had been melting down the baptismal font, a recent gift from Elizabeth, before they hurried from Holyrood. Dunbar was the last place where they were together before their bitter severance at Carberry Hill. The believed missing items did not show up when Bothwell landed at Orkney, nor later when his Danish captors took possession of his fugitive ship. When he was hurriedly packing for his voyage amidst private disorder in the castle at Dunbar the cautious thought may have occurred to him not to carry diamonds on a dangerous voyage to an uncertain destination, but to leave them concealed in a place to which he might never be able to return was an equal hazard. To hide them in a place to which he or friends might return secretly was the safest course. As Lord Admiral of Scotland, and with some experience already as an amateur pirate, he would surely be aware of the lair at the mouth of the Firth only twelve miles from Dunbar. On his way out he may have tarried here and hidden the jewels. This is all the more probable because there is a hint that Mary Queen of Scots had some link with Fast Castle through Margaret Seton, the sister of one of her four Maries. Margaret Seton was the first wife of our Robert Logan's father and the young mistress of Fast Castle for a time. The hint is that Fast Castle was a discreet channel of the Queen of Scots for communication with France even during her reign, and after her abdication and imprisonment it became, as will be noticed presently, a bolt-hole and escape hatch for the North of England Catholic Earls who rebelled against Elizabeth on her behalf. This brings up the other possibility, that the dowry income of the Queen of Scots (managed by her agent Morgan in Paris and remitted by him secretly and regularly to finance her schemes of escape) may sometimes have passed through Fast Castle and may sometimes have been hidden there.

Since we have mentioned in the bridal jewels of the Queen of Scots and her dowry funds it seems a pity to leave out the most celebrated item of all, the casket letters. Apart from the eternal debate about the letters themselves—genuine or forgeries?—the mystery about what happened to them and the casket remains.

The last man known to have possessed both casket and letters was Gowrie, who enticed young King James to Ruthven Castle and kept him prisoner for ten months. After Gowrie was executed for further plotting, a six hour notice to vacate Fast Castle was served on its keepers who had been his allies. Those named in the warrent were Robert Logan, Agnes Gray, his mother, and Robert Lyon of Balduky, his new step-father. It was, incidentally, Agnes Gray's nephew and Logan's cousin, the Master of Gray, who restored the Gowrie estates to the family when he came to power. The intriguing point is that, sixteen years after Gowrie's execution and the accompanying seizure and search of Fast Castle, the succeeding Earl of Gowrie arranged to visit Fast Castle under conditions of great secrecy. The Queen's silver casket had disappeared not long before his father's death. Could the older Gowrie have taken it there? Was the casket the object of the government's search of Fast Castle after Gowrie's execution? Was it the object of young Gowrie's search at the castle sixteen years later?

If we follow the casket story through, and the associated story of Gowrie elder, we may see some probabilities emerging. Mary Stuart's Bothwell sent his valet George Dalgleish to collect the casket at Edinburgh Castle, after his own flight from Carberry Hill, according to the Earl of Morton's sworn statement indeed. The valet was admitted by the Governor, Sir James Balfour, and allowed to remove some of Bothwell's personal gear. While Morton was sitting at dinner with Secretary Maitland 'a certain man' came and told him about the removal of the articles and so Morton sent his two nephews, Archibald and Robert Douglas, and another man in search of the valet. Robert Douglas caught up with him in the Potter Row and found him in possession of some charters of Bothwell's lands. In custody he swore this was all he had removed, but when they put him in a torture engine he remembered something else—he went back to the Potter Row with Robert and revealed the casket.

The next day it was opened in the presence of Atholl, Mar, Glencairn, Morton himself, Maitland of Lethington and others, and the letters were inspected. Then the casket was subsequently taken to England for the inspection of Elizabeth's Commissioners, with the object of establishing Mary's complicity with Bothwell in the murder of her husband, Darnley. It was brought back by Moray and remained in his charge during his regency, passing on his death to the Regent Lennox and then to the Regent Morton; it was their warrent for power, justifying them for taking the Crown from the Queen and ruling in her son's name.

After Morton's execution one of his servants, Sandy Jordan, brought the casket to the Earl of Gowrie when he was briefly the most powerful man in the land and held the young king in custody. It was at this time that both Queen Elizabeth and the Queen of Scots developed a sudden interest in the casket's whereabouts, about sixteen years after it was discovered in the Potter Row.

The English ambassador, Bowes, pressed Gowrie to give up the casket to Elizabeth with the promise of 'princely thanks and gratuity'. This offer was made after his agents had failed in attempts to steal it. Gowrie, who was importuned by Bowes at Holyrood, said he would look for it at home, as if he were not sure what he had done with it or whether he had ever got it. Bowes, however, proved it had come into his hands and warned him he was in danger while he kept it; he said the Queen of Scots had given out lately her demand to receive the letters which she declared were counterfeits held by her rebels. With her demand she had coupled the threat to use 'great and effectual powers' to obtain them and whoever held them would be in danger, no one would be suffered to keep them. Gowrie simply put him off, and ignored the promised reward of Elizabeth and the threatened vengeance of Mary. He said D'Aubigny had tried to get them while he held sway and the King now knew where they were and he would have to get consent.

Then Gowrie's hour of crisis came. The King slipped the lead and Arran rose to power. Gowrie was granted an uneasy remission, while his confederates fled. He applied for the King's licence to go abroad, but he was uncertain about what might happen to his lands and castles in his absence and lingered with his pictures in the new built gallery of Gowrie House at Perth. He went to Dundee and was on and off the ship that was to carry him into exile. Eventually it became clear that he was hesitating on the edge of a new plot. Arran got wind of it and Gowrie was given fifteen days to sail. Still he delayed, until it was too late. Arran despatched Colonel Stewart to Dundee with a hundred troopers and, after a brief siege of his Dundee house, the Earl was seized and taken prisoner. His friends were scattered as soon as they came together and there was nothing to save him. He was hustled immediately after sentence from the court room to the scaffold.

The apparent indecision on the quayside at Dundee had a reason from the beginning. Gowrie would have been much safer in one of his own strongholds than at Dundee port, but while he was messing about in ships his agent, John Colville, was in England plotting with Elizabeth's secretary, Walsingham. As a result, Elizabeth had sent up Lords Claud and John Hamilton to the Borders to be in readiness and Gowrie's licence to sail was apparently obtained to cover up communication with the Hamiltons on the English frontier. Descent from the Tay to the Berwickshire coast was simple. Gowrie doubtless made the voyage to confer with the Hamiltons near Berwick, probably at Fast Castle, without his absence from Dundee being noticed and this, or suspicion of it, would account for Arran's seizure of Fast Castle after Gowrie's arrest.

There was an ominous menace to King James in the Hamiltons' arrival at the Borders after long exile in England. Walsingham had come up from London personally after Gowrie lost his grip on the young King and had met the liberated monarch and his new favourite, Arran. He reported back to Burghley, Elizabeth's chief minister: 'You will easily find there is no hope of recovery of this young prince, who, I doubt, will become a dangerous enemy. There is no one thing will serve better to bridle him than for Her Majesty to use the Hamiltons.' The Hamiltons were the claimants to the Crown of Scotland, if James Stewart's life were forfeited or if his title could be challenged.

Gowrie's second plot, therefore was not another attempt to cage the King—that promised only another frustration—this time it was a move to replacing him. Like a lightning flash in the night, Walsingham's words about the Hamiltons revealed the reason for the attempts of Ambassador Bowes to buy or steal the casket letters from Gowrie. The idea was to use them to fault the young James Stuart's title to his crown if he became really obstreperous: the formula was the casket letters plus the Hamiltons. A hint of this dark design had evidently reached the Queen of Scots in prison and had stirred her to unfathomable fury and the direst threats. If the casket letters were to serve as witness against her son's title to the Crown it meant they were to demonstrate he was a bastard and she was to be accused anew of murdering Darnley and that this time she was to wear also the prior offence of making him father another man's child.

Elizabeth was hardly the person to scruple about taking matters thus far if hard pressed; she was herself menaced in this style. The French Guises had a plan to 'associate' Mary and her son James in a joint claim to the English Crown, and all on the Catholic assumption that she, Elizabeth was illegitimate. The Papal Bull on the point was venomous enough. Why should she not return the compliment and further discredit the mother and tilt her son's throne with the twin charges of cuckoldry and bastardy? 

The secret weapon of the casket letters was deadly enough to achieve this purpose if backed by unscrupulous will and power. It had carried the Queen's discredit so far as to rob her of the Crown. The Regents had kept the casket in turn to consolidate that purpose, but they had a vested interest in seeing that the Queen's alleged shame did not reflect on her son's legitimacy, since they ruled in his name. Now they were all dead, however, and it could be represented that their self-interest had prevented proper conclusions regarding her son's illegitimacy from being drawn. The letters could be subject to new constructions, the casket could be found to contain other letters which Morton had subtracted. Subtraction and addition seemed to be the main thing about the casket collection of letters anyway.

The plot involving Gowrie, the Hamiltons and the casket letters, with John Colville and Walsingham in the background seemed to collapse completely. But the young King appeared to have received the message. Thereafter he became 'bridled', in Walsingham's sense, and under Arran and the newcomer, the Master of Gray, his policy began to take the direction of the 'league' with England.

The question still remains: What happened to the casket? It seems that Gowrie was too ardent a collector to part with it, too much the connoisseur. He collected pictures and castles and experimented in architecture—and he collected Stewart secrets. It is obvious that before Bowes tried to steal the casket and before Walsingham urged Burghley in desperation to use the Hamiltons, Gowrie was aware of the value of such aids to power in relation to the young Stewart. He had been with his father, Lord Ruthven, at the slaying of Riccio in Holyrood when Ruthven imputed that the child Mary carried was not Darnley's. Gowrie appears to have held to this. A tract which circulated later in Perthshire and elaborated the story that James was David Riccio's child was attributed to Colville, Gowrie's man, and among the followers of Gowrie's ally, Bothwell, doggerel lines about Seigneur Davy were popular. On a fatal occasion, much later, a crowd gathered outside Gowrie House in Perth after a young Earl of Gowrie had been slain along with his teenage brother. The King was inside and the mob called out in anger: 'Come down thou son of Seigneur Davy!' James's 'Italianate paternity' was a Gowrie by-word.

Besides, Gowrie went with Lord Lindsay to Lochleven to compel Mary Stewart to sign the instrument of her abdication, and at the ceremony of the crowning of her son he bore witness, along with Lindsay, that it was an act of free will. Already, then, he had experience of using Stewart secrets to subdue the royal will and make it conform 'freely' with the demands of himself and his friends. With the young James Stewart the pressure must have been easier to apply and it is significant that even after James escaped from the Earl he appeared to remain under his thumb. Gowrie's accomplices all fled but he remained on at Court, although he had been the ringleader.

When he was arrested for the second plot he staked everything on a private audience. To obtain it he wrote offering to disclose privily the details of the plot, backed by England, to get both the King and his mother out of the way. If the audience had taken place he would surely have stressed how vulnerable the casket and other secrets made the King's crown and life—the precious casket would have been thrown on the scale as barter for another pardon.

But this letter only incriminated him further; the big brotherly presence of Arran stiffened the King's resistance to blackmail. At Gowrie's trial the jury found him guilty and he told them cryptically they would know better hereafter and urged his judges to spare his estates after his life was declared forfeit. Insofar as he had put the casket beyond the King's reach, he may have hoped it would be a power working for him 'hereafter', ensuring his family their inheritance. Perhaps it did. The estates were declared forfeit and at first Lady Gowrie was brutally treated; she sought an audience with the King but was driven out of the palace, in the street outside she knelt in the King's path and Arran steered the King out of her way and literally walked over her. But when Arran was supplanted by the Master of Gray, cousin to the owner of Fast Castle, the Gowrie estates were restored. A hint of the hidden casket and its destructive potentialities may have helped Gray's persuasion, and may have helped Gray himself to power.

Some probabilities have emerged, as suggested, from this final instalment of the casket story and the last chapter of Gowrie. The meeting of Gowrie with the Hamiltons near the Border is virtually confirmed in a despatch of Ambassador Bowes to Elizabeth's chief minister, Burghley, on March 4th, 1584. 'Gowrie', he wrote, 'has abandoned all thought of concession.' He added: 'the ground and matter of the purpose are known to very few'. No concession! With the Hamiltons at hand this meant the King's overthrow and replacement and the 'ground and matter known to the very few' pointed strongly to the casket letters. What else?

It may be advanced as a strong probability, therefore, that Gowrie met the Hamiltons at Fast Castle and brought the casket letters with him to provide the 'ground and matter' which would be sent on to England as had been done before. It was the one place near the Borders to which he could come by sea, without his movements being observed, and the place belonged to the friends of his ally and fellow conspirator, Bothwell; it suited equally well the secret movements of the Hamiltons. The castle's use for the conference of the 'very few' has some confirmation in its seizure after Gowrie's arrest.

If Gowrie brought the casket to Fast Castle not long before his execution it would not, apparently be the first time since there is evidence to this effect in the trial in England of Norfolk for the marriage plot with the Queen of Scots. Secretary Maitland was at Fast Castle in September, 1568 and there he took out the letters from the casket and had his wife copy them. The copies were sent by Robert Melville to the Queen of Scots in Bolton. (The copyist was, incidentally, Mary Fleming, one of the Queen's four Marys.) The purpose in sending them was to reveal to the Queen the matter that was to be used against her at the conference of Elizabeth's Commissioners in York. This evidence was part of the confession of Mary's ambassador, Leslie, the Bishop of Ross, when he was a prisoner in the Tower and was used in Norfolk's trial as stated.

It was at the time when Secretary Maitland had switched his allegiance back to Mary, but was still trusted by the Lords who had deposed her. Presumably the casket was being held by him, in his continuing office of Secretary, to be sent down to the York conference of the Commissioners and for the same reason of proximity it could have been left at Fast Castle by Gowrie nearly sixteen years later. If James had been deposed like his mother then the casket with extra letters could have gone down to another York conference to vindicate the action as before. History, however, did not obligingly repeat itself in that particular.

There is no other final fact known about the casket, other than that Gowrie held it when he had the young king in his power. When forfeiture of his castles was imminent its removal to a safe place of hiding would be one of his urgent cares. In his second plot involving a threat to James's crown through the Hamiltons it was necessary that the safe place for the letters should be accessible and near where the plot was being hatched. At a moment's notice this weapon had to be unsheathed like a political sword. About the time of Gowrie's death, then, there are no stronger pointers in any direction than those in the direction of Fast Castle, which had served as a repository for the casket before. Indeed there are no other pointers at all.

To round off the possibilities of hidden wealth and hidden secrets at Fast Castle, but not to close the record, there was a certain ship of the Armada—the solitary one that put in at the south-east of Scotland during the fleet's circuitous return to Spain. It was commanded by Admiral Gomez de Medina who had lost about twenty hulks near Fair Isle between Orkney and Shetland and had salvaged one half-seaworthy ship to work his way back down the coast. He chose to look in, when he and his crew were near exhaustion, at Anstruther, although such a man might have been expected to know that most of the coast he had passed on the way was in the control of the Catholic Earl Huntly and his friends, who would have extended warm hospitality.

They were 'for the maist part young berdless men' recorded the minister, James Melville, 'trauchled and hungered'. As well as getting a sermon against popery from Melville, Lopaz got for his men two days kail, pottage and fish which set them up again. For his part, he did not return the coin of religious disputation but held that they had set out against England because the country was a nest of pirates who constantly afflicted them. On that tack his crew must have aroused sympathy amongst Anstruther seamen; they too had been much afflicted by English pirates, so much that they had lately carried out a reprisal and brought back four of the species and hanged them. They were probably not the same pirates as the fellows who had annoyed them and may not even have been pirates at all, but it helped to even up the score.

Why did Lopez pick on Anstruther as a place of succour? Perhaps it signifies something that, looking across the mouth of the Forth beyond the intervening Island of May, one's gaze is slanted towards Fast Castle Head. Could it be that Lopez had salvaged not only men from the wrecked hulks at Fair Isle but also valuables and had made for Fast Castle as a safe deposit for his collection? Spanish captains had put in at that secret harbour before and Lopez may have been one of them. The Huntly coast on the other hand was not favoured by the underground agents of Spain for landing money— the Catholic Earls were too greedy, as one agent, who will come into our story, had occasion to complain. It may also be significant that Logan, the Lord of Fast Castle, owned a mill property in Anstruther, one of his isolated possessions. Having unloaded a precious cargo at Logan's castle did the Spaniards then repair to Anstruther to Logan's friends and Logan's mill in order to ship the sacks of flour that would sustain their voyage home?

One other incident connected with the passing of the Armada remains to be mentioned. Colonel Sempill, Philip's special secret agent in Scotland, who will also come into our story, was in Edinburgh when the Armada was sailing north. Sempill took a boat to the mouth of the Forth and kept a rendezvous with a Spanish pinnace whose mother ship, it seems, was in the vicinity. When he returned he was arrested, but there is no record that he came back with either documents or money from the ship. If he was the recipient of either, they were safely in the bank at Fast Castle before he returned. Lopez and Colonel Sempill appear to link the Armada, and perhaps some Armada gold, with Wolf's Crag. At the very least they hint that the neighbourhood was not unknown to Spanish mariners.

Armada gold, pirate and wrecker's treasure ancient and not so ancient, highwayman's loot, the bridal jewels of a queen, money hidden to aid a queen's escape and the famous lost casket received by Bothwell from Mary Queen of Scots—these are all in the catalogue of Fast Castle's possible secrets. Name the kind of pois you are in search of and it may be there. If you don't find what you are looking for you may find something better. Something yet more fabulous remains to be mentioned in its proper place, something incomparably better.

The point, however, is not what we might find but precisely what were the searchers looking for—Napier, Bothwell, Gowrie and the king of the castle, Robert Logan? Their individual motivation has to be sought in their individual careers and their joint motivation in the happenings of their time. If we can find a pointer to some contemporary secret in which they could all have shared, or could all have had hint of, then we shall be on our way to identifying the Fast Castle treasure. The history of the castle and the life story of the castle owner may provide an informative start. Therefore we cross the drawbridge, following the golden string.

# 3  False Castle. Enigma and variations

THE SUSPICIOUS thing about the beginning of Fast Castle history is that it has none. There is no record or legend proclaiming when it was first built or pronouncing upon the period when it became established as castle or habitation. There has been no serious speculation either. It springs to life abruptly after the battle of Halidon Hill in 1333 which was an English revenge for Bannockburn; about this time Robert Benhale and a band of Englishmen seized Fast Castle as part of the revenge.

It was not Fast Castle then but Faux Castle; it never has been Fast Castle except in misnomer or modern retrospect. The Norman adjective became corrupted or transplanted into the Scottish Faus and lapsed further into Fas. The sense of the word increases the enigma of the castle's origin and early role, and also increases our curiosity. At the same time it supplies a clue—the only one available —the French name reflects the settlement of the district of Coldingham in the first half of the twelfth century by Anglo-Norman families. These included the Lamertons, Mordingtons, Lumsdaines, Prenderguests and others. They received their charters from the benevolent David I, while the Coldingham Priory owed its charters to the mother church of Durham. So the castle's name at least, if not the castle itself, is unlikely to have pre-dated the arrival of those Anglo-Norman barons.

Next, the clue points to Edward de Auldcambus, one of the settlers. The ancient parish to which he acquired a title and from which he derived his name has been subsequently described as a golden bowl. At harvest the term 'golden' is opposite; the rim of the bowl is supplied by the ground rising up to Coldingham Moor and by the cliff tops rising from the North Sea and the encircling eminences of the Lammermoors. Edward was the first recorded proprietor of the bowl and was also our friend cited in the last chapter, Edward the wrecker. If this Edward who lured ships to their doom conducted his nefarious trade from the top of our familiar Wolf's Crag, this would very well qualify the castle there to be known as Faux Castle. Not that Edward would be likely to give his own castle a bad name in his own tongue, but his mocking Norman friends might well have done so. The French merchant sailors passing the crag on their way into the Forth could have learned to recognise the castle by this name also, and would no doubt add a much stronger description of the castle owner. After the wrecker was brought to justice the name would gain wider circulation, and would stick.

The credibility of our speculation is strengthened by the cruel fact that even in our times the measured mile of coast line that takes in Fast Castle has an evil reputation for wrecks. It is a natural grave-yard for ships under natural hazards and not much art would be needed on the top of them to make certain of disasters. It seems then that we are beginning to fill up part of the blank in Fast Castle's early history; one of its lost or suppressed memories is related to its shameful role as a wrecker's castle.

There is the objection to this that Fast Castle lies a half a mile or so beyond the Auldcambus barony which belonged to Edward the Wrecker and half a mile or so into the adjacent barony or parish of Coldingham. This is a very slight objection. Today the Auldcambus barony with its farms is joined to that same corner of Coldingham parish; the modern owners, the Dunglass Estates, possess the titles to Auldcambus but also own the adjacent Dowlaw Farm within Coldingham parish on which Fast Castle's ruin stands, and which was once the home farm of the castle. The same pattern applied in the middle of the fifteenth century when the Home family took over the lands in these parts; they acquired the Auldcambus barony plus Fast Castle with its home farms. The pattern almost certainly applied in the days of Edward de Auldcambus, too, and originated with him.

It conformed, of course, with the general feudal pattern; the Nor-man settler needed not only his tributary lands within his barony but also his demesne comprising his home farms and his baronial seat or castle. In the case of the barony of Auldcambus there is no site corresponding with this requirement, apart from Fast Castle in the adjoining corner of the monks' lands of Coldingham Priory. In this corner there was no other baron to compete with Edward de Auldcambus for the castle site. The Prior was the baron of the Priory lands and he lived miles away at the Priory. It may be added that the rights of the Coldingham monks to all of the lands near Fast Castle were so ambiguous that nearly a hundred and fifty years later David II ordered an inquiry to decide what the rights and tenures were in this very neighbourhood.

If Edward the Wrecker was Baron of Auldcambus and also Lord

of Fast Castle, what followed after he was removed? In our note on his fate in the previous chapter we explained that the Prior of Coldingham found the bag of gold to ransom his life and in exchange took away his titles to Auldcambus. Thereafter the land was feued by the monks to the Templars and it is to be assumed that they marched into Fast Castle too, after the crestfallen Edward shambled out. There is a strong hint that the Norman's eviction was a contrived one—to let the Templars in and to provide a new revenue for the Coldingham monks. Doubtless the charge of wrecking was well founded, but no more than it could have been against many another honest baron. The monks were suspiciously at hand to put up his ransom and hustle him into his 'little particles' of compensatory land, without which he would have faced another death. Instead of gratitude, however, a burning sense of grievance remained in the family until Edward's grandson, David Lumsdaine, took the matter up with the Pope. The family name changed to Lumsdaine because that is what the little particles were 'commonly called', as the Pope explained in his letter summarising the family's complaint.

There was no suggestion that the nearby castle home-farm of Dowlaw was part of the 'little particles' of compensation the Lumsdaines received. This strengthens the idea that the Templars moved into Dowlaw and Fast Castle when they took over Auldcambus from Edward the Wrecker. But there is the suggestion that the Templars as well as the monks were involved in the Lumsdaine family complaint to the Pope since Edward's grandson took his complaint over the head of the mother church of the Coldingham monks—the See of Durham—and in the normal way a bishop would have been the person to try to interest in the matter. But then the Pope was a bishop, in particular, he was the bishop of the entire Templar Order and the sole person to resolve any complaint against the Order or its members. David Lumsdaine's temerity was probably based on the circumstances that his dispute involved both the monks and the Templars, now installed in the family lands, and against the Templars there was only one court to which he could appeal.

For the Scottish Templars of that distant day no place could have seemed to bring them nearer to their spiritual home, Jerusalem, than Fast Castle. There was a distant reflection from the Mediterranean in the castle's image—far away in the Middle Sea, the red-cross knights were busy raising strong fortresses on just such formidable rocks. The most famous was the Pilgrim's Castle at Acre built around 1195 on a fearsome promontory jutting into the sea, about the same time that the Templars moved into the area of Wolf's Crag. Of course there was no need to build a stronghold against the infidels near the North Sea, but there was some indication that these craggy sites served a ritual purpose as well as defence, and the ritual on the North Sea would be no different from that in the Mediterranean. In addition, a site such as Fast Castle's lent itself to clandestine coming and going and conventicles. Secrecy was one of the chief charges against the Order at the time of its persecution and the main cause of popular mistrust.

If our speculations are considered to have a firm foundation, the castle that vanished for a century and a half will have some of its hidden life revealed, although it is necessary to use imagination to fill in the details. Through an imaginative eye we can observe the place astir on nights of storm or mist as the wreckers place their snares or bring in the cargo of a broken ship at dawn and hoist it to the top of the crag. (Part of the wrecker's job would be to stow it away in clever hiding places, and this, of course, is within our terms of reference.) After a time the actors change, but not the scene, and the villains are replaced, by men perhaps gentler in language and bearing, but for their ideal's sake every bit as murderous. Some are quick shadows who appear after the splash of oars and the creaking of timbers in the harbour below. There are conventicles and mystic rites within the more silent stone chambers and. . . . Could it be that at some time there was talk and business that would have interested the gold searchers, Robert Logan and John Napier, as well as ourselves?

Apart from imaginative exercises respecting detail we may now be able to understand better why the castle did not become a focus of Border warfare until relatively late on. Its occupation by the Templars who had a unified 'British' organisation and discipline would raise it above the battle. True, it was not above the battle in the suppression and desertion of the heroic Wallace, but in a divided Scotland this was not yet total treason, on the other hand, this enhanced Fast Castle's immunity from the unwelcome English attentions that came later. Our reconstruction also supplies a rational explanation of the castle's name. Through its wrecker owner it got a dubious name, Faux Castle; the misty affairs of the Templars gave the name a new, dark nuance, the castle then became 'false' in the sense of being mysteriously deep and indefinably dangerous behind its everyday exterior. Finally, our restored history links Fast Castle with a stirring incident in the story of Scotland and Bruce.

In 1317 Bruce encamped his army in Auldcambus. From the explanations we have given this virtually means that in 1317 Bruce was at Fast Castle; the tents of his army may have been pitched in the fields of the Auldcambus bowl or on its sea braes, but almost certainly the castle would have served as the operational head-quarters of the King and his staff. Supplies or secret reports may have been brought into its harbour and an assault along the coast quietly planned there, while the making of war engines and general preparation for the seige of Berwick was going on. During this time a messenger came to the King with a letter from the Pope command-ing him to make a truce with England, but the King refused delivery on the grounds that it was improperly addressed—it ignored his coronation. On his way back to Berwick from his fruitless mission the Papal messenger was disrespectfully treated, was in fact beaten up; if his Holiness did not feel the blows he acutely felt the affront, and not for the first time Bruce was spiritually cast to the devil—excommunicated.

It was not too much to suggest that the company Bruce was then keeping heightened his pride and unyielding resistance towards Papal authority and helped to increase the force of his rebuff. This company around the King included the fraternity of the Knights Templars by then under the joint designation of the Templars and St John. It was in an enclave of the Templars that Bruce had en-camped his army and, if our theory is accepted, at a castle of the Templars that he was preparing his military plans.

Adversity made Bruce the leader of Scotland's national struggle and the Templars his bedfellows. The Order had previously fought on the side of Edward I against Wallace and paid dearly for what-ever honour or dishonour it involved. At the battle of Falkirk in 1298 both the Master of the Temple in London and his Vice-Regent, the Preceptor of Scotland, died in the English cause, but the Order, or its scattered brethren, transferred their support to Scotland when Bruce took up the sword. The plain reason was that simul-taneously with Bruce they had become outlaws, suffering the ful-minations of the Pope and the persecution of feudal monarchs, notably Philip the Fair of France but also, before long, Edward II of England too. Before the persecution their treasuries were freely plundered but the pressure was building up, and in their crisis of 1307, which coincided roughly with Bruce's crisis after slaying the Comyn, they quickly linked up with their Scottish friends.

It was natural that, while Bruce was confined to the west of Scotland, Templar refugees and underground emissaries would sail from France round Ireland to join his camp and land in places like Mull; also that they would travel to their Edinburgh confreres of the Order in Scotland by the east coast route and land at or near Fast Castle, thus causing a new reason for the shroud of secrecy over the castle. Ten years later, when Bruce was in camp in the Templar enclave of Auldcambus the cause for secrecy had not lessened. The Order was by then universally dissolved by Papal decree and its property transferred to the Knights of St John. While sadly weakened elsewhere by imprisonment, burnings and torture, in Scotland it had gained greatly in secret strength and in influence within Church and State, especially as the power round the Throne. The reaction against the Papal legate within Bruce's camp at Auldcambus, therefore was not merely the hard feeling of a king whose dignity had suffered slight, it was also the hard feeling of men whose comrades and leaders had been burned at the stake or spared to rot in dungeons. The knocks for the Pope's messenger were also an expression of the feelings of the Templars, who had removed the red cross from their vestments to wear it on their still more secret hearts.

As far as military glories go, Fast Castle was too small to earn many. The vaunt was that twelve men within its walls could withstand the siege of an army—but what army in its right mind would settle down to sweat it out with twelve men? It was left usually to 'a band of Englishmen' or 'a band of Scots', as the case might be, to neutralise its nuisance value; if their strength was not equal to a quick result they fell back on patience and stratagem, which was always effective in the end. After the serious Scots defeat at Halidon Hill in 1333 an English 'band' seized the castle, as we have mentioned, and it was again seized for the English in 1402; the return match in 1410 got the Scot Patrick Dunbar in and the Englishman Thomas Holden, whom we have already listed in our catalogue of pirates, out.

Our interest is drawn more to the changes in castle ownership. The Lumsdaines, the descendants of Edward de Auldcambus, appear to have lost even their 'little particles' near to the castle by now referred to as West Lumsdaine, the century after their appeal to the Pope. In their place a charter was conferred on one Michael Angus, although kinsmen of theirs still had lands, called East Lumsdaine, further along the cliffs. The ambiguity and dispute over tenure of land round the castle led to the inquiry ordered by David II in 1364, which has been mentioned, and this had the effect of strengthening the position of the Coldingham monks in the castle area. Consequently, the castle itself and the Dowlaw home farm were clearly at the disposal of the monks at the beginning of the following century. In 1419 Haliburton was not only their tenant in the castle but also their accomplice: the 2,000 merks which the Coldingham Prior, Drax, obtained by highway assault were conveyed to Haliburton for safe keeping at Fast Castle. By 1431 the monks had installed one of the Lumsdaines as a free tenant of the castle, and a Lumsdaine received £6 13 4 from the Scottish Exchequer a few years later for keeping the castle in time of war.

There were more masterful people about with designs on the castle, however, and against their strength the monks were as straw. These men belonged to the family of Home; from the moment they assert their rights to Fast Castle we go straight forward to the times and tribulations of the castle owner, Robert Logan. It was William Barton 'messenger and mandatory of our holy father the Pope' who described the Homes as 'masterful persons', referring in particular to Patrick and John Home, near kinsmen of the Lord Home, who had entered the Priory of Coldingham and excluded the Prior and the monks. No officer of the Crown was bold enough, he said, to serve a writ upon them, and added that for fear of death he dared not seek their persons. The Pope, on account of this offence against the monks, excommunicated the two young men in 1467. It was during this time, or soon after, that the Homes acquired the lands which the Coldingham monks took over from Edward the wrecker—Auldcambus and also Fast Castle and its home farms. They negotiated from a position of strength, although it helped, too, that their kinsman, Alexander Home, was hereditary Bailie or Protector of the Priory lands. The transaction was 'regularised' by the ceding of the family acres at Houndswood.

As a result of these transactions, whatever may be made of them, Sir Patrick Home was the king of the castle at the end of the century, and he appears to have been the Patrick who, with his brother John, put the fear of death into the Pope's messenger around 1467. He is first designated as Baron of Fast Castle on deeds on which his name appeared in 1488 and 1489. He was a politician by then and later a diplomatist and, in all the circumstances, we may be forgiven for thinking that his urgent need of the castle had something to do with his career. He was made one of the Lords Auditors of Causes and Complaints (which seems fair enough considering his creative talents in this field); he served as a Commissioner for Scotland in peace or truce negotiations with England and journeyed on Government missions to London and Spain. His second wife was Isobel Forman, sister of the celebrated Abbot Forman who also moved in high circles of Church and State.

There is one cause or complaint that may have weighed on the mind of our Lord Auditor of Causes and Complaints even if it never came up for trial. It concerned the King. James III was also interested in Coldingham Priory, and employed his authority to annex the revenues of the Priory to his own Chapel Royal in Stirling Castle. The Homes resisted his exactions and this precipitated an Act of Parliament in 1488 framed to deal with those who threatened the King's revenue from this source. Probably it was not only the Kings' financial interest in Coldingham Priory that disturbed the Homes, but this sign of his aim to assert military and political authority in the area. The rage to possess Fast Castle, which the Homes had wrested from the Priory, was perhaps being exhibited again, this time by James III.

To meet the threat, the Homes made a Border alliance with the Hepburns and together Homes and Hepburns rallied a large following of lords and barons, including Angus, Gray, Argyle, Drummond and Hailes. The King's strength was mainly in the north. The rebels seized the fifteen year old Prince James at Stirling and then put his father to flight at the Battle of Sauchieburn. Not only did the King choose to fight there, near Bannockburn, but he hopefully armed himself with the sword of the Bruce as his principal talisman, just as he sustained himself with the best astrologers. The sword, however fell from his uncertain hand and clattered on the battlefield. He learned that the strength of the Bruce cult resided in the living power, or lay with those who possessed the living furnace and crucibles for producing new glittering weapons. Even the Bruce himself had been warned at Arbroath that he was not irreplaceable and Edward I was taught that though he stole the most ancient symbol of all, the stone of destiny, he could not by that dead magic alone ensure dominion. For James III the lesson of the fallen sword came rather late; he fled to a nearby mill for concealment but was betrayed by his grazing horse and sought out and killed.

Subsequently Alexander, Master of Home, was made Great Chamberlain, when the young King James IV was crowned at the age of sixteen. This ascendancy of the Homes under the new King, of course, helped the political and diplomatic career of Patrick Home of Fast Castle. Simultaneous with the rise to power of the Homes and their friends, a considerable treasure that James III had amassed in Edinburgh castle was seized, and supplies further food for our speculations concerning the Fast Castle pois. (Sir Patrick's son, Cuthbert, must have benefited from the family ascendancy too, and the next two or three links after Cuthbert are absolutely vital to our story. Cuthbert's heirs were his two daughters, the elder of whom married a Logan. Our Robert Logan was the grandson of this union.)

In 1503, Margaret Tudor, sister of the prince who became Henry VIII, crossed the Scottish Border on her way to Edinburgh for her nuptials with James IV. She had a large English retinue which was joined by a larger Scottish escort; the happy cavalcade proceeded across the two leagues of the Coldingham Moor late in the day until they reached Fast Castle. Patrick Home and his wife, Isobel Forman, were there to take care of the princess and her personal suite. The rest bedded down back in Coldingham village and returned in the morning when the scene of pomp was renewed. A thousand Scots were assembled, 'five hundred mounted on horses of great price and well appointed', while the princess herself mounted a pure white pony and wore a rich riding dress. The footmen on either side of her had jackets embroidered with portcullises and her Scottish hosts 'shot more ordnance' from the castle walls—the thunder among the cliffs must have been deafening. John Young, the Somerset Herald, was there and saw and heard it all.

This was Fast Castle joy; it was mingled with deep misery. At the same time a group of English hostages were rotting in Fast Castle's dungeons. The men had been delivered by Princess Margaret's father, Henry VII, because they were related to or allied with English raiders who had killed Sir Robert Ker, the Scottish Warden of the Marches and Master of Ordnance; the main killer was one named Heron whose brother had been sent into Scotland in chains as a pledge that the chief culprit would eventually be found and delivered. Ten years later the ledger with the unsettled Heron account still lay open. Margaret Tudor's husband, the Scottish king, quarrelled with her brother about this unsettled account, about the killing of his chief sea commander, Andrew Barton, and the seizure of the splendid ship the *Lion* and about the fact that Henry had not delivered to his sister Margaret the jewels willed to her by her father. There was also the larger quarrel, the European power struggle, in which Henry was against France and James was deeply committed on France's side. King James had offered his services as commander of the Venetian fleet and army to lead a new crusade, but his services were not required in that quarter. France had bemused the monarch with promised support for the mystic Scottish dream of Jerusalem which had flickered before the eyes of Bruce before he died and had never quite faded. The major power cleavage and this major dream sharpened the dispute about the unsurrendered felon, the family jewels, the seized ship and the like. As a result, in place of the chivalrous king's golden dream of Jerusalem regained, the corpse-strewn vista of Flodden Field unfolded like a cemetery nightmare.

Lord Dacre wrote to the English Lords in Council after the battle claiming that 'Cuthbert Home of Fast Castle was slain by me and my folks on the field of Brankston [Flodden]'. Poor Cuthbert had returned home to his inheritance in 1510 and Lord Dacre and his folks killed him at Flodden in September 1513. His curious career makes us long to know even a quarter of what he was up to. Holinshed records that he returned via Flanders by sea with the newly-made Archbishop of St Andrews, the King's bastard son; he had joined the Archbishop there after travelling through a great part of Christendom 'and moreover passing into Turkey came to the Emperor of Turkey at the city of Cairo, who retained him in his service and gave him good entertainment'. According to Holinshed, Cuthbert remained at the court in Cairo until he learned that Fast Castle had fallen to him by lawful succession, although there were eight persons before him in the succession who had all died since he left home. If Cuthbert was Sir Patrick's son, as Holinshed declares, it seems to imply the preposterous sudden death of eight elder brothers. The other strange thing is the report that 47 sacks of wool, each weighing 640 lbs, had to be shipped from Leith by Cuthbert's father for gold to pay a ransom to allow him to get back home—but Cuthbert is said to have resolved to come home only after news of his father's death.

Behind the contradictions there seems to lie the truth that Cuthbert leapt over a gap in the succession in order to land in Fast Castle. He appears to embody the recurrent passion for possession that centred round our castle on the crag: David Lumsdaine dragged the Pope into the conflict over these debateable lands, someone else brought David II into the dispute a century later, and in the next century again the Homes themselves were at war with the monks, the Pope, and the King, Cuthbert Home's short cut to the succession has the same relevance. Plunging into the future from Cuthbert's present we have a late example of the urge for possession of the castle supplied by a Home descendant of the seventeenth century: in 1644 the Earl of Home was fined £24,000 Scots because he had violently dispossessed Sir Patrick Hepburn of the lands of Fast Castle and Wester Lumsdaine. Was there some specific and common factor behind the rage for possession of all these violent and disputatious men?

The most intriguing episode of Cuthbert Home's career may be called 'a Scotsman at the Court of the Turkish Emperor'. Bearing in mind that his father was a diplomat who had carried out missions in England and Spain, the son may be credited with some kind of unofficial mission in Cairo where, significantly, he was well entertained and retained for a time in the Emperor's service. What service? He came home with the Archbishop of St Andrews, who was joyfully received on his return from Flanders. Both came home when the war alliances and preparations were maturing and Abbot Forman, Patrick Home's father-in-law, was also busy coming and going on pregnant missions. As well as his journey to Cairo, Cuthbert travelled widely through Christendom and other missions may have been involved. At no point does it seem, however, that Cuthbert's mission at Cairo could fit in with any mission he might have within Christendom, or with the missions of Forman, the Archbishop of St Andrews or any other secret diplomat. Surely the fundamental cleavage was between Islam and Christendom and the idealistic basis of James IV's foreign policy was a new crusade which deepened that cleavage? Yet things are not ever what they seem in diplomacy.

The disclosure of a late sixteenth century plot in Malta was recently made possible by opening the archives of the island's Inquisition. This plot has a strange resemblance to the activities of the Scots diplomats at the beginning of the same century. The essence of it was that the island would be subject to a naval action by English and French ships which would have the secret support of the French contingent of the Knights of St John and of the Order's Grand Master, Verdalle. Nominally, the island was the sovereign territory of the St John Knights but politically it was subject to Spain and by being taken over thus it would come under French and English protection and the link with Spain would be broken. But this was not all. The brunt of the assault on the island was to be borne by the Turkish army and navy; and the essence of the plot uncovered by the Inquisition was that England's spymaster, Walsingham, had sent agents into the Mediterranean to plan the joint operation with the Sultan of Turkey and the other parties concerned.

In the light of this revelation we may be less disposed to look on Cuthbert Home as a peculiar Scot with a taste for travel and exotic or Oriental life. Rather does he appear as a trend-setter in diplomacy, a man as deep as England's spymaster, Walsingham, living and plotting seventy years before Walsingham's time. Similarly, the chivalrous and crusading prince James IV appears no more as a residual figure of Bruce's days, but a man of the future obsessed with playing a leading role in the cockpit of the world-changing struggle for commercial power, and seeking to put himself at the head of the Venetian army and fleet. Failing in this, he built his own fleet to send into the Mediterranean and began building his own alliances. The motive and inspiration were supplied by a present historical necessity, not simply an old dream; Western Europe was demanding life more abundant and was threatened with death, and the fall of Constantinople had fouled the trade channel with the East. In Cuthbert's day, and James's, Portugal's efforts to establish the new route to the East by the Cape were still tentative as was Spain's exploitation of the New World, and so a return to Jerusalem and the re-opening of the old trade routes remained the primary solution, especially for Spain and Portugal's rivals.

Only if conceived in the old terms of a renewed war between Christendom and Islam was the old solution Quixotic and outmoded; in terms of expanding part of Christendom in the West in exchange for the prizes in the East it became practical politics—or practical, if treacherous, diplomacy. That an alliance with Cairo was the key to expansion, and the formula for suppressing a rival appears to have entered the minds of Cuthbert Home and James IV in 1510 as insidiously as those of Walsingham and Elizabeth in 1580. Since England was travelling the road of Spain on the earlier date, the collision at Flodden was all the more inevitable, but not from chivalrous folly.

Cuthbert Home's ports of call within Christendom can only be conjectured, but it is not improbable that the Scottish dove landed on the island of Rhodes, headquarters of the Knights of St John, which had a Scottish chapter. About forty years later the Scottish knights, under their leader Sir John Sandilands, took part against the old Church in the upheaval of the Reformation. The Hospitallers of St John had absorbed the property of the Templars under Papal decree and also some of the Templars themselves. The plot of 1580 just referred to suggests that in some degree the Templars had secretly absorbed St John in Malta. In Scotland, where the Bruce tradition and the Templar tradition marched hand in hand, this was even more likely. The Templars and their successors knew that their downfall was made possible by the final loss of Jerusalem but that to open the golden gates again, even by composition with the Turks, would restore their international power. That was why the dream of Jerusalem died hard in the circle round the Scottish Throne.

Doubtless their circle worked with a larger one and there was a deep mystic cult allied with power vistas and growing material advantages behind it. Cuthbert Home's travels through Christendom and Egypt have the appearance of a journey through these labyrinths of power and international intrigue. It is significant that he arrived home with Alexander Stewart, bastard son of James IV, who was both Abbot of Dunfermline and Archbishop of St Andrews. At exactly this time the Pope finally disjoined Coldingham Priory from Durham Abbey and placed it under Dunfermline, and so the Dunfermline Abbot and fellow traveller of Cuthbert Home became Prior of Coldingham too; the returning Master of Fast Castle seemed to be the good neighbour or friend of half the world, the King, his natural son, the Pope and the Sultan.

This supplies part of the solution to the enigma of Fast Castle— the early invisible and unchronicled history to which we have responded with the theory of Templar occupation. The subsequent enigma of the rage for possession of the castle has a like answer—it was required for some kind of continuation of its early veiled use and tradition. The secret diplomacy of both Patrick Home and Cuthbert prospered after the Homes and their friends captured the monarchy, and Fast Castle appears to have been an adjunct to their power at home and the advance of the world ambitions of their circle.

It would be a mistake to think that the castle lost its esoteric character when Cuthbert Home was carried away lifeless from Flodden leaving his cares behind him on the battlefield. There was a military interlude while Alexander, the third Lord Home, took over the castle on behalf of friend Cuthbert's widow and daughters, but two years later this Home was declared an outlaw and the Scottish Regent placed a garrison in the castle. The Homes snatched it back long enough to level its walls, then, when more permanently restored to their possession in 1521, they rebuilt it. The military story continues during the wars with England in the forties, and the castle fell into English hands soon after the battle of Pinkie in 1547. Thomas Gower, the Marshal of Berwick, who was made the castle governor knew the Border well, and seemed to have a notion for the castle. His superior officer the Earl of Rutland informed him in 1549 that Somerset had ordered Fast Castle to be destroyed and abandoned. This prompted Gower to write to Rutland urging him to move the English Council and Somerset to grant the castle a reprieve; he stressed that it was important for storing supplies and conveying them by sea and put in a plea for enjoying the house and lands himself. It was neither destroyed this time, nor did it fall to Mr Gower for the Homes organised a party of young men to take it by stratagem. That ended its military career, except for a spell twenty years later when it was occupied by an English garrison with the consent of the Scottish Regent Morton. A plan of the castle, as it was when Gower coveted it, was made under the direction of the Earl of Rutland in 1549, the last year of its hostile and unauthorised occupation.

When the castle fell to the English in 1547 it belonged to the Logans of Restalrig. Indeed the castle owner was Rogert Logan, the father of our Robert who signed the treasure contract with John Napier. Our Logan's father had just been charged, by the Privy Council, in May 1547, with the keeping of the Dowlaw balefire. The Dowlaw height towered directly over Fast Castle crag and was one of a chain of fiery warnings of enemy approach stretching from the Border into the heart of Scotland. St Abb's Head was the nearest to the enemy country, next was Dowlaw above Fast Castle, then followed Dounlaw, a Lammermoor peak above Spott, followed by the coastal cone North Berwick Law, followed by Traprain Law, a buried treasure site, and on to Arthur's Seat presiding over Holyrood Palace and the capital city; another hilltop to the west carried the warning as far as Linlithgow Palace. The glaring balefire on Dowlaw at night throwing its glow and flame on the dashing waves, the ebony cliffs and naked tower must have looked like a large wall torch thoughtfully provided to illuminate an interesting corner of inferno. Alas, the Dowlaw balefire was not of much avail even to the castle under its nose.

The entry of the Logans into possession of Fast Castle after the death of Cuthbert Home was a guarantee that it did not lose its mysteries. It was our Logan's grandfather, Sir Robert Logan, who married the heiress of Cuthbert Home, his daughter Elizabeth; it was in the same way, by marriage to an heiress, that a Logan ancestor had acquired the valuable lands of Restalrig. The Restalrigs or Lestalrics were an ancient family who had held the barony of Lestalric

45

along with the town of Leith since 1124; in 1382 a Sir Robert Logan married the Lestalric heiress and their son married a daughter of King Robert II. The Logans shared in the mystique that thickened round the Scottish throne at the time of Robert I, and had their place in the inner temple. The favourite family name of Robert for their first born reflected their links with this time. Before acquiring Restalrig their main land base was the barony of Grugar in Ayrshire, and it was as descendants of Fergus, Lord of Galloway and Carrick, that they originally bore some significance which was increased by their association with Bruce in that cradle of his power. After the King had died two of the Logans were chosen for the small band of knights elected to carry the royal heart to the Holy land.

Their departure was attended by high and elaborate ceremony. The strangeness of it is accepted by us as a matter of course because we look on it as characteristic of a strange and distant time, but it must have been a contradiction and anomaly even then—the casting away of the precious relic and of the lives of the men. If the main mission on which the knights set out was to entomb the heart in a holy place they would have avoided the risk of battle for a season; on the other hand, if they had been bent mainly on fighting the Moors they would have laid aside the relic safely for a time. All that seems certain is that what they did was not a careless accident—they planned it that way. A friend of the present writer has solved the riddle for himself by deciding it was a ritual suicide. In that case the overt aim must have been to keep alive by a striking deed the vision of Jerusalem and everything it symbolised for their sect.

The two Logans who thus died, apparently sacrificially, in Spain have the honour of mention by Barbour in his history of *The Brus*:

> 'The Gud Lord Douglas thair was slayne
> And William Suncler syne alsua
> And othir worthy knichtis twa.'

The two worthy knights are then named, Sir Robert and Sir William Logan. As a result of their dedication the Logans shared not only in the Bruce mystique but in the enduring pattern of power associated with it. We credit the continuation of ideologies and political affinities for centuries on end in our modern swift-moving age. Yet in a slower and more traditional age we are blind to the enduring patterns of power and the continuity of ideas partly because they do not take the shapes of our own time and partly because power and its inspiration were then more deeply veiled. Even with this customary blindness it is easy to see that the Logan acquisition of the important Scottish maritime area of Leith and Restalrig and their marriage into the Royal House were not lucky accidents. Nor was the marriage later on to the heiress of Cuthbert Home and the inheritance of Fast Castle a mere matter of the luck of the Logans.

We may assume then, that Fast Castle was a fortress of the Templars in its shadowy days, and we find grounds for the further assumption that it continued in the same tradition. The castle owners, Patrick and Cuthbert Home, apparently attempted to adapt James IV's revival of crusading aims to sixteenth century conditions and the Logans later joined with the Homes in maintaining links with international centres of intrigue. They dedicated the castle to conspiracy and the habits that marked it in the period of Templar occupation. Fast Castle was at the beginning, and remained, an esoteric castle and place of conspiracy, continuing the same use and tradition much as does a sanctuary or a temple. But temple of a sort it perhaps was and remained—a sanctuary also and an unsuspected power-house. At no time was this more apparent than in its final phase in the last third of the sixteenth century when much happened that was fateful to Scotland, but chiefly under the surface. It was also the period that encompassed the careers of our Fast Castle treasure hunters, the young Earl of Gowrie, John Napier, Francis Bothwell and the last Baron of Restalrig and Fast Castle, Robert Logan.

# 4 Robert Logan, a destined conspirator

ROBERT LOGAN, last Baron of Restalrig and Fast Castle, was a boy of six when his father died in 1561. His mother, Lady Agnes Gray, then married Lord Home. The boy was thereby tied to the Homes by a double knot: through his grandfather's marriage to Cuthbert Home's daughter and through his mother's second marriage to the fifth Lord Home. As a result of this later marriage there was a son and heir to Lord Home, and young Logan was brought up with this half-brother and under the guardianship of his step-father, who was meantime the Lord of Fast Castle. It was while Lord Home was Lord of the castle that an important visitor called (probably the most important visitor since Margaret Tudor had bed and breakfast at the castle in 1503), Sir Nicholas Throgmorton, ambassador of Queen Elizabeth of England. Throgmorton wrote to Elizabeth's Minister, Cecil, on July 11th 1567, from Berwick, and said, 'This day I take my journey towards the Faux Castle where the deputy wardens to the Lord Hume do receive me'. The Scottish Secretary, Maitland of Lethington, had written to Throgmorton on the 8th saying he would meet him at Coldingham and lead him to the castle—he had added a warning about the hospitality, 'You can have no good cheer, yet I dare well assure youm you shall be welcome'.

In a way, Throgmorton's visit was linked with Margaret Tudor's visit at the beginning the century. When James IV was killed at Flodden, his wife Margaret was left with an infant in her arms who grew up and reigned as James V. But the uncertain feudal loyalties to the Crown, made more disgracefully uncertain by the eroding influence of the English Reformation on the Scottish Catholic Monarchy, quite broke his heart and he died of melancholy. This time the heir was a girl only six days old—Mary Stewart, the granddaughter of Margaret Tudor. It was events in the life of Mary Stewart that brought Throgmorton to Fast Castle, sent in haste by the Queen of England because Margaret Tudor's granddaughter was now a queen and a queen in trouble. She was shut up in Lochleven Castle accused of helping to blow up her husband in order to marry another man and both her crown and life were in danger.

This shocking crisis threatened Queen Elizabeth too. It might prompt the French to send an army into Scotland to quell the rebellious Lords who had locked up their Queen. The French army might restore the Queen in Scotland and try to make good her claim to the Crown of England while they were on the scene or, alternatively, they might try to perform the service of securing the Double Crown for her infant son and make themselves caretakers for him on both sides of the border. The initial reaction of Elizabeth was to restore the status quo at all costs, to get back to the day before yesterday; this was Throgmorton's brief, along with the secret idea of having the young prince moved to England as insurance.

On the evening of his arrival at the castle the English ambassador had a meeting with three men representing the Lords who had shut up the Queen at Lochleven. There was his host, Alexander, fifth Lord Home, step-father of our Robert Logan and custodian of the castle in his minority, there was also William Maitland of Lethington, the Queen's Secretary, and Sir James Melville, a member of the Privy Council. The next morning Throgmorton sent a despatch back to Cecil, Elizabeth's Minister, saying that he had been treated well but adding 'according to the state of the place which is fitter to lodge prisoners than folk at liberty'—the downstairs ghosts of the hostages had apparently cast a chill on the upstairs hospitality. Apart from the formal diplomatic representations by Throgmorton, the Fast Castle talks appeared to establish a rapport between the ambassador on the one side and Lethington and Lord Home on the other which bore fruit later. After their talks they rode to Edinburgh and were there escorted into the city by four hundred horsemen, but although he stayed long and had many more talks, Throgmorton was not permitted to see the captive Queen.

The Queen of Scots was spirited out of Lochleven Castle, the unsuccessful battle on her behalf was fought at Langside and she escaped to asylum—which proved to be lifelong imprisonment—in England. Before long, the first attempt at her rescue and elevation to the English Throne was made by the North of England Catholic nobility. It failed and the Earls of Northumberland and Westmoreland and 'divers others of the principal rebels' fled to Scotland. This brought Fast Castle back into the picture. In December 1569, Queen Elizabeth sounded an alarm to George Carey in Berwick concerning the fugitive rebels. 'It is vehemently suspected,' she wrote, 'that the said Earls and their accomplices will either be conveyed to the west coast of Scotland; or else by help of Lord Home will put into Fast Castle, there to remain until they escape by sea. Which we rather suspect because we understand that the Lord Home has of late victualled the said castle.' A few weeks later, on January 9th of 1570, the Queen's cousin, Lord Hunsdon, wrote to the Scottish Regent, Morton, declaring that 'the Countess of Northumberland has been received at Home Castle where she is yet, unless conveyed this day to Fast Castle. The queen,' Lord Hunsdon threatened, 'will make Lord Home repent of his folly.'

This threat was not long delayed in its fulfilment. On May 5th, 1570, the Earl of Sussex wrote to Elizabeth from Scottish soil and reported that Fast Castle had been seized. Two thousand English soldiers were involved under Sir William Drury. The ten retainers of Lord Home holding the castle gave up without a shot, on promise of their lives—they may have heard that a dozen men could hold the castle against an army, but they were two short. Sussex in his despatch referred to the castle as the place 'where your rebels have been most maintained,' adding that he had placed certain shot inside until the Queen's pleasure should be made known. He explained that he found the castle did not belong to Lord Home but was 'the rightful inheritance of the Lord of Restalrig, now a ward and son of Lady Home by a former husband.' The Queen replied that the castle should be kept and guarded at her command, and their Scottish friends should be persuaded that it was done in their interest.

Young Logan was not disposed to think so and was not out of harmony with his guardian in allowing Elizabeth's rebels the use of his inherited stronghold, as was shown when he presently entered the castle of Edinburgh along with his stepfather, Home, to help to hold it for the Queen of Scots. Secretary Maitland was another who joined the last-ditchers of the Queen of Scots. Home and Maitland had taken part at Fast Castle in the first secret talks with Ambassador Throgmorton fresh from England, and they were both parties to breaking up the shot-gun marriage between Mary Stewart and Bothwell, which they were prepared to put in that light. They had concurred in her forced abdication and the coronation of her infant son, James, but with her separation from Bothwell achieved and apparently permanent they renewed their allegiance; indeed, they began plotting for the marriage of Mary to England's premier nobleman, the Duke of Norfolk, with the backstairs help of their friend, Throgmorton.

This scheme was chiefly the brain-child of Secretary Maitland and had the consent of the Queen of Scots in captivity. There was more than consent; it inspired her to new romantic and regal heights in her correspondence with Norfolk. Things advanced so far that Throgmorton wrote saying that a powerful and numerous party in England had been won for the scheme and it only remained for Secretary Maitland to come to the English Court and break the affair to Elizabeth. (It has already been mentioned that Secretary Maitland made his first move at renewing his service to the Queen of Scots when he secretly sent her copies of the casket letters from Fast Castle, according to Mary's ambassador, the Bishop of Ross.)

Others broke the affair to Elizabeth and saved Maitland the embarassment for by this time the scheme had also received the blessing of the French and Spanish courts. It was one of the several shocks of Elizabeth's life. The leaders of her nobility were aligning themselves with the Scottish claimant to her crown with the backing of the Catholic rulers of Europe who regarded her merely as illegitimate. The result was that Norfolk landed in the Tower and the Regent Moray, who was in power in Scotland, in order to assuage the wrath of Elizabeth, promptly put Maitland, too, under restraint. He had him charged with a hand in murdering Mary's husband, Darnley, and he intended to make the charge stick.

Those holding Edinburgh Castle for the Queen of Scots, however, came to Maitland's rescue. Kirkcaldy of Grange, who commanded the castle, permanently transferred Maitland to his care, within the castle walls. Lord Home, Maitland's partner at the Fast Castle talks, did his bit too; he turned up in Edinburgh on the date of Maitland's trial with a sufficient force of border horsemen to ensure the charge was deserted by Regent Moray and, in the absence of the accusers, an acquittal was claimed. The siege of the castle was drawn a little tighter under three short-lived Regents, but it was eventually the longer-living Regent Morton who broke the deadlock. He made a bargain with Elizabeth to send in Sir William Drury from Berwick with fifteen hundred English soldiers by land and heavy assault batteries by sea. The defenders nevertheless hung on; a banner of defiance was raised on David's Tower, the castle's highest point, and help from France was believed to be on the way. The English batteries were planted all round the rock, two of them on the present line of Princes Street (then a green ridge) and one near the west end of the present thoroughfare. By 23rd May, 1573 the guns of the defenders had been silenced and the castle walls were beginning to turn to sand as prophesied by John Knox. Drury computed that nearly three thousand great shot had by then been poured into the castle and its ramparts. When the truce came and surrender terms were discussed, the garrison was promised life and liberty, all except nine persons. The English general, Drury, might have wavered even concerning the nine, but Regent Morton was out for blood. The nine included the castle commander, Kirkcaldy of Grange, the Queen of Scots Secretary Maitland and Lord Home with his stepson Robert Logan. Kirkcaldy was executed; Maitland, the Secretary, died in prison, by his own hand it was said; Home, a sick man, was allowed to expire in peace, and young Logan, apparently because he was only eighteen, was spared.

Perhaps he was spared because of his resourceful mother, the Lady Agnes Gray who had already persuaded Sir William Drury that she would have Fast Castle back. Drury wrote from Restalrig, the seat of the Logans, to further this suit with Elizabeth. Elizabeth in turn wrote to Regent Morton saying she understood Lord Home's wife was no party to her husband's doings and the 'poor lady' ought to have good assurance of the right of Fast Castle to her and her heirs. The Scottish Regent Morton received Fast Castle from the hands of the English garrison a few months after Drury presented him with the ruins of Edinburgh Castle. The 'poor lady', Logan's mother, had the rights of herself and her heirs restored, as Elizabeth had urged and three years after the Edinburgh Castle surrender Robert Logan, being of age, took possession in the legal sense of his Fast Castle inheritance. Neither his estate nor his person remained under penalty or restraint for harbouring Elizabeth's rebels or for his part in the last stand on behalf of the Queen of Scots.

Once in the hands of Robert Logan deeper shadows closed round Fast Castle and the place itself was lit up by only occasional shafts of official light. It was not Logan's regular place of residence. He had Gunsgreen House, about ten miles away at Eyemouth, which served better for his drinking and sociable occasion, his yuletide feasts and the like. The family seat was at Restalrig and he had some howf in the Canongate also, but like his step-father, Home, he victualled Fast Castle for occasional use.

If the castle's recorded connections with events are few, there are many distinct links of the castle-owner with the history of his time, with contemporary plots and plotters. Logan's first connection with conspiracy was rather by way of a counter-plot: when King James was still a youth and his mother had been a prisoner in England for over ten years, the Duke of Guise sent the King's cousin, Esmé Stuart or D'Aubigny, from France to captivate and corrupt him, and gather into his hands the reigns of power. Almost overnight D'Aubigny became Earl of Lennox, proof of his success, and his aide, James Stewart, became Earl of Arran; between them these two hustled Morton the one-time regent to the gallows. Behind their success loomed an invasion threat from France. Queen Elizabeth frantically incited a counter-plot led by the elder Gowrie, Mar and the Master of Glamis; the youthful King was made virtual prisoner at Gowrie's castle of Ruthven, otherwise Huntingtower. This Ruthven raid caused Guise's agent, Lennox, to return hastily to France.

In the sequel the King regained his liberty and Gowrie was executed at the close of the second instalment of the plot (as we recounted when discussing his custody of the casket letters). Lennox was prevented from returning by illness and died in France. Arran, his lieutenant and successor, showed his hand in Gowrie's execution and also in a warrant issued for the delivery of Fast Castle, which was suspected of some connection with Gowrie's plotting. The order was issued to Robert Logan, Lady Agnes Gray (his mother) and Thomas Lyon of Balduky (his new step-father). This was Logan's first new brush with danger since he escaped the death penalty after his march with the vanquished out of Edinburgh Castle.

Both he and the castle were drawn into deeper conspiracy when a new figure moved towards the footlights, the Master of Gray, another man out of France, who had gone there after he left St. Andrews at sixteen, and, like Lennox, was an agent of the Duke of Guise; he was also a link with the Queen of Scots in prison. He harboured the Jesuit, Father Holt, in his Edinburgh house and went on a secret mission to the Duke of Guise, on the King's behalf, along with the staunch Catholic agent, Graham of Fintry. His first mission for the King had been to bring from France the young son of Lennox, the deceased favourite.

The Master of Gray possessed the renaissance male ornamentation and beauty on which the young King fed; his dazzling aura ensured easy entry into the King's good graces, and into Arran's. To ingratiate himself further with both he spilled over the secrets of Guise and the political secrets of the Queen of Scots. In consequence the Master was entrusted by Arran and the young King with a private mission to Elizabeth to secure for King James a special 'league' with England. The Master was proudly introduced by

Arran to Elizabeth's cousin, Lord Hunsdon, at a border conference and thereafter he was left to descend on London to complete his delicate mission with the English Queen and her Ministers. So persuasive was Gray that he not only obtained top level agreement on the 'league' between Elizabeth and James, but further agreement that he should be the 'league's' future instrument in Scotland. Arran, on his advice, was to be eliminated as too venal and one too inclined towards France to be trusted.

To give effect to this new twist it was arranged that Mar, Glamis and others who had helped Gowrie to kidnap James would get English help to march back into Scotland. At the same time, Gray would collect extra strength for them on the Border, including the young Francis Stewart, Earl of Bothwell, who has been introduced as a Fast Castle treasure hunter. With Bothwell was the new Lord Home, and along with him Robert Logan. These two, Home and Logan, had different fathers but the same mother, Lady Agnes Gray; through her they were related to the leader of the plot, the Master of Gray who was, therefore, a cousin of both.

Bothwell, Home and Logan rallied forces at Kelso; and Angus, Mar, Glamis and the rest advanced over the border to join them. The combination was effective and by the time they reached Stirling, where Arran was with the King, the rebel army was eight thousand strong. Arran fled and the King accepted his new Ministers.

While Gray was in London promoting the plot Logan wrote to him and also conducted an intimate and gossipy correspondence with Gray's collaborator, Archibald Douglas. Douglas was the nephew of the one-time Regent Morton, and one of the two brothers who unearthed the casket letters in the Potter Row. He had fled to England when his uncle was belatedly seized for the murder of the King's father, Darnley. This Archibald was said to have been involved too —at any rate his servant testified on the scaffold that he saw him return from the Kirk o'Fields explosion minus a shoe and coated in lime and dust. To reinstate himself in Scotland, Archibald began to work clandestinely for the Queen of Scots in prison and for the agents of Guise, when they were in the ascendant, but he anticipated Gray in transferring his services to Elizabeth's spymaster, Walsingham. In one of his letters to Douglas, Robert Logan asked him to recommend his service to 'that able man Secretary Walsingham whom he holds in higher regard than all the noblemen in England and whom his master, the Earl of Bothwell, loves entirely well.' Logan appears to have obtained the recommendation he sought.

After the Master of Gray returned to Edinburgh, Logan received a cipher number '876++' enabling him to correspond secretly with Secretary Walsingham. His role, if there was no other, was to receive letters for the Master of Gray from Walsingham. His control of the post road from Berwick ensured that these secret letters never fell into any other hands, anyway not in Scotland.

Immediately after Arran was driven out, the English ambassador arrived to complete the negotiation of the 'league' with the Master of Gray and his friends, now in power. The ambassador was empowered at the same time to raise with the King, on Queen Elizabeth's behalf, the delicate matter of terminating the exile of Archibald Douglas. Despite the undertones of regicide in this case, the King was accommodating, and agreed on a trial that would have regard to Douglas's 'surety'.

When the trial came round, Robert Logan and other Logans were members of the packed jury which cleared their friend Archibald Douglas. Laundered and stainless Douglas returned to London as Scotland's ambassador and Logan continued to act as a two-way channel of intelligence for him. The 'league' with England which Gray had laboured for came almost immediately under strain; Mary Queen of Scots was put on trial and the shadow of the axe was on the wall. The Master of Gray set out on a mission of intercession to Elizabeth's court—he could not evade it—and Robert Logan was a member of his suite on the journey. For Logan to go was in character with the part he had played in the last stand for the Queen at Edinburgh Castle. Without hypocrisy he certainly could be associated with the attempt to save the Queen's life when he had nearly rendered his own on her behalf. The open record of the dialogue between Elizabeth and Gray also points to some sincerity on the part of Gray in the endeavour to avert the execution. Independent testimony confirms that he acted on the mission as a true 'Scottisman', as he vowed he would.

Naturally, however, in the revulsion after Mary Stewart's execution Gray incurred most of the odium, having been the chief architect of the 'league' with England and having failed in his mission to save the Queen's life. King James allowed him to slide, happy to have a scapegoat. Gray's fate was similar to that of Elizabeth's Secretary, Davison, who was ruined by his royal mistress so that she might seem blameless. While Gray's credit went down that of his rival John Maitland rose; but Gray's credit went down in England too. He was now disliked for his spirited dialogue with

Elizabeth and for standing by his co-delegate, Sir Robert Melville, who spoke even more boldly. He was also blamed for an apparent stiffening of the official attitude in Scotland. Leicester, who had been his friend, was now among those who sought his injury and sent to Scotland a copy of a confidential letter from Gray which showed that he favoured the private ending of the Scottish Queen's life if her fate was sealed. In that respect so did Elizabeth, but she could find no candidate for this private commision.

Richard Douglas wrote to his uncle Archibald, the ambassador in London, and referred to Leicester's betrayal of the Master of Gray. The nephew told his uncle that Restalrig would let him know more fully about the matter and would also reveal the Master's mind. Restalrig, otherwise Logan, not only informed Ambassador Douglas on the point but wrote concerning it to Elizabeth's Secretary, Walsingham. Writing over his English cipher number '876++', Logan reported to Walsingham that he had found the Master of Gray greatly altered towards England. Being inquisitive to understand, he went on, he had caused the Master to dilate, 'as in all things he is plain with me'. It was the copy of Gray's private letter to Leicester that was behind everything he had learned. It had been shown to the King to bring about Gray's disgrace. The Baron of Restalrig and Fast Castle then proceeded to veiled blackmail and a transparent hocus-pocus on behalf of his cousin. He wrote, 'Fear not of anything that the Master can attempt against your estate. I shall be able to cause you to anticipate.' He meant, 'Tremble in case the Master attempts to do you some evil turn with Elizabeth. I will let you know what's coming to you.' That was the personal blackmail part. The hocus-pocus consisted in a promise of the important things his Lordship would get to know through Logan if Gray remained at the King's elbow. 'I am esteemed participant in all his proceedings,' he harped and added 'if he be fallen I cannot goodly stand to do your Lordship any service or pleasure.' Having conveyed to Walsingham that both he and England had a vested interest in saving the Master, Logan indicated the simple course of getting Leicester to write to Gray, repudiating the compromising letter. To stress the gravity of the situation he mentioned the anti-English pasquils and placards freely in evidence in Edinburgh and urged Walsingham to reply quickly.

Andrew Lang, the Scottish historian, made a study of Robert Logan's character in connection with the Gowrie mystery and treated this letter as proof that Logan was a treacherous and worthless fellow since he was here offering to act the spy on his cousin, Gray, and turn over entrusted secrets to the English secret service. Walsingham, the English spy chief, was not quite so simple minded. He did not rush to save Gray and make sure of these precious secrets—no reply arrived at Fast Castle either from him or from Leicester.

The following month Logan wrote again to Walsingham, 'No answer yet,' he complained. 'True it is,' he went on by way of proclaiming the consequences, 'that the Master had become a very great enemy to your Queen's Majesty, your country and all your proceedings.' He elaborated that he, Logan, had been sent with letters of credit by Gray to the Catholic Earl of Huntly in the north east, to enable Gray to recover his old standing with the Catholics. A plot was proposed to seize the King and to make a treaty with France on the basis of liberty of Catholic conscience in Scotland. He, Logan, had worked on Huntly to this purpose and found him more than willing. Huntly had promised that his most special agent, Captain Ker, a vehement Roman Catholic, would follow on Logan's heels for a conference with him and the Master.

Poury Ogilvie, a double agent of King James and Queen Elizabeth, also reported to Walsingham Gray's overtures to the Catholic Earl of Huntly, in which Logan was the go-between. Chancellor Maitland spilled the information too, representing that he had beguiled Fintry into giving way the secret. All sources in Scotland were anxious to inform Walsingham of Catholic plots to make his flesh creep in view of the impending war with Spain. Logan's motive was to bid up Gray's price, the King's to enhance the value of his good will for England in her coming conflict with Spain.

When it came to the reckoning for Gray it was not Leicester's letter that pulled him down; his accuser was Sir William Stewart, brother of Arran whom Gray had overthrown. Stewart raked up everything, past and present, to the Master's discredit, but especially he alleged that Gray had tried to interfere with the mandate which he, Stewart, had received from the King for a mission to Paris. Gray was banished. He was given a month to leave the country from 24th May (the execution at Fotheringay had been in February) and he was out of the country by June 7th. Logan, Francis Bothwell and Lord Home pledged themselves jointly to the tune of £40,000 that he would remain away as long as the King wished. In fact, a pardon was sent to him in Paris in the autumn and he was free to return, but he stayed on for a time before he returned to become again keeper of the King's wardrobe. Logan's share of the surety for his cousin belies any belief that he was ready to betray him or his secrets for a few pounds to Walsingham, the spy master. Like his manoeuvre to have Leicester's enmity reversed, his signature to the £40,000 bond was evidence of how close he stood to Gray.

At the time of Gray's decline and betrayal by Leicester, Logan became fully involved in Gray's reversion to the old policy of intrigue with the Catholic factions and powers. He carried out the confidential mission to the Scottish Catholic potentate, Huntly, and arranged to meet the vehement Catholic agent, Ker, for discussions in detail up until the summer of the year before the Armada. That year and the next, Gray was plotting in Paris, while Bothwell in Scotland was proclaiming openly for an alliance with Spain and working for it secretly, and Douglas was believed to be engaged in similar mole-like activities in London. Logan was in league with all three.

It was with Bothwell now, more than with Gray, that Logan appeared to be associating—'my master Bothwell', as he had described him in his letter to Archibald Douglas three years earlier. Bothwell's importance was increasing while Gray's declined, even after his return and as already mentioned, it was on account of his dealings with Bothwell that Logan was denounced by the Privy Council.

The strongest pointer to Logan's activities in the period following his dealings with Gray is provided by a later event—the secret visit to Fast Castle in February 1598 of George Ker, who had escaped in 1593 from Edinburgh Castle. Later Ker left for the Continent, departing the country probably by the way he now returned. (He was the leading figure of the sensational conspiracy of late 1592 known as the affair of the Spanish 'blanks'.) His homing instinct had brought him across the sea straight to the castle on the crag. It was John Colville, the agent at one time of the elder Gowrie and later Bothwell's right hand man, who reported the return of George Ker in 1598. By this time Colville was spying for the English government, and his report was confirmed in an intercepted letter which Ker had sent from Calais. The letter was to inform a friend he had bargained with a Burntisland skipper, John Brown, to take him from Calais and land him either at Fast Castle or Eyemouth.

The eventual return of the Catholic conspirator, Ker, to Fast Castle made it plain that Logan's business with the Catholic Earl of Huntly on the eve of the Armada had matured. Logan, like his Lord Bothwell, had put a foot in the Catholic camp. The alignment was entirely political: Bothwell was a Protestant Lord, although the King belonged to the devil's kirk of witchcraft and magic; Logan was an indifferent, who liked to conclude his letters by invoking 'Christ's holy protection' for the rogue to whom he was writing. Huntly, for his part, was a faithful Catholic who had subscribed to the Protestant confession to get closer to the King and make himself Captain of the Royal Guard. The Master of Gray was equally happy at mass in Paris or singing psalms with Lord Hunsdon at Foulden Kirk near the Border.

All the main moments in Robert Logan's career of conspiracy, except the crowning episode of the Gowrie plot, have been given a passing glance. All of it has been misrepresented or misunderstood: Logan has been represented as having a sheer love of plotting for plotting's sake—or plotting for the sake of paltry gain and selling his friends and their secrets. His code signature '876++' in the files of spymaster Walsingham is considered conclusive proof of his venality and treachery. But this was not the man, for instead of betraying friends he was ever at hand to serve and save them, and repeatedly pledged his credit on their behalf. So far from owing money, the highest in the land were heavily in his debt when he died and to their discredit they evaded payment by helping on the processess that led to his obloquy and forfeiture. His plotting followed a consistent political pattern and was not unprincipled. As a youth, along with his step-father, he helped the escape of the northern rebels via Fast Castle, because they had risen on behalf of the Queen of Scots; and he was a last-ditcher for the Queen inside Edinburgh Castle. When the schemes of the Queen's Guisian friends in Paris threatened to isolate and subvert Scotland he went with the political swing towards the 'league' with England, and he was an active agent for the 'league' under his cousin Gray. When the 'league' suffered crisis in the trial of Mary Stewart and the cavalier treatment of the Scottish mercy deputation on which he served, he was naturally associated with the patriotic protest and the return swing of the pendulum. At the same time the danger to England threatened by the Armada opened new opportunities for dealing with both France and Spain and for re-asserting an independent Scottish foreign policy. Like others, including the King himself, Logan regarded this as a Scottish opportunity, and went in for foreign affairs, necessarily clandestine.

A rugged patriotism may be observed throughout the man's career. If he was 'a favourer of thieves reputed,' it was his affinity with Border freedom and lawlessness coming uppermost; he was related through drink to common, rough living humanity and took time off to be a human being, so that he appears as a 'good fellow' even in the eyes of a political spy. But there was something more about the rugged conspirator—there was an ingredient of destiny. It was not merely inclination or accident that opened to him in youth the experience and knowledge of Northumberland earls smuggled out of Fast Castle's secluded harbour, of the castle serving for secret talks with Throgmorton leading to the Norfolk marriage plot, of Secretary Maitland closeted there while his wife copied out the casket letters for secret transmission to the dethroned Queen of Scots. That, and the endless conspiratorial talk that naturally accompanied the cooped up days of the Edinburgh Castle siege, were all something he was born into, but besides these he had the relationship of confidant, even in matters of life and death, with important people like Minister Gray, Ambassador Douglas, the Earl of Bothwell and the Gowries which seemed to be pre-ordained, as was also, apparently, his relationship with Walsingham, the head of the English secret service. There was an occasion, too, when a visitor called and was informed he was away to Dalkeith on business with the King. There are strong hints that Logan's conspiracies were not a personal matter at all but were evidence of a hidden brotherhood of his day in which he occupied a position of importance, probably hereditary.

We have already insisted that it was not the luck of the Logans that enabled them to marry into the royal house, to travel in the company of death and the Bruce casket, to acquire the maritime estate of Restalrig—which is not without esoteric features in its landmarks—or to inherit Fast Castle. To this we would only add, it is hoped credibly, that Robert Logan, the last baron of Restalrig and Fast Castle, inherited his conspirator's role along with his mystery castle—his intrigues were his destiny to a very great degree. In the end, the tragedy of the Gowries in which he had so essential a part, drove him to revolt against that destiny and, embittered, to reply to his wife's protest that if he had all the lands between the Orient and the Occident he would sell them or give them away.

If the man Logan is considered seriously in this light, then his treasure hunt with Napier will appear in a more serious light too. It is partly the misreading of his character that has brought ridicule and some contempt on his contract with Napier. A man who was supposed to make all sorts of shifts to get money for drink, including the sale of his friends, might predictably be a treasure seeker and many other adventuresome things. He was even charged posthumously with being a burglar and stealing someone's plate; in his lifetime as well, an attempt was made to associate him with an alleged crime of two of his servants, a connection that would hardly turn a man into a criminal to-day.

# 5 *The calendar clue to the search*

THE CONSPIRACIES which the Fast Castle searchers were mixed up in supply a clue to what they were looking for, and so does the calendar for 1594, a year which reeked with invasion plots and the odour of Spanish gold. The very month the treasure contract was signed Scotland was agog with invasion rumours and astounded by a sensational event which occurred at Aberdeen, where a Spanish ship entered the port on July 16th and disembarked several passengers, including known Jesuits and a papal legate carrying secret papers and ten thousand crowns in Spanish gold. Because they attempted to detain the money and some of the men, the town and port officials were terrorised and the town nearly burnt down. The image of Spanish gold could not have been far from the thought of Robert Logan and John Napier, therefore, when they met to discuss the treasure of Fast Castle.

It was Father Gordon, the Jesuit uncle of the Earl of Huntly, who was recognised by the port officials. His companions proved to be Father William Crichton, another Scottish Jesuit, George Sampiretti and three English priests. Out of respect for, or fear of, the Earl of Huntly, Gordon and his Scots companion were not molested, but the magistrates detained Sampiretti and the three Englishmen. The latter were in trouble because they carried no credentials or passports from Queen Elizabeth; the former owed his difficulty to the fact that he was well supplied with credentials—from the Pope. The ten thousand crowns were also seized along with a letter said to be addressed to King James.

While the ministers were murmuring the Earls of Angus and Errol acted. They gathered together some retainers and made a forthright demand for the release of the men and the money. Within three days they were joined by the Earl of Huntly and a joint protest was then made to the magistrates against interference with liberty; it was evidently considered a case which came under the Arbroath declaration. By now the protesting earls were joined by several hundred mounted spearmen who began to burn down the town, and very soon the magistrates yielded and gave up the prisoners and the gold.

This was a climax. Earlier in the year the General Assembly of the Kirk passed a resolution which warned that the Spaniard had never ceased to plot the invasion of the island since the dispersal of his Armada six years before. There were many rumours and reports of Jesuits entering the country and Spanish ships arriving with subversive gold: vigilante forces rushed to Kirkcudbright on one such report concerning a Spanish ship; a similar fire brigade dash to Callander took place on news that subversive gold had turned up there. In April a Spanish ship was really seen at Montrose; the ship went aground and the Kirk sounded the alarm, but too late to make any fruitful search or arrests. Later the ministers alleged that gold had been removed from the grounded ship by the country's enemies and that the seditionists who had arrived with the money had been in secret conference with their friends in the area.

There is reason to believe that these events not only coloured the thoughts of Logan and Napier but may have prompted and directed them in their decision to search Fast Castle. An agent could have called at the castle, either from the Montrose ship or put ashore from the Aberdeen ship before it sailed up the coast. Indeed, these quiet calls at lonely parts of the coast were the rule, and sensational appearances at Aberdeen, Montrose or Kircudbright the exception. Another Scottish Jesuit, Father Abercromby, laid down this rule very firmly: he said it was never judicious to arrive at a town, and that he himself always disembarked at his grandfather's castle by the sea. There was a list of quiet places and, of course, Fast Castle was one of them, as the Privy Council came to believe. An agent at the time of all these Jesuit visitations could either have given Logan cause to seek out Napier to undertake the Fast Castle search, or have given Napier cause to go to Logan by conveying a secret report from Spain to the gold-smuggling Chisholms who were Napier's relatives.

What makes this speculation acute is that the search agreement coincided with the return of the Jesuits Gordon and Crichton who were leaders in the invasion business, part of which was concerned with landing invasion gold. If there was need for Spanish agents to come to Scotland to inquire into gold that may have been hidden too well, none could have been more qualified than these two who, with others, had organised the invasion plot known as the affair of the Spanish 'blanks', which had come to light about eighteen months earlier. Crichton had been in Scotland in the year of Armada and had attempted to organise an impromptu invasion when the Spanish ships were retreating by the northern route round Scotland. He had set out then for the Western Isles with the authority of Scottish Catholic earls in order to contact the Spanish admirals and persuade them to halt the retreat and make a stand on Scottish soil until joined by native Catholic forces, but the winds and tides had raced faster than his jaded nag could carry him. Next, he was in Spain at the court of Philip from where he wrote to Father Gordon in the Huntly stronghold to say he had opened the Spanish King's eyes to the way he had been deceived by the English Catholics, and had won him round to a new plan to invade England through Scottish soil. This was followed by what came to be known as the 'blanks' plot, which was in two parts: first, money was to be sent to organise supplies for the invading forces and to raise a supporting Scottish force and then, later, the Spanish troops were to sail. There were indications that the first part of this plan had been carried out and that the invasion gold had been delivered, but hidden too well. There were indications too that money raised for earlier invasion plans may have been salted away to await the day of decision.

We need to delve into the background of all the contemporary Scottish invasion plans to discover for ourselves all the factors that may have prompted the Fast Castle search. If we follow Father Crichton's rich career as an invasion organiser it will take us right back to the time his involvement began in the first year of the reign of Mary Queen of Scots. The Pope's legate, Nicholas de Gouda, travelled that year from Antwerp to Scotland in the company of Father Edmund Hay, a relative of the Earl of Errol. From Hay's home in the north they came down to Edinburgh and, dismissing their guard outside the town, they stole across the fields and cautiously proceeded along the town walls to make an unobserved entry. Next day they entered Holyrood Palace with the same furtiveness and were received by the Queen—an audience made possible only because the courtiers were at that hour spellbound under the pulpit of John Knox. The nineteen-year-old girl told the nuncio that she could offer nothing but her own personal loyalty to the Faith, to the point of death, and that she was afraid no Scottish bishops of the old church would be able to attend the Council of Trent. According to Gouda, the Queen declined to give him a safe conduct because it would only invite his murder, instead she put a young priest at his service, William Crichton. Crichton and Father Hay got Gouda safely away after dressing him up as a sailor and rowing him out to a ship some miles offshore. They embarked with him, and along with Crichton went other young emigrants including another Hay, a Tyrie, an Abercromby and a Murdoch. Within a few years all these young Scots emigrants had joined the Society of Jesus; although there were no Scottish delegates to the Council of Trent there was his alternative Scottish contribution to the counter-reformation.

Crichton's talent for organising invasions remained hidden for about twenty years. Then one day General Aquaviva, the head of the Jesuits, commanded him to give a report on Scottish affairs to a meeting in Rome. This report pleased the General and brought Crichton to the notice of the Pope and, consequently, he was selected for a mission to Scotland, after a briefing in France from the Duke of Guise and the English Catholic leader Father Parsons, and advice from Mary Stewart's ambassador in Paris, Beaton, the Archbishop of Glasgow. He was to promote plans to free the Queen of Scots from her English captivity and gain access to her son, still a minor; he was also to convey instructions to Esmé Stuart, otherwise D'Aubigny, otherwise the Earl of Lennox, who was the King's cousin and had been sent by Guise to Holyrood where he had become established as the boy king's idol. The letter for Lennox contained plans for Spanish and French landings in Scotland as a preliminary to the invasion of England. The English Catholic leader Father Parsons, had high hopes of Crichton's mission and, at that time, high hopes of support in Scotland. 'Our chief hope is in Scotland', he wrote to General Aquaviva, 'on it depends the conversion not only of England but of all the North of Europe.' It was the execution of the ironclad Morton by Lennox and Arran that seemed to open the floodgates of Catholic restoration.

In Scotland Crichton was received warmly by Lord Seton at Seton House near Edinburgh and then was smuggled into Holyrood and remained hidden in a secret chamber for three days during which time the invasion plans were discussed and articles were drawn up by the priest and signed by Lennox. Everybody was excited when Crichton got back to Paris. He reported to Parsons, Ambassador Beaton and Guise and to the Scots Jesuits, including those who had sailed away with him from Scotland so long ago. While Crichton travelled to Rome to exhibit his plans to the Pope, Father Parsons went jubilantly off to Madrid to report them to King Philip. Alas the plans languished. In the impatient priest's own words, what should have been carried out in two months was spread over two years and, in the meantime, the Earl of Gowrie had, by

August 1582, kidnapped the young king and sent Lennox, the agent of Guise, scuttling back to France.

About two years after the Gowrie coup, however, when Gowrie was dead and the young king free again, invasion was once more in the air. Archbishop Beaton wrote from Paris to Pope Gregory XIII urging him to desire General Aquaviva of the Jesuits to send Crichton and Gordon back to Scotland. They set sail but their Scottish ship was captured on the way by Dutch pirates. The merchant who had commissioned the ship convinced the Dutchmen that he was a friend and ally, but he denounced the priests in order not to strain their charity too far. Then, remembering the long sharp sword of the Earl of Huntly, he withdrew his denunciation of the member of the clan Gordon leaving the Jesuit Crichton, the only victim in their hands, to be taken a prisoner to Ostend where there was a hue and cry arising from the assassination of the Prince of Orange, allegedly by Jesuits. Crichton could not have arrived at a more opportune time for the local hangman. The gallows was promptly set up in his honour but, just to prove that truth was stronger than fiction, an English Government agent intervened to have him sent on to London for the sake of the information that might be extracted from him. Walsingham, the English spymaster, extracted from Crichton the information that he was returning to Scotland with a new set of invasion plans. The spymaster was able to explain in a letter to his friend Sir Ralph Sadler that when the priest was seized on the ship he pulled some papers out of his pocket and tore them up and cast them into the sea. Like the landlubber he was, however, he threw the pieces against the wind and they blew back in his face and so were picked up, pieced together and studied. Crichton spent the next couple of years in the Tower. When he was released by arrangement with Walsingham, Morgan, the Paris agent of Mary Stewart, suspected he had supplied much information as the price of his liberty and said so in a letter to the Queen which was critical of the Jesuits in general. This could well have been so as Crichton disliked the English Catholics; the English Catholics in exile, on the other hand, disliked, or many of them did, the Spanish policies of their leaders. Walsingham specialised in exploiting all these inner conflicts and mutual betrayals.

The young king himself, while Crichton was in the Tower, became a dabbler in invasion plans. Before the switch to the 'league' with England he chiefly employed the Master of Gray and David Graham of Fintry as his secret agents for intriguing with the

Catholic leaders at home and abroad. Father Holt, the Jesuit, who lived with Robert Logan's cousin, Gray, in Edinburgh for a while, reported this to his superiors, 'he enjoins Gray and Fintry', he wrote, 'to use no concealment in their efforts on behalf of the Catholic cause, promising them protection'. Indeed, at this time the eighteen-year-old James sent Gray and Fintry on a mission to Paris and despatched Lord Seton abroad to negotiate both with the King of France and the Pope, he dangled the bait of his conversion and sought to raise money to attack England—well, sought to raise money.

In 1584, however, the invasion outlook changed, and not just because the invasion specialist, Father Crichton, was languished in the Tower. The Duke of Guise who had sent his agents into Scotland suddenly gave up all interest external to France, because the protestant Henry of Navarre had come to the French throne and presented him with enough internal problems. At the same time Philip of Spain became disenchanted with the prospect of the conversion of James VI. Philip's minions, Dr Allen and Father Parsons, proclaimed simultaneously to their followers that an invasion from Scotland would only stiffen the national resistance of the English, it was better to welcome their Spanish friends and liberators on English beaches. And King James? He was moving towards the English 'league'. A close season set in for invasions from Scottish soil.

It was the face of Spain, really, that was behind every mask worn by the plotters. In the earliest days of Jesuit penetration of the island the Spanish Ambassador in London, Mendoza, was inspirer of everything; Father Parsons sent the Englishman, Holt, and the Welshman, Watt, up to Lord Seton's house in Scotland for meetings with important men, but it was really Mendoza who was prying into Scottish affairs. Parsons had been shaken by the arrest and execution of his co-worker Campion (the Campion canonised in our day), his own printing press was seized and he narrowly escaped. Refuge was provided in Mendoza's house and he walked in Mendoza's garden. When he eventually fled to Rouen he was detached from the French interest and effectively espaniolated, returning later to give priority to the Scottish mission under Mendoza's direction.

Mendoza's interest in Scotland, however, pre-dated his dealings with Parsons, for in 1578, before the Jesuits came to England or Scotland, he was advised by King Philip to keep an eye on the Scots and on the Scots Queen in captivity. Mendoza then learned through his opposite number in Paris, Vargas, that Mary Stewart had intimated her desision to put herself, her son and her alienated realm of Scotland under Spanish protection; she had secretly conveyed the decision to her ambassador in Paris, Beaton, who communicated it to the Spaniard, Vargas.

The Guisian plots and Jesuit activities in Scotland had both, therefore, been a façade behind which Spanish policy was furthered in Scotland, but this indirect intervention did not fully satisfy Philip that he would be in a position to control the results. For that reason he had pulled back from supporting the invasion plans signed by Lennox and Crichton in Holyrood. It was not merely ineptitude, as Crichton thought, but the fear that France would reap the dividends and bring both Scotland and England within the French orbit— even Guise, though an ally, was not to be trusted. To resolve the uncertainties and build up a clear cut Spanish conquest of England, King Philip began from 1584 to prepare on several fronts. His ambassador at the Vatican, Olivares, attacked the Scottish way to the conquest of England as of small value and discounted any hope of the genuine conversion of King James; he ran counter to French policy in relation to Scotland and also the alignment between France and the Vatican. The accession of Pope Sixtus strengthened Olivares' hand. At the same time, the English Catholic leaders were made sure of and this further strengthened the Spanish line at Rome and cloaked the purely Imperialist Spanish designs. Allen was presented with an Abbey at Naples and provided with a handsome pension by King Philip—as Olivares had observed it was desirable to 'lay under an obligation the man who was to lead the whole dance'.

Another significant and ominous preparation on Philip's part, reaching beyond Mary Stewart's grave, was that he planned, as a descendant of the House of Lancaster, eventually to present his claim to the English crown in place of hers. His plans for the man who was to lead the whole dance, Dr Allen, had long shadows too; he was being groomed for his three-cornered hat while the Queen still lived so that, as Cardinal of England, he might replace the Queen as the rallying figure. It is not surprising, perhaps, that at one point Mendoza discouraged the Queen from making a private escape and King Philip approved his wisdom since in Mary Stewart's end Philip saw his beginning.

The agent in Spain of the Queen of Scots, Sir Francis Englefield, warned King Philip of the suspicion he was arousing and urged him 'to prosecute the long intended enterprise for the delivery of the Scottish queen out of prison . . . if she perish (which is now most likely) it cannot be but very scandalous and infamous to his Catholic Majesty. He, being after the Queen of Scotland the nearest Catholic that is to be found of the royal blood, will ever be subject to the false suspicion and calumniation of leaving and abandoning the good queen to be devoured by her enemies, in order to make the more open to his own claim and interest.' Englefield's appeal to the Spanish Monarch's conscience was made just before the final and inexorable legal processes were set in motion which brought the Scottish Queen to the block. Dr Allen received his cardinal's hat six months after the Queen's death, in the summer of 1587; he had had some difficulty just before then in restraining Philip from trying on the English Crown in the shadow, by formal assertion of his right. 'When God has given victory to your majesty,' Allen wrote, 'your relationship to the royal House of Lancaster may be justly pleaded in Parliament.' He declared it was unsafe to begin the war on dynastic grounds but whatever was acquired in a just war was lawfully possessed.

For himself, Allen aimed to possess the authority spiritual of the Archbishop of Canterbury and the power temporal of the English Chancellor. He did a great deal of shadow-cabinet making, on some of which Philip and his General, Parma, indulgently smiled. How simply he would manage Philip's claim to the Crown he explained in a few words: the cause would be pleaded in Parliament, he, as Archbishop of Canterbury and Legate of the Apostolic See, would have the right of first vote of the whole realm and his lead would be followed by all the bishops and Catholic nobles. There would be no other voters, he averred, because of the previous 'death or dismissal of the heretics'—except for the heretics, it all seemed perfectly trouble free and painless.

Although Philip and the English Catholic leaders brushed the Scots to one side in the major preparations for the 'sacred expedition', the Guisian interest and the Scots involved were not wholly ignored. Philip certainly wanted to hear no more about King James's conversion, which could cut off his own hand outstretched for the English Crown, but he saw the need for a Scottish sideshow or diversion to aid the Armada. Scottish developments revealed that there was some common ground here on which he could meet the Scots and their friends.

Father Gordon arrived in Scotland after being separated from Crichton on the ship seized by the Dutch. The next year, 1585, we hear of him in a letter sent by Beaton, Mary Stewart's Paris ambassador, to General Claudius Aquaviva, head of the Society of Jesus, in which Beaton reported that Gordon and Father Holt were both at the house of his nephew, Graham of Fintry, near Dundee. Later the same year it was Father Tyrie, acting as Beaton's assistant, who reported to the Jesuit General that Fathers Hay and Gordon were in the north of Scotland with the Earl of Huntly, and Fathers Holt and Dury in the west with the Earl of Morton, Lord Maxwell. Early the following year, 1586, Father Tyrie reported further to his General concerning the four Jesuits resident in Scotland and mentioned that Lord Claud Hamilton, recently won to the Catholic faith, was coming over from France and that from him they had great hopes of assistance.

An outline emerges from these bare reports to General Aquaviva concerning the Scottish Jesuit network: Gordon and Hay are seen to be cultivating their native north east, where their relatives, Huntly and Errol, were powerful Catholic overlords, while the Englishman, Holt, maintained contact with the Earl of Morton, otherwise Lord Maxwell, in the south west. Thereby both the north east and south west coasts were kept open for their overseas friends. Graham of Fintry apparently provided them with a general base and a bridge with the Lowlands, while the coming of Lord Hamilton promised to strengthen their position. Father Tyrie in Paris was their liaison with Rome and their link, too, with Mary Stewart via her ambassador, Beaton.

Through the eyes of the Queen of Scots, remote and cut off as she was, we get a remarkable vision of the dramatic potentialities in this rather dull looking set-up. Writing to her English friend, Charles Paget, early in 1586 she said, 'I desire that you should essay if the King of Spain has intention to set on England . . . In case that he deliberate to set on the Queen of England, esteeming it necessary that he assure himself also of Scotland, I have thought good that you enter with the ambassador of Spain in these overtures following.' The Queen then went on to outline her clear and forceful programme: she would work to win her son's support of the King of Spain's enterprise, but failing in this she would promote a strict league between the Scottish Catholic noblemen and their adherents to aid the King of Spain. They would need to be supplied with men and money, but not overmuch of either because there were plenty of men within the country and a little money went a long way there. She would prepare the means to make her son a hostage in the hands of the King of Spain or of the Pope—the best hostage that she and the lords of Scotland could give for the performance of that which depended on them. In his place a regent must be established, having commission and power from her and from her son whose agreement she thought could easily be secured once he was in the hands of the lords. For this office she found none so fit as the Lord Claud Hamilton; she could not yet write to Lord Claud herself, she explained, for want of a cipher alphabet between them, but she now enclosed one for his future use.

This was irony of ironies in relation to the fate prescribed for King James. Only two years ealier Elizabeth, in the interests of England, had made some move through Gowrie to remove his spindly shanks and hips from the seat of Scottish kings and replace them with the broader beam of a Hamilton. Now, in the interests of Spain, the Queen Mother was as ruthlessly plotting the same thing to replace James Stewart with a Hamilton.

Once the Queen had opposed her half-brother, later the Regent Moray, in his scheme to eliminate the Hamiltons from the succession by an Act of Parliament or other instrument, and had vehemently asserted their rights of birth and blood by which alone she had become Queen herself, but now she was proposing to bring these rights into dangerous proximity to the throne. The removal of her son and a regency were unconditional, even if he supported Spain, but it was scarcely conceivable that once the power switch to the Hamiltons had been made it would ever be reversed in James's favour. The Queen Mother made no stipulation on this point but merely insisted that he would be given his 'liberty' when she desired it, or, after her death, he would be allowed to return 'to this isle' provided he was then a Catholic and it was then his desire. Conditional 'liberty' or 'return to the isle' had not much to do with James's restoration. All this profited Mary Stewart nothing, for she was on her way to the block before it all matured. Nevertheless, a great deal of it began to take shape: the 'strict league' of the Scottish Catholic noblemen drew together, including Lord Claud Hamilton along with the Earl of Huntly from the Catholic north east and the Earl of Morton from the Catholic south west. These were the first stealthy steps in the direction of controlling the King's person, which led eventually to Huntly commanding the King's Bodyguard.

The most positive pointers to progress in the plot were in the discussions with Spain which the Queen of Scots had envisaged, about men and money. The Catholic lords, Huntly, Morton and Hamilton sent an agent with letters of credit and a plan to Paris in the summer of 1586, not long after the Queen of Scots had outlined her plan to Paget. In their plan, which the Duke of Guise commended to Mendoza, the Scottish lords promised James's conversion, and undertook to hold several ports open for the use of the Spanish fleet near the Borders. They requested a sum of one hundred and fifty thousand crowns for organising supplies and forces, but to show their office was a bona fide one, and not a ruse to come by Spanish money, they declared they had no desire to handle all the money at once—they wished only that it should be ready and deposited within reach. For its bearing on hidden gold this provision is especially worthy of note.

The bearer of this plan was Robert Bruce, a former secretary of Beaton, ambassador of the Queen of Scots in France. Mendoza, the Spanish ambassador, sent Bruce on to Spain where he expounded the plan with enthusiasm. The promise of King James's conversion naturally did not cause his enthusiasm to be echoed by King Philip who, however, did examine the military aspect of it and, contemplating a force of four thousand landing in Scotland as a useful diversion, referred the matter to Parma, his general in the Netherlands, for his view.

In November, Bruce was waiting in Paris for a decision; they were waiting in Scotland too and growing impatient. (The trial of the Queen of Scots at Fotheringay had ended, and the English parliament was pressing for her execution.) Bruce received letters from Scotland urging an instant decision. Mendoza, who supported Bruce, pressed Madrid for an answer. Eventually the answer came— after the death of the Queen of Scots in February—King Philip accepted the offer of help from the Scots.

# 6  Gold for the Armada diversion

THE DESIGNS of King Philip and the English Catholic leaders Allen and Parsons were such that they desired only a hole and corner arrangement with the Scots; a Scottish Catholic monarchy or regency recognised by the Vatican and France would only have raised obstacles to Spanish imperialist plans. As it was, the Spanish ambassador talked the Pope to a standstill on the question of Mary Stewart's successor as claimant to the English Crown and, without disclosing his sovereign's hand, he gained the essential point that the decision would emerge out of Spain's political wisdom.

Following the Spanish decision to organise some Scottish aid the agent, Bruce, again began to negotiate on behalf of the Catholic lords, Huntly, Hamilton and Maxwell. This time his conference, because of its purely military bearing, was with the commander of the Spanish forces in the Netherlands, Parma, whom he met at the end of March, 1587. What emerged from their talks, ostensibly at least, was a scheme to charter thirty ships in the Baltic which were supposedly to load a wheat cargo for Scotland; after loading at Danzig, however, they were to make for Dunkirk and there discharge the wheat cargo for the supply of Parma's army, and in place of the wheat Parma's soldiers were to sail in the ships for Scottish ports. Bruce received ten thousand crowns and set out on his mission.

Meanwhile Father Crichton had been released from the Tower, and was soon after reported to be in Rome where he was said to have gone secretly on behalf of King James. He then returned to Scotland to resume his links with Huntly and the other Catholic earls and to work with his Jesuit colleagues, Fathers Gordon, Holt and Hay. He marked his return by converting the Earl of Crawford; this carried the Jesuit penetration near to the King's Bodyguard and into the royal bedchamber—young Alexander Lindsay, the brother of the converted Crawford, became a King's favourite, to the damage of Chancellor Maitland, and it was expected that young Lindsay would replace the Master of Glamis as Captain of the King's Bodyguard. Lord Home declared that the new favourite was 'the King's only minion and conceit, his nightly bedfellow.'

In this phase of his work Crichton came into contact with the underground agent, Bruce, who in time informed Parma that in dispensing money entrusted to him he had associated himself with Father William Crichton, Jesuit, 'a very honest man, and very wise'. As Bruce was trying to explain away why he had not consulted Graham of Fintry in his money matters, as instructed, he naturally stressed the honesty and wisdom of Fintry's substitute. By the time he met Crichton, Bruce was working with Francis, Earl of Bothwell, concerning whom he supplied glowing reports to his superiors, describing his 'waging' of soldiers as part of the preparation to take over the Border ports for the Armada's coming. The thirty wheat ships to bring in the Spanish troops, however, had somehow dropped out of the picture. The whole summer of 1587 had slipped past, and in that time there had been no sign of Bruce or the wheat-ships, nor in the autumn either. He was said to have been held up in Brittany and eventually it was decided that the Baltic would be frozen over before the ships could be brought out, so Parma called the whole thing off. When the Armada sailed the next year the wheat ships were forgotten.

A more realistic picture of the whole invasion plan and of its Scottish aspect was supplied by the Earl of Leicester, writing from Flushing to Queen Elizabeth in November, 1587. He described Parma's preparation by sea as 'the greatest that ever was and not likely to be all for these part (England) but rather part for Scotland'. He added that King James's instruments steadily laboured to have men sent to Scotland by Parma. He warned the Queen that 'the world was never so dangerous and never so full of treasons and treacheries as at that day'.

If the dangerous world did not come up with thirty Baltic troop carriers disguised as wheat-ships, what was Bruce's summer mission of the pre-Armada year on which he spent his ten thousand crowns? Apparently the Duke of Parma was satisfied with the work his agent had done, because the next year he was paying him five thousand crowns in fee and forty crowns monthly in expenses. There was, of course, the other half of the request Bruce had made on behalf of Maxwell, Hamilton and Huntly, namely the money that was to be available, if not accessible, before the men—one hundred and fifty thousand crowns—that may have been Bruce's real assignment while he was missing during the summer 'in Brittany' or, while he was diverting spies and encouraging them to scan the horizon for the ghost Armada of wheat ships, others may have quietly delivered the gold.

Presently Bruce was working with another important agent, Colonel Sempill, a Scottish soldier of fortune, who had been in the service of the Prince of Orange but on the advice of the Queen of Scots transferred his allegiance to the Prince's enemy, King Philip, and in doing so took with him the regiments he commanded and the important forts he controlled. He subsequently rose high in Philip's military service and esteem, despite an initial mistrust for being a Scot. Sempill was sent by the Spanish King on a special mission to Scotland at the beginning of the Armada year, accompanied by Maxwell, the Earl of Morton, who had been sent out of the country for his intrigues and was still without royal licence to return, and provided with five thousand crowns. Before his departure the colonel had consultations with the Spanish ambassador, Mendoza, and with the Duke of Parma, and came away with letters for King James, setting sail with Maxwell from Gravelines.

When they arrived the King was nearly at the end of a long waiting game. During the preceding summer he had allowed patriotic feeling to rise against England on account of his mother's death and encouraged unofficial missions to European camps and courts—Crichton to Rome, Bruce to Madrid, Gray and young Seton to Paris, Captain William Stewart to Parma in the Netherlands. As Leicester said, his agents worked steadily. Maitland, his chief Minister, had at the same time entered into close communication with Huntly's party through Graham, the Laird of Fintry, and there was report of Fintry being made Secretary when Maitland became Chancellor.

In London, the King had allowed the ambassador, Archibald Douglas, to follow a non-committal policy of drawing offers from Queen Elizabeth to mollify him for his mother's death and secure his good will against the impending Spanish invasion. Richard Douglas, the nephew of Archibald, had written in June, 1597 to his uncle describing King James's attitude at that stage and conveying the King's instructions. His letter referred to 'the discourse you had with her Majesty [Elizabeth] and counsellors touching offers to be made to her Majesty by them.' Richard went on to say 'he esteemed very well of your diligence, but could not but marvel of this long delay. Always he approves your opinion in saying you know nothing able to satisfy him unless it were a public declaration of his succession to the crown, failing issue of that Queen's own body. He is not so disprovided of means at home, nor of foreign friendship (seeing he is solicited both by France and Spain with great promises) but he were able to repair the wrong affered to him . . . you may be assured he cannot be long restrained.'

By September 1587, however, James had partly dismounted from his high dudgeon and was being more cautious. He now conveyed to the ambassador that he would not become the suitor himself and make proposals, but neither would he 'cut off all dealing'. He would abstain from all things that might 'offend or irritate that country.'

The truth was that, by the time Sempill arrived early in 1588 with his letters from Philip and Parma, King James had maintained his attitude of exhausted patience towards Elizabeth too long to feel safe, unless there was now some great new offer to be grasped from all the missions he had encouraged to change his posture. But there was not, and could not be, any such great new offer in the letters Sempill carried. James wanted the assurance of the English succession, as his ambassador Douglas had stressed to Elizabeth; since Philip was in the market for the English Crown himself he had no assurance of this kind to give James. Indeed, Philip was hastening the plans for the English invasion because the Pope was considering a French scheme for Elizabeth's conversion which might save the Vatican's promised million pound share of the bill for the 'sacred expedition'.

The letters brought by Sempill were necessarily an anti-climax to all the time and labour spent on clandestine missions by King James, whose reaction was soon made manifest. He made a descent on the west Border where Maxwell, in defiance of the order of banishment, was proceeding to build up forces to keep the coast open for Spain. Lochmaben Castle was captured and its captain and six men hanged; Maxwell himself was pursued and made prisoner. The report by Richard Douglas to his uncle, the ambassador in London, clarifies the objective: referring to the assault on Lochmaben castle Richard said, 'the cause that moved his Majesty to desire cannon from Carlisle for dinging of that house was not that he could not bring his own safely thither . . . but being then in great expectation to be well used by the Queen he thought he would give them the proof of his friendly mind.' The request for the friendly cannon from Carlisle advertised the King's serious intention to open up the English negotiations at the eleventh hour, after the long period of stand-offishness and parade of secret diplomacy with the Catholic powers. Negotiations soon followed with the English ambassador, Ashby, producing mainly an assurance that the trial of the Queen of Scots had not prejudiced any rights James had to the English succession and a promise of a yearly English pension of £5,000. These promises and assurances were puffed up by the winds that filled the Armada's sails and there was a later deflation on the promise side after the Armada had passed by.

The King's blow at Maxwell was intended at the same time as a rebuff to King Philip and his special agent, Sempill, for their disappointing offers. Could the conspirators at this stage have averted the blow at Maxwell by carrying out the seizure of the King which had been part of his mother's plan? There was evidence of some such design immediately before Maxwell got back to the country with Colonel Sempill. Gatherings of strength representing the followers of Huntly and Lord Claud Hamilton and also Lord Maxwell's faction from the south west, took place near Edinburgh in February of the Armada year; their ostensible purpose was to see justice done in the case of a kinsman of Huntly, the Laird of Gicht, accused of murder. Richard Douglas, however, reported to the ambassador in London that 'their forces are dissolved and everyone retired whence he came.'

Probably Sempill's secret arrival or an instruction from him averted the showdown. It was not in the Spanish interest to have a new government in Scotland, headed by a regent, which might have immediate recognition from the Vatican and France, since this could have produced barriers to Philip's arbitrary and unilateral actions. At the same time, such a government might have provoked military entry of English forces into Scotland, making the Spanish landings in Scotland more hazardous instead of less so. A fluid situation best suited Spanish invasion strategy.

The King's blow at Maxwell did not seem to disturb the promising prospect for the conspirators. Sempill and Bruce had confidence as shown by facts that came to light, that they could free Maxwell whenever they desired. The King made no move to arrest Sempill who had entered the country along with Maxwell, having re-established his credit with London and Elizabeth, James allowed all the other preparations to welcome the Spaniards to go forward.

There was thus the curious situation in which the Scottish plotters with Spain were half encouraged and half repressed by the King while the Armada was still round the corner. On the gold front the position continued healthy: Sempill and Maxwell came in with money (five thousand crowns), Bruce had received money (ten thousand crowns plus his own fees and expenses), Francis Bothwell participated to an unspecified extent and John Chisholm, brother of an officer of the royal household, came in with funds in August (ten thousand crowns) and brought in a similar sum again by the end of the year. There was also another hint of invasion gold, something resembling the one hundred and fifty thousand crowns that Maxwell, Huntly and Hamilton had requested for the big day. A spy of Walsingham reported to London in June, 1588, the year of the Armada, that another million had gone to France 'whereof, like enough, a part may go to Scotland'; Walsingham considered the report serious enough to file and it remains to-day among his papers. The English spy had as his informant someone with the conspiracy name of the 'Cavalier'. The 'Cavalier' had added that he thought part was for Scotland because five days before a man of Maxwell, the Earl of Morton, had come to Madrid from France and then hurriedly returned. There is no record of Bruce being in France at this time, and he was certainly agent of Maxwell, Huntly and Hamilton, but so was Graham of Fintry, Bruce's co-worker in the underground and his superior, and according to a letter from his kinsman, Judge Graham of Halyards, to Ambassador Douglas in London, Graham was in France at this time.

There were thus two occasions presenting some semblance of arrangements to ship the invasion gold to Scotland. One was when Bruce disappeared during the summer of 1587 and was said vaguely to be in 'Brittany' when he should have been in the Baltic chartering the wheat-ships. The other was when Graham of Fintry went to France, and apparently also Madrid, in the spring and early summer of the Armada year, at the time another million was said to have gone to France, part maybe for Scotland.

Sempill's presence in Scotland suggests that the invasion gold had become a fact, however shipped. He was one of Spain's important military leaders, his Scottish origin was incidental, and he was there to seize the Border ports for Spain. That is why he arrived with Maxwell who could command the south west coast and why he provided Francis Bothwell with the means to 'wage' soldiers to command the coast above the eastern border. Cognisant of his strategic purpose, King James called in Carlisle cannon to 'ding doon' Lochmaben Castle in the west while he reached out for Maxwell and placed him within restraining walls. But both the King and Sempill refrained from pressing matters to a premature decision before the Armada struggle was joined; James gave himself the option to change his policy if Spain looked like winning and Sempill remained to see that Spain did win.

The failure of Parma to embark his troops and mount the invasion because of the Armada defeats altered everything. It meant the war chest which Sempill had been ready to open remained closed—the invasion gold was frozen. This, perhaps, was the reason for the impromptu attempt by Father Crichton and the Scottish Catholic earls to halt the Armada at the Western Isles. They would have had all the more confidence in this gesture if the war chest had already been delivered, and it would also explain why Huntly and the other pro-Spanish noblemen addressed letters to Parma which all carried a pre-echo of the Jacobean refrain, 'Will ye no' come back again'. When it came to the later stage of planning this return in the form of the 'blanks' plot, the gold for the landings then may not have required shipment but only authorisation for its use; an order to the trusted custodian to open the war chest was perhaps the only requirement for this part of the plan.

# 7 Elizabeth thinks she is dreaming and James kisses his traitors

JAMES CONTINUED his ambivalent attitude after the dispersal of the Armada. He ordered the arrest of Colonel Sempill, the Spanish military agent, it is true, but it was a benevolent arrest. Sempill had sailed to the entrance of the Forth when the Armada was passing by for the purpose of communicating with a Spanish pinnace, and was arrested on his return to Leith. The Earl of Huntly secured his release, but he was taken again, on the King's order, and confined under guard in Robert Gourlay's house. It could not put the King in peril from Spain to imprison Sempill since the danger was past, nor could it defeat Sempill's major plans because they had all gone adrift in the general miscarriage, but it increased King James's credit with Elizabeth, or robbed her of a rejoinder to the complaints which he began to voice, that she was not keeping to the bargain made by her ambassador, Ashby, during the English hour of danger. The demonstration of Sempill's arrest having been made, however, the underground agent, Bruce, was allowed to bribe his guard and restore him to liberty. After conference with his noble Catholic friends, Sempill left the country, charging Robert Bruce and Graham of Fintry to continue the work. Before long he was sending letters to the King in the underground mail bag, demonstrating that there were no hard feelings.

There is the usual romantic story associated with his escape. A beautiful lady brought him three large pies one of which contained a silken rope with which he lowered himself to the ground from the top of seven storeys. The agent, Bruce, however, never debited the cost of any pies or rope against the Duke of Parma's benevolent fund, only the four hundred crowns of the bribe. He wrote to the Duke saying, ' the four hundred crowns employed for the deliverance of Colonel Sempill I have put in compt.' He went on to say that Lord Maxwell in prison was greatly pleased with the care it pleased the Duke to take of him. 'In case they should annoy him,' he assured Parma, 'or if it was presently requisite for the weal of our cause to deliver him, we have every means to get him out of prison.'

The only reason why Robert Bruce did not deliver Maxwell 'extra-ordinarily', was that he meant to solicit the lords, his friends, to procure his liberty from the King very soon. It was merely a question of whether Maxwell should walk out of Edinburgh Castle after dusk or in broad light of day.

The lords who might procure Maxwell's liberty from the King included, of course, the recently converted Crawford whose young brother, Lindsay, was the King's favourite. There was also Huntly, who had just become Captain of the King's bodyguard in place of Glamis and instead of young Lindsay, who had been tipped by court gossips. James was not amusing himself in advancing Huntly. He went further and promoted the young man's marriage to the sister of the Earl of Lennox. The King had brought over from France both these children of his mature first favourite D'Aubigny who had fascinated him at an impressionable age and later became Earl of Lennox. It was not simply as a tribute to his idol's memory; the more Stewarts there were around him with a near claim to the Throne the more he might discourage the Hamiltons from the dangerous thought that only one thread required to be cut, only one life extinguished. With Claud Hamilton looming large in the Catholic camp and with his nephew, Huntly, leading it, it seemed sensible to detatch Huntly from the Hamiltons and link him with the Stewarts through love and marriage—a form of insurance for life and crown. It was wise enough when the Queen Mother's plan to have Hamilton made the Catholic regent is remembered, and also the earlier plot of the Gowries to bring in the Hamiltons. James pushed his wisdom and his luck a little further by persuading Huntly to subscribe to the Protestant Confession of Faith.

To Queen Elizabeth it seemed that in making Huntly Captain of his Guard he had pushed matters to the verge of self-destruction. The madness of it all apalled her when she read a letter written by Huntly, on 24th January, 1589, and addressed to the Duke of Parma. In this Huntly said that after the departure of Colonel Sempill he had found himself so pressed on every hand that he had subscribed, but not with his heart, to their Confession of Faith. It had either been that or leaving the country or taking to the field against the King's forces augmented by help from England. 'With the returning of your army to Spain,' he bewailed, 'all help was taken from us.' The consolation was that he had now such credit with his Majesty that he had broken his former guard and established his own men about the King's person. 'Their captains are also mine,' Huntly exulted in his epistle. 'I may ever be master of his person; and, your forces being arrived, spoil the heretics of his authority, and fortify and assure our enterprises.'

Elizabeth's minions had seized Sempill's servant, Pringle, who was bearing this and other letters abroad. She still had a sense of shock when she sat down and communicated the discoveries to King James. 'Good Lord!' she wrote, 'Methinke I do but dream. No King a week would bear this.' She exhorted him suddenly to 'clap them all in safer custody than some others had been which had bred their laughter.' She had clearly read Robert Bruce's letter to Parma, too, in which he reported the modest cost for freeing Sempill and spoke of the ease with which he could deliver Lord Maxwell either 'extraordinarily' or by court influence.

All of the intercepted letters must have been disturbing to the English Queen who had just a few months since drawn a sigh of relief with the return of what was left of the Spanish fleet. The principal letter was addressed to King Philip by the three leading Scottish noblemen, Huntly, Maxwell and Claud Hamilton. The letter expressed their great regret that they had not seen the desired effects from His Majesty's preparations. They had been ready to welcome his army with sufficient forces for the peaceful receiving of them. They went on to declare that the Armada would not have found half so many friends in England, for all that was spoken by the English Catholic refugees abroad who by unchristian envy minimised the Scottish aid to magnify their own and to advance themselves in his Spanish Majesty's credit. Wooing Philip in earnest, the noble lords referred him to his own subjects who had been here, concerning the advantage of landing in these parts. The equipping of one galliasse to come to them, they urged, would be more fruitful than having ten on the sea; the English forces should be left to stay on the sea unfought.

Before the Armada sailed, in April 1588, Elizabeth's chief Minister, Lord Burghley, had confirmed the reality of this danger of war by land. He was writing to Elizabeth's Council to propose that Lord Hunsdon should be urgently sent to Berwick and money sent to bribe someone to seize Francis Bothwell before he took complete command of the Borders for the Spanish. 'If this fire be presently quenched in Scotland,' he said, 'her Majesty need fear no offence by Spain or Flanders. Otherwise surely the danger by foreign war will speedily come from thence, where with surety they may make wars without resistance by sea.' Now, when all that seemed past, the peril was coming to life again in this Scottish supplication to Philip to renew the invasion attempt on cheap and easy terms. The seriousness with which the English government viewed the content of the intercepted letters was reflected not only in Elizabeth's letter to King James, but also in a letter signed by all the members of the inner Council—Walsingham, Hunsdon, Hatton and Hensley—instructing their ambassador, Ashby, how to handle the matter. He was given translated and deciphered versions of the letters along with a cipher alphabet and was instructed to press James to apprehend all the conspirators at one time and put them in safer custody than Morton and others had been. He was also to stress that the harbouring of Jesuits like Crichton had been the root of the conspiracies and the sooner they were committed to the seas the better. To prevent alarm from being spread among the conspirators, he was given an innocuous commission requiring his presence at the Scottish Privy Council and then suddenly he was to produce the letters.

The conspirators were clapped in custody suddenly but not very permanently. Huntly was present at the Council when the letters were read and offered to enter into ward until he was tried. The choice of confinement was left to him and he chose Edinburgh Castle. The next day, according to the Kirk chronicler, Calderwood, the King and the Chancellor went up to the castle and dined with Huntly. 'The King kissed him often and protested he knew he was innocent.' In a few days Huntly was ordered to return to his own country in the north east and, as he was departing, Lord Claud Hamilton entered the castle to answer for his part. While this was going on the provost gave private warning to the burgesses to have their armour and their weapons by them in their booths. It was not a needless precaution since Huntly, had two hundred Gordon kinsmen to escort him down the street when he left the castle. Although Huntly appeared to be loath to leave town he came round in the end to arranging a sort of farewell banquet at Janet Flockhart's house to emphasise that he and the King were still friends. They went out hunting on the day of the banquet and were joined in the fields by the Earl of Errol, another correspondent of the Duke of Parma. But somebody brought a report to Huntly that the burgesses had put on their armour, and in consequence he decided to take the road north without his dinner. Errol and he made a great effort to persuade the King to throw in his lot openly with them—and Parma—but the King refused and warned them that if they tried to command his company by force they would never have his heart and he would be revenged in time. He returned alone to Janet Flockhart's house; it seemed a shame to waste a good dinner.

Before the dust and stir produced by the intercepted letters finally settled there was a spring confrontation between Huntly's followers, two thousand strong, and the King's forces of one thousand at Bridge of Dee. Errol, who was there with Huntly, urged him to fight, but the leader probably saw beyond this battle to the next one against England; he withdrew and later surrendered. Francis Bothwell, meantime, was mustering his Border followers at Dalkeith and rode with three hundred horsemen to Restalrig, his friend Logan's place (it was at Restalrig, too, that he paraded his final force of skirmishers a few years later—apparently he was always sure of some encouragement there); Bothwell also gave himself up without a fight. The mildest trials for treason followed: Huntly was examined privately in the garden at the back of the Council-house before the King and a few of his councillors; Bothwell and the Earl of Crawford were arraigned more publicly inside the Tolbooth. Huntly was committed to Borthwick Castle, Bothwell to Tantallon and Crawford to St. Andrews, but they were all out in a few months to meet the King's bride who was expected from Denmark in the autumn. When storms delayed her and prompted the King gallantly to go and bring her across the dangerous seas, Bothwell, the recent conspirator, was left in military charge of his kingdom along with the Earl of Lennox. For the wedding festivities Lord Maxwell, the subject of the Duke of Parma's loving solicitude, was also released.

At the time of their trials, on May 31st, 1589, a great ship of the Queen of England appeared in Leith. It was to help in suppressing the horrible treason in Scotland which Elizabeth had brought to light. If the crew of the great English ship were counting on seeing traitors heads roll in the dust their pleasure was sadly spoiled. The same day, also, Elizabeth's cousin Lord Hunsdon arrived to encourage the King's steadfastness against the Spanish plotters, and with him came the Master of Gray.

Gray had by now worked his way round, temporarily at least, to his strong anti-Spanish standpoint. Indeed, the previous summer when the Armada crisis was at its height he had sought to become Queen Elizabeth's agent in confounding the Spanish knavish tricks in Scotland. Lord Burghley, the chief Minister, however, thought he was up to no good. Now, following the sensation of the intercepted letters, Gray's services were at the disposal of the English Queen again. Before leaving for Scotland with Hunsdon he wrote to Queen

Elizabeth urging a letter of credit to King James which she had promised. 'The sooner he has his despatches the better will go her Majesty's affairs in Scotland' he promised, but in the next month an agent was writing to London saying Gray had gained little credit at the Scottish Court on his return.

Presently the Master himself, in a report to Lord Burghley, confirmed his lack of success in stirring up feeling against the Spanish faction. The King, he stated, was showing himself negligent in punishing the conspirators and his dealing with them would daily increase, Huntly had still the support of the King's natural inclination and so had the others, their confinement was lax and they would soon be free. Such was Gray's unpromising report.

Hopes for a new invasion plan were at the heart of the intercepted letters, the post-Armada sensation. Before the year was out all who entertained such hopes in Scotland were as free as formerly to conspire in that direction. The Kirk had stirred and agitated, and Elizabeth and her ambassadors had fumed and fretted and pressed, but the results were meagre. The Privy Council, the month following the opening of the letters, had, as Elizabeth had urged, passed an Act against Jesuits and seminary priests, naming Fathers Gordon, Crichton, Hay and others and ordering them furth of the realm. Henceforward when they came it had to be by stealth, unless they arrived in Aberdeen and could be greeted by Huntly.

Nothing was greatly disturbed either in the darkest corners of the Spanish plotting, illuminated by the intercepted letters, relating to the operations of the underground agents.

# 8  Who was custodian of the invasion gold?

THERE WERE some striking revelations concerning the underground organisation in the intercepted letters. Prison breaks and bribes for the purpose were referred to as a matter of routine, as was the underground post which brought letters to such high-placed people as Bothwell and even secret mail to the King. (It suffered a bad breakdown, however, through Sempill's servant, Pringle. Chris Hatton and Francis Walsingham of England were willing to send this unfortunate postman up to Berwick so that King James could try his hand, or his thumbscrews, to extract more information.) Illegal entry, it appeared, was a simple procedure. One way, Bruce explained, was to land near Seton House and look in there. Seton House had opened its hospitable gates to the plotters ever since the Welsh priest, Watts, and the English Jesuit, Holt, had been sent by Father Parsons and Ambassador Mendoza to break the ground in Scotland.

Perhaps the most sinister scheme was that which Bruce, according to his report, was in process of elaborating. He said the Jesuit Fathers were making great gains in Scotland and as soon as a lord or other person of importance was converted they inclined him in affection to the King of Spain as a 'thing inseparable'. For every Catholic lord a councillor was chosen. The councillors were to meet to advance the cause and communicate the instructions of their lords, while the lords, in turn, bound themselves to carry out the instructions of the council. 'Always,' he added, 'they will know nothing of our intelligences nor our final intentions, but only according to the exigencies of the affairs in hand, and that superficially and without discovering ourselves over far.' This scheme of a secret council of shadows linked with the nobility revealed a design to lead them on in the King of Spain's service beyond their knowledge and understanding of the imperialist aims involved. It also expressed a basic mistrust of the Catholic earls who had a big stake in the country and so much to lose that they might at any time defect and betray 'intelligences'. The other cause for mistrust was the suspicion that the noble lords were largely concerned with obtaining Spanish gold.

'I have much to do,' Bruce reported to Parma, 'to moderate the appetite that some Catholic lords have to handle the money presently for the hope they give of some pretended occasions, which will never fall out.' He went on to explain that the three who had first offered their services to King Philip, and had sent him on his mission nearly three years before, expected that all the money that came should be divided between them immediately after arrival. The three were, of course, Huntly, Claud Hamilton and Lord Maxwell. Besides them there were a great number of others, Bruce declared, who were prepared to put themselves under a direct obligation to the King of Spain for money received, but they did not want to be obliged for it to the three and bound to them in service. Lord Maxwell, Bruce informed, had hitherto been contented with reasons given and Huntly had never shown himself susceptible to money but he had been induced by the example of Claud Hamilton, his uncle, who was 'covetous of gear'. When, however, John Chisholm had brought six thousand three hundred and sixty crowns of the sun to Huntly's house at Dunfermline, along with three thousand seven hundred Spanish pistolets, Bruce had persuaded Huntly that the money must be held in reserve; one part of the money, he said, was hidden in Lord Livingstone's house and the other part was in Edinburgh in good enough security.

Bruce found reasons for side-stepping Parma's command to consult with Graham of Fintry and dispense the money jointly with him. He said Fintry was warded within Dundee for the present and could not go outside its ports; he did not say why he could not go to the laird in Dundee if the laird could not come to him. In default, he said he was associating himself in the matter with Father Crichton and would also consult Sir James Chisholm, brother of the Chisholm who brought the money.

Colonel Sempill was dispenser of the funds up until the time he departed and he had left a small residue in his sister's hands to be taken over by Bruce, who referred to this in a letter to Sempill and also expressed his obligation for five hundred crowns wages allowed to him with forty crowns monthly for expenses. 'If thought expedient,' he added, 'you may procure increase thereof from the King of Spain when you go to him.' In the same breath, he asked to have command, or the like that they had spoken of, when the time shall come to begin our enterprise', that is to prepare for the invasion. From this it appears that Bruce was anxious to establish himself as the leader now that Sempill was gone. He informed Sempill they might be able to take the government of the country into their hands but not without a greater abundance of money, and vowed that nobody would ever know about it through him until the time came to use it. He was anxious to control a larger war chest for such greater efforts as seizing the government and supporting the landings. It is thus implicit in this letter that whatever hand Bruce may have had in the shipping of the invasion gold during his original mission the knowledge of its concealment was not vested in him; if the one hundred and fifty thousand crowns solicited, or something corresponding to it, had been hidden away ready for the day as was proposed, he had still to find his way into the secret and this he was probably trying to do.

Who then was the custodian of the major war chest, if not Bruce? Our thoughts naturally turn to the other man Parma trusted with Spanish gold—Graham of Fintry, who made the voyage to France in the spring when 'another million' had been sent from Spain into France, part of it likely to pass to Scotland.

Bruce's letters contain an undertone of jealousy and malice towards his comrades as patent as his ambition and this ill-will reached Fintry obliquely. First, he evaded the command to share the disbursement of funds with Fintry by making the one sided excuse that Fintry could not come to him. More directly, there was an attack on Father Tyrie, who arrived along with John Chisholm with the last consignment of crowns and pistolets, and was accused of being negative towards Bruce's messenger sent specially to ask if he had something that required talk between them. A further accusation was that Tyrie had failed to deliver a letter from Colonel Sempill to King James and he (Bruce), had been compelled to bring it to the King's notice by getting Bothwell to show His Majesty a copy of the letter, as if the copy had been enclosed with the letter Bothwell had received from Sempill in the same delivery. Bruce sent on to Sempill the explanation of these matters about which Father Tyrie had written to him and alleged it was full of shifts. Tyrie had written that he was really in earnest about meeting Bruce, but the messenger had merely asked about letters for him. As to Sempill's letter for the King, although he had shown it to him, the King had refused to receive it because of displeasure with Sempill's behaviour when last here. But he understood His Majesty was now in a better frame of mind and content that correspondence between him and the Duke of Parma would increase, and had signified that he would receive Sempill's letter from Tyrie on his return to Edinburgh.

The worm in it all, apparently, for Bruce was that Father Tyrie had gone to Dundee for close conference with Fintry instead of seeking out Bruce first. Added to this was the fact that Tyrie and Fintry together were closely associated with the King's sector of the Spanish plotting and in general with the deeper levels of intrigue of Parma's agents.

Tyrie wrote his explanation to Bruce from Fintry's place. Tracing it back, Tyrie and Graham of Fintry had been near the heart of the affair all through. Likewise from early on Fintry had been a link between the King and the Catholic continent; when James escaped from Gowrie's servitude he sent a letter to the Duke of Guise exulting in his smartness and Fintry was reputed to have been the bearer. Bowes, the English ambassador, noticed and reported a long conference at this time between the King and Fintry, when the latter got back from France. In the same year the General Assembly of the Kirk denounced Fintry as an insidious influence at Court. It was not long after this that Fintry's uncle, Archbishop Beaton, in Paris, appealed to the General of the Society of Jesus to send Gordon, Hay, Crichton and Tyrie to Scotland to support Father Holt and others there. Crichton, as we noticed, fell among pirates on the way and landed in the Tower, but the main network was established. Tyrie was retained near Beaton in Paris as a liaison while Beaton's nephew, Fintry, was the co-ordinator in Scotland, his home serving as headquarters.

Out of this grew the offer of Scottish support for the Armada made in the names of Huntly, Hamilton and Maxwell. It corresponded with the plan sketched by the Queen of Scots only months before her trial. So far were the activities of the conspirators bound up at this stage with the Queen's fate that Fintry made desperate efforts to get inside news of the charges and evidence against the Queen. He pumped the Master of Gray hard, according to a letter from Gray to Archibald Douglas in which he said he thought it might not be unmeet to enter into an information deal with Fintry, but Fintry would have very little out of him if he did not learn part of his purpose. He left it to Douglas to ascertain from the spymaster, Walsingham, how far he should go in this deal. Fintry wished to probe so far that he joined Archibald Douglas on the road to London when Douglas was taking up his official duties as ambassador.

The picture that forms of Fintry is one of a simple man, at least compared with the cleverness of Gray, the scheming and calculating nature of Chancellor Maitland or the deceitfulness of the King. He opposed the shiftiness and self-concerned anxieties of others with a quiet stability and he remained permanently in the centre of the enterprise he was organising. It was perhaps this rock-of-ages quality that caused him to be so often the target of the Kirk's denunciation, but in consolation it earned him the trust of the Catholic leaders on the continent whom he served, his uncle Beaton, the Duke of Guise and finally the Duke of Parma. Parma's command to Bruce to bring Fintry in on the distribution of the crowns and pistolets marked Fintry as the man above suspicion. The hastening of Father Tyrie to Broughty for conference with Fintry, after his meeting with the King, provides similar evidence.

It is clear that Graham of Fintry was the pivot of the whole conspiracy. The Catholic noblemen with their allies, like Bothwell, were the political and military leaders, and the conspiracy would not exist without them, although even the most powerful of their number, Huntly, had his moments of weakness and inconstancy (Bruce declared that his constancy, on the other hand was due to the influence of Fintry and himself). Sempill was a military leader imported for a season and not to be reckoned a permanent element in the plot. The Jesuits were too conscious of the aura of their order and were liable to self-delusion, and for that reason the Spanish promoters had their reservations concerning them. There were auxiliary gentlemen like John Chisholm who brought in money during the Armada year, George Ker who later became a courier, and Sir James Chisholm who was the brother of John and valuable because he was an officer of the King's household, but they had other occupations in life than conspiracy. Bruce and Graham were the two dedicated professional conspirators, as Sempill realised when he left them to continue the work, and as Parma also recognised. Of the two, Graham had the deeper roots in the affair, the stronger connections, the more stable character. With Bruce, the rot was already setting in; he was factious towards Tyrie, obliquely jealous of Graham, censorious in reporting dealings with the earls, fawning in relation to Parma and Sempill, greedy for increase of pay and ambitious and anxious to control the whole project and its funds. His desertion, which took place about two years later, was already foreshadowed in the intercepted letters—written not long after the Armada's return.

If Parma and King Philip responded to the appeal of Hamilton, Huntly and Maxwell for a secret invasion fund of one hundred and fifty thousand crowns, an appeal backed in principle by the Queen of Scots in her last days, and if one man had the special custody of that money until the hour of need arose, then that man was surely David Graham of Fintry.

# 9  The golden string links Bothwell and Fintry

THE GOLDEN string has led us to the Laird of Fintry, the underground leader, and we now find it leading back to Fast Castle and its treasure hunters, particularly the Earl of Bothwell. At the stage in the evolution of the Spanish plots when all the plotters were free again to celebrate the King's wedding, we see a significant connection coming to light between Fintry and Bothwell. It was one which the King observed too and it caused him much annoyance.

Francis Bothwell was the nephew of the Bothwell associated with the downfall of the Queen of Scots; his father was the bastard son of James V who married that other Bothwell's sister, Lady Jean Hepburn. James V had bestowed the commendatorship of Coldingham on his natural son, John Stewart, and James VI confirmed the son of John Stewart, Francis Bothwell, in the inheritance and honours associated with his father and the Hepburns. Francis Bothwell was, therefore, a Stewart whose proximity to the Crown was weakened by his father's illegitimacy. If, as suspected, King James's conception was not very legitimate, Francis Bothwell's connections with the Throne were then as honourable, and this may have explained the aggressive attitude of Francis and the defensive, sometimes panic-stricken, attitude of James which developed during the conflict between them. Francis always conveyed the impression that he saw right through James; and in his rumbustious assaults on the royal palaces and his Rabelaisian mockery of the monarch he lowered the royal arcanum to the level of a comic make-believe.

In power terms, this Earl of Bothwell drew his strength from the alliance between Homes and Hepburns which had been formidable enough to overthrow James III and take his son James IV in tow. The Logans were later partners in this alliance and it was Francis Bothwell, Lord Home and his half-brother, Robert Logan, who rallied the Border forces against James's Minister, Arran, and compelled the King to accept the Government of the Master of Gray. In the confrontation at Stirling on that occasion the King turned to Bothwell and said reproachfully, 'As for you Francis, who has stirred up your unquiet spirit? When did I ever wrong you?' Bothwell thought he had been wronged by being kept out of Court until he composed his differences with the man in power, Arran, whom he hated. Before joining the Master of Gray against Arran, he had a hand in the second instalment of Gowrie's plot which aimed to dispose of Arran and, apparently James also, because the rival Hamiltons were brought up to the Border to get a tempting view of the Throne on that occasion. When the Master of Gray fell, typically it was Bothwell, Lord Home and Robert Logan who signed the bond, pledging under a heavy money penalty to themselves, that Gray would remain abroad. Typically it was Bothwell who encountered Arran's brother, Captain Stewart, in the Royal Mile after the latter had produced Gray's downfall, and killed him.

Perhaps the ghost of the Queen of Scots later came between Bothwell and James, as Arran had done. The treaty which James completed with Elizabeth had left out all mention of his mother and nothing was provided for her safety. After her execution Bothwell appeared at court in armour and delared that his mail suit was the only fitting mourning for the occasion. Before the execution James had inquired of a group of courtiers what should be done in face of his mother's danger, and Bothwell had answered boldly, 'If your majesty suffers the process to proceed, I think, my liege, you should be hanged yourself the day after.'

It was out of the tragic event of Fotheringay that the real cleavage developed. Bothwell took the occasion of the Queen's death to declare openly in favour of an alliance of Scotland with Spain against England, Protestant lord though he was. Then he became involved with Colonel Sempill and with the underground agent Bruce, who sent a glowing report on his work and worth to the Duke of Parma. It seems that King James was not entirely ignorant of Bothwell's military intrigues with Sempill, just as it is transparent that James had dealings with Sempill himself and tolerated his military mission during the Armada crisis. On the one hand, he crushed Maxwell's preparations in the south west, but on the other he gave Bothwell a commission to 'wage' soldiers for the pacification of the Isles when it was patent that Bothwell was recruiting his thousand men to seize the Border port of Eyemouth and keep open the eastern marches for Parma's entry into England. This, however, was when the King was backing both sides to win; it was Bothwell's persistence in this alignment with Spain that produced the mischief.

Even Bothwell's part in the Bridge of Dee affair, when Huntly put up his fists to the King but did not come to blows, was of no great importance. Bothwell disbanded his three hundred men then and came quietly in with the rest to receive the royal mercy. A month or two of the sea air at Tantallon Castle ensued, and set him up for his commission to govern the land along with Lennox during the King's winter absence in Denmark. Then, when the King and his Chancellor were both absent, Bothwell committed his totally unpardonable offences. First was his intercession for Graham of Fintry at the Kirk General Assembly in March, not long before the King's return. The Moderator and the Brethern were proceeding with the matter of Fintry's excommunication, which, of course, involved a form of civil outlawry as well, when Bothwell joined with the Earl of Montrose, head of Fintry's clan, in a strong intercession on the laird's behalf. Bothwell pressed his plea so hard that the Assembly, mildly accommodating at first, took umbrage. In consequence, he asked them to conceive no ill opinion of him and promised he would speak to Fintry no more—instead he did something rather more heinous: as Eastern Governor he persuaded James Scrymgeour, Constable of Dundee, to restore Fintry to Mains Castle, although he had been removed on the King's order. This resembled his splendid effort to placate the Kirk the preceding November, just after the King left the country, when he humbled himself in the Little Kirk in the forenoon and in the Great Kirk in the afternoon, both times confessing to a dissolute life and promising to be a different man in time to come. The same night, alas, he 'ravished a daughter of Gowrie out of Dirleton'—perhaps dwelling on his sins twice in one day made him realise how attractive they were. Bothwell's moral slip, however, probably did not feature in the reckoning on the King's return, although his kindly intervention for Graham of Fintry certainly did because of the secret dealing with the underground organiser which it betrayed.

His behaviour advertised strong and continuing links with the Spanish conspiracy in other ways. In January, Claud Hamilton, the Setons and Father Crichton's proselyte, the Earl of Crawford, foregathered in Edinburgh with many others of their persuasion. Calderwood records that 'the sight of so many uncouth faces' gave rise to alarm that Edinburgh was about to be seized and caused the burgesses to gird on their swords because it was accompanied by a rumour that some of Parma's ships were due at Leith. Bothwell took the burgesses to task for arming and keeping a strait watch without cause and without his authority, but the Provost and magistrates asserted their privilege to be on guard and were supported by Robert Bruce, the minister, who had been invested by the King with some civil authority. Thomas Duncan of Leith strengthened the suspicion of some ill design by reporting that John Knolls of Aberdeen had been to Parma as a courier and was back with some secret orders.

To crown it all, a Spanish ship suspected of bringing gold to Parma's correspondents arrived at Wigton. The captain of the ship along with a Scots pilot, an Englishman and three Spaniards were brought to Edinburgh out of the thirty or so persons on board, but they were soon allowed to go, except for the Scotsman who was detained in Edinburgh Castle for a while. King James, it appears, was livid at Bothwell's leniency towards the Spanish captain and his associates. Chancellor Maitland wrote to minister Bruce from Denmark on the strength of what news had reached them, saying that the late barque from Spain exposed the dissimulated hypocrisy of some, and that the King took very hardly the freeing of the captain and the Scots pilot. He had written home in an attempt to have them examined by torture, for he was convinced there was more in their errand than was confessed. The Chancellor added that he had heard also that a start was being made to revive the 'band' of the Brig of Dee, meaning the confederacy of Huntly, Bothwell and the rest which had confronted the King in arms the year before. Presumably the substance for this was a meeting of the 'northland conspirators' held in Kincardine under cover of the baptism of Lord Home's child. Bothwell had been there.

The royal voyage back from Denmark took place in April and James arrived at Leith with his bride on May 1st. The castle and the ships in the Forth were firing off guns with rare abandon when the welcoming party received them at the head of the stone stairway of the harbour. Bothwell, Lennox and Mar were to the fore, but it was not long before the King took the welcoming smile off Bothwell's face at least. Bowes saw the shadow pass over Bothwell after words exchanged between him and the King; he thought the earl was irritated by the apparent ingratitude of his royal master, for which he was inclined to blame Chancellor Maitland. It was remarked that Bothwell's indulgence towards Fintry was the main cause of the King's displeasure.

Yet soon after his homecoming the King himself was being blamed by the Kirk for encouragement of the idolators, and with some cause. By September, following his return in May, the Kirkcaldy Presbytery wrote to the Edinburgh Presbytery complaining that the magistrates of Burntisland had refused to arrest Huntly's Jesuit uncle, James Gordon, although desired to do so by the local minister. The reason was that the magistrates found the Jesuit Father Gordon in possession of a warrant from the King to reside there—as far as the King was concerned, the Privy Council Acts against Jesuits and seminary priests were scraps of paper.

James was arrogating to himself the royal right to be soft towards the Jesuits and the Spanish faction as long as they seemed to be in accord with his secret diplomacy, and were under his control. His new rift with Bothwell was not on account of the Earl's continued association with Spanish conspiracy, but because Bothwell appeared to be betraying the King's special sector of the plot. It was in the belief, apparently, that Bothwell could be trusted with his special Spanish interests, as well as with the defence of the realm, that the King had sailed happily away leaving Bothwell in command. The intercepted letters of the previous year had shown that the King assured Father Tyrie of his desire to continue clandestine dealing with Parma and Colonel Sempill. The letters of the agent Bruce had shown also that Bruce and Bothwell had acted together in drawing the King's attention to a letter from Sempill which Bruce alleged that Father Tyrie had tried to suppress. Out of this deviousness the King had apparently been made to believe that Bothwell and Bruce would look after his sector of the Spanish plot and inform him regularly of anything to his detriment contrived by Father Tyrie and Fintry. In the end, Bruce did openly play the role of informer against Fintry to the King and had probably played this role secretly all along from the date he supplied the King with the alleged suppressed letter. With Bothwell it was different. The restoration of Fintry to Mains Castle and the attempt to save him from excommunication, almost as soon as the King's face was set towards Denmark and his back was turned on Scotland, were proof that Bothwell had other loyalties within the conspiracy circle. Spies' reports, no doubt added to the King's picture of Bothwell's deep complicity with the chief underground organiser, Fintry, and taken together with the freeing of a Spanish ship by Bothwell, the absent King was thrown into a state of anxiety and rage. He was probably not worried about the Spanish ship bringing in money—perhaps his real fear was that the ship had come to remove money, that the invasion gold deposited for the Armada sideshow was on its way back to Spain or was being removed to a safer place. There were later indications that the King considered he had a proprietary interest in this gold; at any rate he attempted to rush orders to Scotland to torture the captain and the Scottish pilot and get to the bottom of the whole affair.

In the post-Armada situation it had become vital for the King to curb drastically, if not to eradicate entirely, the private diplomatic dealings of the Scottish Catholic earls with Spain, whose Armada defeat was his gain. King Philip had lost hope of winning England through internal support and of controlling France in the same way. English Catholic participation in the rebuff to the Armada had brought home this fact to the English Catholic leaders, Cardinal Allen and Father Parsons, as well as to Philip. With France failure had been spelt for Spain in the same year by the assassination of the brothers, the Duke of Guise and the Cardinal of Lorraine, through whose agency Philip had hoped for eventual domination.

Chancellor Maitland impressed on the English agent Fowler the meaning of this sombre fall of the curtain on the House of Guise. 'Your queen thinks she has lost in Guise a great enemy, and my master a great friend. Be assured it is not so. For a long time the King had no dealings with Guise: he loved him not. But, mark me, this will make the King of Spain seek my master; for by the Duke of Guise that King thought to have had all France at his devotion except the Protestants, to have subdued even them ere long, and to have been so strong as to have had his revenge on England without our help here. But now Scotland is his only card to play against England and this you will see ere long.' Maitland had begun to build a policy on that expectation and the King's instinct followed the road shown. The first need was to prevent Philip buying Scotland cheaply as an oddment offered by some hungry trafficker. Some precautions of this kind had been taken in advance of the Armada failure, when Philip still believed he could go straight to his goal and needed only a minor diversion in Scotland. The ports and coast of the south west of Scotland that were to have been kept open by Maxwell for the Spanish incomers were fairly effectively closed. The blow at Maxwell had been well timed and well aimed, because it was here that most of the preparation to welcome the strangers had been made; as early as 1586, when the Queen of Scots was still alive, the Master of Gray reported that Maxwell had received his first gold and with it had raised five hundred footmen and fifty horses.

Now, the next most urgent task for King James, even if belatedly approached, was to put that part of the Scottish east coast above the English Border beyond the danger of an easy snatch. Then he, and he alone, would be able to sell the Scottish postern to Spain to allow their accounts to be settled with the English who were playing havoc with Spanish shipping and trade and with Spain's Netherlands dependencies. His price? There was only one figure and that was the relinquishing by Philip of his claim to the English Crown and the recognition of the right of James Stewart. Alternatively, the threat of selling the Scottish postern to Spain would be used to compel Elizabeth to acknowledge the right of James Stewart.

Of course, there remained the Catholic north east coast where invaders might be welcomed by Huntly and his allies. Here the danger could be contained for a time, however, and in the early stage of the double game for the Double Crown it was necessary to have Huntly as a bridge with Spain to offset the pressure of the English Court and the Kirk.

It was pre-ordained that after the blow at Maxwell, the next should fall on Bothwell, if King James was to control the Scottish postern himself. Bothwell's intuition had enabled him to see his peril as far back as the time when the purge of the south west had been in progress, when Maxwell had been imprisoned and the ruthless mercenary officer, Sir William Stewart, let loose on the area to pacify it with hangings. Only weeks later Stewart's fatal quarrel with Bothwell had occurred in The Royal Mile. James at that time had been furious, but it was not the best time to call for a reckoning. Bothwell had his followers under arms for the bogus expedition to the Isles and had allies in the Catholic earls and the Armada had set sail and might at any time appear round the corner, so the settlement was postponed. When, later, it appeared that Bothwell might faithfully manage the King's sector of the Spanish conspiracy, and hold the rest in check, he had been made Military Governor in the King's absence, but it had given the King and the Chancellor in Denmark anxious moments and convinced them both otherwise. The intercession for Fintry, the baptismal party at Kincardine and the Spanish ship at Wigton finally settled the question.

In the suspended account with Bothwell the King had cause to remember not only his killing of Captain Stewart, but also the death of the good and holy Protestant Earl of Angus. He died of a disease which contained an element of inevitablity—witchcraft. Thus within a few weeks his two main agents against the pro-Spanish faction in the south west had been disposed of, the one by assassination and the other by black magic. Who could be more suspect of the black magic murder than the Border earl who had slain Stewart? There were many witches and warlocks in the Border country and it became known that one of them, Richard Graham, had been consulted by Francis Bothwell—twenty times it was said. When Bothwell eventually made his formal and legal defence he declared he had twice only consulted with Ninian Chirnside and that was for the charitable object of saving Angus from the curse of which he was dying, and at his wife's solicitation, but the time would come when Bothwell's lieutenant, Colville, would say that he made black white in confirming Bothwell's story. Whether Bothwell's dabbling was in black or white magic, whether he hoped to kill Angus this way or to save his life, the reckoning for everthing began to be made in the winter after the King's return from Denmark. Unfortunate witches, not from the blasted heath, but from Tranent, Haddington and Edinburgh closes were dragged screaming by the hair of the head into politics. The line of questioning, reinforced by thumb screws and other ghastly 'truth' extractors, was not aimed at establishing Bothwell's black magic conspiracy to destroy Angus, although this was almost certainly the inspiration of the proceedings; the torturers and examiners were given the task of extracting confessions implicating Bothwell in black magic plots to kill the King. It was not desirable to try Bothwell on any count that might rouse the loyalty of the Spanish faction. Indeed it was not desirable to try him at all. The object was to get him quietly out of the way, by his own concurrence if possible.

The witches went to the stake denying their confessions extracted under torture but, by promise of pardon according to Bothwell, Richard Graham's accusation of Bothwell was made to stand. In April 1591, therefore, Bothwell was locked up in Edinburgh Castle charged with black magic attempts to kill the King in Denmark and on the North Sea. It was a lurid way of dressing up the somewhat less colourful offences committed by the Earl when the King was in Denmark—attendance at the Kincardine baptism and the like.

When after two or three months the lords began to ask questions about Bothwell's trial, for which King James and Chancellor Maitland were by no means prepared, the Chancellor visited Bothwell in his prison-house and offered a bargain: he might have his life and also security of his estates if he retired into permanent exile. The same night Bothwell gave his answer, by escaping through the roof. For the next three years James quarrelled with the Kirk and the English court about his priorities; they held it was his first duty to suppress the Catholic earls in the north and abandon his own clandestine dealing with Spain. They gave comfort and help to Bothwell. James stuck to his original strategy of completing the destruction of Bothwell's faction while falling back on the Catholic north for comfort and keeping open a bridge with the Catholic powers for succour in desperation. Although the outlawed Bothwell became a serious menace by falling back on the support of the Kirk and the English court, this very switch was a gain for the royal policy, since it destroyed Bothwell as a leader of the Spanish faction. He was compelled to apologise abjectly for his former Spanish alignment, and thereby the King was assisted in containing the Spanish faction within the North. It lost its alarming aspect of pre-Armada days, when Maxwell backed by Claud Hamilton held the west, Bothwell was mobilising in the east and Huntly was preparing an easy descent on Leith Port. (Of course, the King himself was to be annexed then, along with the seaports.)

Even before the imprisonment of Bothwell the King renewed the harassment of David Graham of Fintry, now an excommunicate, by subjecting him in 1590 to a period of house arrest with his kinsman, Judge Graham of Halyards, who was under heavy penalty if he failed to act as efficient jailer. Fintry, the Master of Angus and the Bailiff of Errol were haled before the Privy Council in June 1591, while Bothwell was still under lock and key. They were charged with giving shelter to Papists, distributing foreign gold and 'waging' soldiers. Ambassador Bowes of England was there, along with Kirk leaders and the King. Bowes made the matter look as grave as he could by divulging that he had a spy's report that Bruce the agent was due back soon with another fifteen thousand crowns of Spanish gold. The spy's report was doubtless a report from Bruce himself, who was in due course the informant about the 'blanks' plot and later warned of the arrival of the Spanish ship at Aberdeen. Although the accused made denials, the King asserted that it was all as true as he was sitting there—Bruce had evidently sent him a mass of information too. There were more restraints on Fintry and his friends and more obligations on their kinsmen to find surety; it seemed not a year passed but Fintry was warded, or excommunicated or made to find surety, then forfeited, then. . . .

Strangely, the King's encouragement of Huntly, on the other hand, continued to grow until it reached incitement to murder. This involved, as victim, the Earl of Moray who was tricked into coming south. Lord Ochiltree swore that he brought Moray to Donibristle by arrangement with the King and the Chancellor to effect a reconciliation with Huntly, and that no one else knew. The firing of the house at Donibristle and the killing of the injured fugitive on the dark shore was a deed that roused great popular anger. The motive attributed to it was that of destroying a potential ally of Bothwell, the King's enemy; it also divided Huntly and Bothwell more deeply and promoted the King's policy of a northern containment. James had to fly from the popular anger to the west and take refuge with Lord John Hamilton. While he was there, one John Naismith was brought in and threatened with torture to testify that Moray had been involved with Bothwell in plots against the King. The stout John refused to collaborate. On the departure of the royal party from Edinburgh the soldiers of the Royal Guard, infected with the mood of rebellion, went on strike for their arrears of pay. They took the Chancellor's trunks and coffers off the pack ponies and carried them back into the palace where a household official had to make a solemn promise to rectify their grievance. At the height of his troubles the King wrote to Huntly to say, 'I have been in such peril and danger of my life, as since I was born I was never in the like. . . . When you come here come not by the ferries. And if you do, accompany yourself, as you respect your preservation.' Before he overcame this crisis, James had to institute some mock justice against Huntly and make a sacrificial lamb of his Chancellor Maitland by sending him from Court.

# 10   *Fintry takes his secret to the Next World*

THE 'BLANKS' plot, which has been mentioned, brought David Graham of Fintry's life story to its last grim chapter. It was also the final invasion plan of Father Crichton—his fourth, if we count his impromptu effort to halt the Armada at the Western Isles. Graham's conspiratorial activities in Scotland spanned the same decade as Crichton's: both were brought back to Scotland from abroad by the false spring of Catholic hope and restoration produced by the apparent success of D'Aubigny (later Earl of Lennox) in his Guisian-inspired conquest of the young James Stuart and the Scottish court, but Graham had been in exile for seven years only against Crichton's twenty. With the Master of Gray, he arrived to serve the imprisoned Queen of Scots as a secret agent, sent by his uncle Beaton who was the Queen's ambassador in Paris. When Bowes of England warned the Earl of Gowrie that he was in danger from Mary Stewart if he kept the casket letters in his custody, the danger was probably represented by Gray and Graham and their shadowy associates.

Graham was first noticed when the young King slipped the leash and escaped from Gowrie. He carried James's jubilant and boastful message which advertised his freedom in Paris, and Bowes noticed that he had a long audience with the King on his return. The Kirk also noticed him as a new and, to them, insidious influence at Court. The French ambassador, Fontenay, jealously observed that he held the purse strings of the Queen of Scots' dowry funds once they were sent to Scotland. As to a certain disbursement of six thousand crowns from this scource, Graham distributed half on instructions from Paris and half at his own discretion, but refused to discuss the matter of the distribution with Fontenay and returned a false and evasive answer to James. Thereupon Fontenay and young James got their heads together, and Fontenay wrote to the Queen of Scots in England saying her son thought it was a great villainy to see her money handled in this fashion, at the discretion and appetite of Glasgow (that is of Beaton in Paris and his nephew in Edinburgh); he was very astonished, Fontenay added, that the Duke of Guise let himself be run by such a man. James, however, knew the buttered side of his bread so well in relation to Beaton and Guise that for all his private complaining about villainy, he held the ring in Fintry's favour whenever there were religious arguments among the courtiers. He also favoured Fintry with his confidence, along with Gray, when it was a matter of another special mission to France.

Graham of Fintry was, of course, shut out in the swing to the 'league' with Elizabeth. His uncle Beaton, in Paris, then arranged with the Pope and General Aquaviva to establish the Jesuit network in Scotland, with Tyrie passing instructions from his side in Paris and Fintry co-ordinating the activities from his home in Scotland. That pattern continued and was the cause of the destructive and consuming jealously of the agent Bruce who had begun his career as a secretary to Beaton. It was the pattern that was in evidence when Tyrie arrived after the Armada and hastened up to Broughty for conference with Fintry, slighting and offending Bruce, who was ignored.

In the few years between, Bruce and Fintry were both busy putting flesh on the bones of the Queen mother's plan for a 'strait league' of the Catholic lords to negotiate a military and financial alliance with Parma. As a 'fly by night' Bruce was more often in evidence as, for the protection of his estate in Scotland, Fintry was forced to limit and conceal his movements, which were only too well studied, as efficiently as possible. This did not prevent him from undertaking a mission to France and Spain on the very eve of the sailing of the Armada, nor from undertaking the long ride to London when the legal process had started against the Queen of Scots, solely to extract information from the ambassador, Douglas, on the way. Following the Queen's death, the fluid situation had enabled him to come close to the Court again and begin an intrigue with Chancellor Maitland. His part in the military plans of Colonel Sempill must have been greater than has appeared, because of his close acquaintance with Bothwell and the fact that he was the one person warded following Sempill's departure. In the matter of his links with Bothwell and the Border coast, his Mains Castle on the Tay served better for inconspicuous movement than a voyage down the Forth or a journey through the Lothians; from Fast Castle on a clear day the Bell Rock glitters at the mouth of the Tay, and on such a wide highway there were no great dangers of recognition.

As has been mentioned in connection with the 'blanks' plot, Crichton wrote from Spain to Father Gordon in Aberdeenshire saying that he had opened King Philip's eye about the deceitful English and won him for a plan of invasion through Scotland. Crichton requested the procuring of as many signatures of Scottish noblemen as possible, on blank papers. On sight of the 'blanks' which were to be filled in by Philip and his officers with guidance from Crichton and Tyrie, an army was to be sent from Spain the following spring, 1593, to sail for Kirkcudbright. Crichton's letter was passed on by Father Gordon to Father Abercromby, who brought it to Fintry in Dunfermline in April before anything was done about it.

Next, Sir James Chisholm came to Fintry and said he had conferred with the earls, including Huntly, at the time of the Parliament in Edinburgh in June and had been accredited by them with the mission of carrying the 'blanks' to Spain since he was bound on a voyage to his uncle in exile, the Catholic Bishop of Dunblane who, abroad, was also Bishop of Vaison. Sir James was brother of the John Chisholm who had two or three times smuggled sums of ten thousand crowns into the country during 1588, the Armada year. Sir James himself had been consulted by Bruce, the agent, concerning the distribution of the gold, or at least Bruce had promised Parma he would consult him in default of consulting Fintry. While the Parliament was meeting in Edinburgh in June, Chisholm collected signatures from Errol and Angus, but for some reason had not got Huntly's although he was dealing with Huntly at this time. It was only when George Ker, son of Lord Newbattle, went up to Huntly's Castle at Strathbogie that copies of Huntly's signature were obtained, and by that time the mission to convey the 'blanks' had been transferred by Chisholm to Ker.

This change was accompanied by increased activity on the part of Father Abercromby, who obtained additional signatures from Angus and Errol as late as October, 1592. There were now two signed 'blanks' available from each of the three earls, Angus, Errol and Huntly. In their subsequent confessions, Ker and Fintry testified that these were to have the eventual form of massive letters with the substance of them to be supplied in Madrid, but later further signatures were in demand for another purpose together with impressions of the noblemen's seals for proclamations. The two proclamation 'blanks' obtained by Father Abercromby were double sheets with the signatures and seals subscribed and affixed in the middle of the open paper. There was the additional signature this time of Patrick Gordon of Auchindoun. Abercromby received Huntly's and Auchindoun's signatures first and then collected those of Errol and Angus in Edinburgh. During this period he conferred with Fintry on several occasions, according to Fintry's confession, and before Ker got ready to go, there was a final conference between Abercromby and Fintry in prison at Stirling Castle, where Fintry had landed in the meantime.

Nearly nine months after the receipt of Crichton's letter, Father Gordon sat down to write his reply to send off with the 'blanks'. 'We have delayed overlong, I grant,' he wrote, 'but we will show you the cause of all.' He warned that next summer many would be bound for other countries and would wait no longer. 'You have gottin all that you desired,' he added, 'therefore make haste.' The 'cause of all' in the matter of the delay was doubtless connected with reluctance to endanger lives and estates by such dangerous and un-limited commitment without knowing whether the Spaniards were also committed, at least to the extent of the invasion gold being al-ready in Scotland. It almost had to be by the winter of 1592–93 if the Spanish army was due to arrive in the spring. Fintry may have given enough assurance on this point in the end, since the eventual completion of both the missive papers and the proclamation sheets seems to say as much. On the other hand, had the Spaniards at their end got everything they desired as Father Gordon averred? Perhaps they had not. They had the signatures of the Catholic earls of the north only, Angus, Errol and Huntly, with Huntly's reinforced by Auchindoun's. This northern one-sidedness was explained by a state-ment that the three earls took upon themselves the burden for all the Catholics of Scotland, for better secrecy. Yet Father Crichton had not asked for secrecy—he had asked for as many pledges as could be obtained. Conspicuously lacking were the signatures of Lord Claud Hamilton who, with Huntly, had set the whole thing in motion six years earlier; all three had signed the 'will ye no' come back again' appeal to Parma as late as the time of the Armada's return.

It was a sign of the success of the King's, or his Chancellor's, policy of containment of the Spanish faction. The outlawing of Both-well in the summer of 1591 had been as timely as the blow at Max-well in the spring of 1588. There were now no easy landings for invaders near the Border, either on the west coast or on the east, and this had the effect of slowing down the tempo of Father Crichton's invasion plans at the Spanish end and curtailing the response in Scot-land. Another evidence of weakness was that someone had can-vassed the King's opinion on the invasion project during the delay; the benefits to his royal estate and his prospects for the Double Crown were the blandishments. He treated the question as a logistic exercise and gravely set down a list of the pros and cons; the cons had it. While he allowed the advantage of the money being ready and the men not far away, he stressed that he could scarcely hold rebellion and invasion at bay in relation to his own realm much less promote them against England. He might in the future, he said, undertake the invasion himself with the help of a small force and the money, 'as mickle or mair'. He was apprehensive about being overwhelmed by too many Spaniards and he laid stress on a small force —he had not the same fears of being overwhelmed by too much money and here he raised no limiting condition. He was for delay, and made it plain that, for him, invasion was on only if he could have his right of succession in England recognised and acknowledged otherwise.

James was to have sent his memo on invasion to the Spanish Court by his own courier, Poury Ogilvie, in the summer of 1592, but Ogilvie's departure was delayed and somehow he King's virtual veto went into the same courier's bag as the 'blanks' which were a *carte blanche* for an immediate invasion entirely on whatever terms would suit the Spaniards. This inclusion of James's memo, as well as the approach to him, was a puzzle. So was Sir James Chisholm's failure to get Huntly's signature at the parliament meeting at Edinburgh in June, as well as his failure to get the others. Indeed, for a time the only signatures obtained were those of Fintry's two neighbours, Angus and Errol, who had been haled before the Privy Council with him the year before for 'waging' soldiers. This was a clear sign that it was Fintry and his immediate friends who were pressing for the die to be cast both in Scotland and in Spain. When Father Gordon said 'make haste', since there were some who would be bound for other countries by the next summer, this applied especially to Fintry. His final sentence had been banishment and he was confined in Stirling Castle until he chose to go; it would seem that, for Fintry, the last chance to use the funds at his command had arrived and the last chance to restore the cause and his own fortunes.

The collector and courier of the 'blanks' had been changed in midstream from Sir James Chisholm to the young George Ker. Father Abercromby and Ker together had stirred themselves to get if not more signatures then more copies, including proclamation signatures, to impress King Philip that those concerned were prepared to have their names posted up in Scotland. The Jesuits, with no worldly estate to imperil and George Ker, a younger son of Lord Newbattle in much the same position, threw themselves on the side of Fintry who had already lost his estate. They won Huntly; Father

Abercromby and Ker made a journey to Strathbogie Castle, and Father Gordon, Crichton's friend, was already there. Auchindoun, Huntly's other adviser, clearly helped them and to strengthen Huntly's resolve risked his own name. Huntly's soul was in the keeping of the Jesuits more than was the case with any of the others; he was full of contrition for having signed the Protestant Confession to obtain the Captaincy of James's Guard, and he was among the last to be brought to the table to sign again. Plainly it was the Jesuits who won this battle for a soul and a signature, as far as Huntly was concerned.

There were signs that Fintry was using his command of the secret of the invasion funds to push matters. Who was resisting him, if the Scottish Jesuits were his main support? In his letter from Stirling Castle he made dark references to people who were trying 'to dress up quarrels' which suggested that he was the target of a number of factions. Events and circumstances point to Sir James Chisholm being a principle obstacle to the underground leader's plans. The agent Bruce alleged to Parma that Father Tyrie was poisoning the mind of King James against the Bishop of Vaison. Tyrie was Fintry's associate and agent of his uncle Beaton in Paris and, if Bruce's tale was true, it advertised a rift between Fintry and the Chisholms, who were Vaison's agents and kinsmen in Scotland.

Sir James Chisholm was an officer of the Royal Household, and although selected by the earls to collect and convey the signatures to Spain, he made no job of the collecting and backed out of the delivering. Having daily access to the King, he could well have canvassed James's opinion on Spanish invasion schemes in order to exhibit to Madrid that the King was not going to be easily taken in tow. It had been the boast of Huntly that, when Parma came, they would be masters and captains of the King's person and would use his authority to strengthen their enterprise. Chisholm was probably determined to show the true picture. When the King's courier, Ogilvie, failed to leave for Spain with the memo, Chisholm appears to have volunteered to transmit the document for the King, it is likely that he said that he would send it through his uncle in Vaison, who was in touch with both the Vatican and the Spanish court.

It was late in December 1592 when young George Ker, distantly related to Father Crichton, prepared to take ship for Spain from the Isle of Cumbrae in the Clyde. He never got outside Scottish waters for Andrew Knox, a Paisley minister, appeared on the quay suddenly with a party of armed parishioners and Glasgow students and descended on the ship. Ker was seized along with his baggage and taken to Edinburgh amidst excitement all the way. The King's memo, however, was officially abstracted before the 'blanks' and the accompanying letters were exhibited to the world, like the letters Queen Elizabeth exposed to the light of day about four years before.

There had been a third threat to the plot all the time, a threat additional to the strategic difficulties and divisions in Scotland and the diminishing confidence in Spain, which was expressed in the demand for the blank pledges. It was the threat of betrayal from within, and it led inevitably to this seizure of Ker and the incriminating 'blanks'. One of the letters Ker carried with the 'blanks', wrapped in the folds of his change of sailor's shirt, was from Dr John Cecil to Father Parsons. Cecil was living at Seton House, which was Liberty Hall to all the conspirators, and had been secretary to Cardinal Allen. A letter announcing his voyage to London was intercepted by Sir Robert Cecil, Burghley's son, which caused his ship to be stopped and searched at sea by HMS *Hope*. In London Dr Cecil made a deal to perform 'good and acceptable services' for Sir Robert Cecil in exchange for his freedom. He then proceeded to Scotland on the mission to which he had been assigned by Father Parsons, but he was now serving two masters. What damaging part Cecil played in the 'blanks' plot cannot be specified. He was later denounced by the plot's organiser Father Crichton as an English intelligencer, but there was a more dangerous informant, Robert Bruce the agent. His communications with Parma and Sempill, which came to light in the letters intercepted by Queen Elizabeth, revealed this. In August 1592, Bowes, the English ambassador, wrote to Lord Burghley saying that a servant of the Bishop of Glasgow in Paris had written to him offering to discover the practices of Spain in Scotland. By November the envious Bruce was back in Scotland. On his arrival he supplied much information to Bowes but he also unburdened himself to King James. In gratitude the King pardoned him for all past crimes including treason, negotiation with foreign princes and distribution of foreign gold. The betrayal of Fintry and Ker was part of the information supplied by Bruce for this pardon. This same Bruce sent on a report to Bowes two years later concerning the Spanish ship that sailed for Aberdeen with Father Gordon, the Papal Nuncio and the ten thousand crowns. Eventually he was put on trial in Flanders as a spy and betrayed, and Father Crichton and George Ker were amongst his accusers. Apart from spying, it appeared to be the function of Bruce, Dr Cecil and other internal enemies of the conspiracy to spread conflict and doubt. Fintry's factional enemies were no doubt stirred up by them.

Between seven and eight on the night of the 31st December 1592, George Ker, the 'blanks' courier, was thrust into the prison house of the Edinburgh Tolbooth after being brought into the city guarded by sixty horsemen and two hundred foot. The next night, Monday, the Earl of Angus one of the signatories of the 'blanks', was put under guard in his own lodging and the following day transferred to Edinburgh Castle by the magistrates on the order of the Privy Council. Graham of Fintry was already in confinement within Stirling Castle.

The King was at Stirling at this time, and letters were sent to him from the ministers and his Council urging his return. He was back by the Wednesday, Ker having been brought into the city on Sunday, and addressed some words of approval to a combined gathering of the magistrates, ministers and members of his Council. But a week later the barons and the ministers were still having to press him, and a deputation led by the minister Bruce, which included John Napier of Merchiston, went down to the Palace with their demands. They were kept waiting an hour and a half and when they were admitted to the great hall James, sitting on a chair covered with velvet, made 'a long and confused harangue' according to Calderwood. He condemned them mainly for meeting without his warrant, saying he knew nothing of it until the Kail Market wives knew of it, but he still promised severity towards the traitors.

Eventually, about the middle of March, the King gathered forces together and pursued the signatories of the 'blanks', Huntly and Errol, who were not yet in custody. He chased them as far as Aberdeen and they retreated into Caithness. The King then returned to Edinburgh and the General Assembly later recorded that 'all these fair shows turned to no effect'. Before the King set out on his canter a placard was nailed to the door of the Tolbooth declaring that Huntly and Errol were in no danger, a recommendation had been made out for their favourable reception in foreign parts if they had to go abroad, and their friends and relatives were invested with their lands which were entirely safe. Another declaration nailed up about the same time alleged that Lords Home and Maxwell, friends of the 'blanks' signatories, were strong at Court and had received money to look after the prisoners in the Tolbooth. These public commentaries were ascribed to Francis Bothwell.

It was in the prison house at the Tolbooth that the real sequel to the 'blanks' plot was enacted, there and at the Mercat Cross, on the scaffold. The King's Privy Council had examined the letters found among Ker's belongings, concealed in the sleeves of a sailor's shirt. They had taken him out of the Tolbooth and questioned him before the King came back from Stirling, but he refused to give any explanations. After the King's return, so Bowes the English ambassador reported, commision was given to 'Justice-clerk Blantyre and George Young to offer him the torture'; Bowes added that many thought he would suffer the torture without confession. But some thought the torture was a pretence and a sham. Mr John Davidson, who wrote a preface for the publication of the intercepted letters, made an entry in his diary for the following May recording that there was a letter to the Prince of Parma which 'touched the King with knowledge and approbation of the trafficking and promise of assistance, etc.' This may have referred to the King's memo on the invasion from the standpoint of his hopes for the Double Crown, the document still extant at Hatfield House, or it may have been something more compromising. Davidson declared it was not thought expendient to publish it; if not, then it was perhaps inexpedient to put the bearer of this compromising document to the torture. Whatever the process, a confession of George Ker emerged.

Fintry's examination followed. Calderwood says Fintry's friends made him drunk to withstand the ordeal, but after his wits returned to him he wrote a confession and sent it to the King, which, although sufficient for his conviction, the King 'would have him to be re-examined and threatened with the torments of the boot'.

The official record shows that Ker's statements were taken on 3rd, 5th and 6th February. The 4th was a Sabbath and it is a testimony to the piety of the official torturer and that of his employers that he did no work on the Lord's day. Fintry was drunk on Monday the 12th and his statements were taken on the 13th and 14th. Both prisoners were in accord that the Spaniards were to land and be assisted, Fintry being more explicit in giving the number at thirty thousand. He stated further that their object was to avenge the death of the Queen of Scots. Both agreed that the purpose of the 'blanks' was to bind the signatories and their followers to help the invaders.

Ker's fate was decided first. Having signed his confession and addressed a letter craving pardon from the King, in which he declared the King's title would not have been harmed and his agreement with the enterprise had not been doubted, he waited. He was duly granted his life and remained confined in Edinburgh Castle but by June he was allowed to escape. For appearance sake his friends, who included the unfailing Samaritan, Lord Seton, and also the Queen, it was said, gave his guard Smeaton a bribe of five hundred marks—for further appearance's sake the King had Smeaton hanged. The cynical Calderwood remarked that on the day of his escape Ker was pursued, but Ker was conducted one way and the pursuers went the other. Next day the minister Balcalquall preached a sermon against such mockery.

On 13th February, while Fintry was still under examination, the Earl of Angus, one of the 'blanks' signatories, likewise escaped from Edinburgh Castle, in advance of Ker. The same Calderwood says that sufficient warning was given to the King, the captain and the constable; but no warning availed.

Two days later Graham of Fintry was turned over by the King to a court of barons and burgesses for a hurried trial. Then, at about two in the afternoon, they took him to the Mercat Cross where he was beheaded. This was far more than many had expected, Calderwood commented. Fintry had supplied the same evidence as Ker; it was more detailed, if anything. He had addressed the same plea to the King for mercy and pardon, but the result was expressed in the difference between death and life. Moysie the notary, writing on the strange outcome said; 'in respect of Mr George's declaration of the truth the King granted him his life. The Laird of Fintry deponit the same and was executed'.

All save Fintry escaped with their lives. Freedom was contrived for Angus and George Ker; Huntly and Errol returned from the wilds of Caithness; and the Jesuit Fathers were unscathed. There was no penalty for the officer of the King's household, Sir James Chisholm. The earlier conspirators, Claud Hamilton, Lord Maxwell and Colonel Sempill never came to any harm. The agent Robert Bruce was pardoned. Francis Bothwell was driven into exile, but for other notorious offences, and he died a natural death. Only the head of David Graham rolled on the scaffold on account of the Spanish plots in Scotland.

What was there to account for this singular execution? It was not due to the clamour of the Kirk or the pressure of the English court because that clamour and pressure were directed against all the conspirators impartially. It was not produced by the design and malice of some instruments of the King. Bowes, the English ambassador, reported home that the King himself had conducted the examination of Ker then hurried forward the examination and trial of Graham. 'The King in this has remained resolute,' he said. 'He was occasioned to stay his journey (to the north in chase of Huntly) for two days for the trial and execution of Fintry.' Bowes declared that Fintry had offered the King fifty thousand pounds to spare his life. It appears that though the King got as much out of Fintry as he extracted from Ker, he was being frustrated. The signed statements from either were largely superflous to him; he knew the gist of the plot from the approach made to him early in the summer when he had drawn up his memo on invasion. He had obtained the whole story in detail since from the defector, Robert Bruce the agent. His examination and torture threat in the case of Ker was a charade; but the examination of Fintry was in deadly earnest. Fintry apparently had information that Ker did not possess and his skull held secrets that Bruce the informer could not impart.

It was strange that King James was at Stirling at the end of December and into early January. (Fintry was imprisoned at Stirling Castle). Or was it so strange considering what was going on? George Ker was being tracked down by Lord Ross, with minister Knox and his Glasgow 'scholars' as his hunting pack and had been turned on to the secret by Ambassador Bowes's intelligence service. In his last letter of the year to Lord Burghley in London, Bowes reported a secret meeting of the Catholic earls. After that meeting Ker was ready to depart with the 'blanks' but was held up a while for a ship. Fintry writing from prison about the delay referred to it picturesquely, 'I am sorry that George has been so long disappointed of his horse. But much better it is not to have hazarded an old gloyd that might have stammered and put him in hazard'. All the time Ker was waiting he was being watched so that when he set out his pursuers were never many steps behind him.

While Bowes and Lord Ross and minister Knox were looking after Ker, the King inspired by the same informer, appears to have decided that Fintry was more worthy of his attention and so he betook himself to Stirling Castle. The interrogation in Fintry's case almost certainly began there before he was ever brought down to the Tolbooth in Edinburgh. At this stage it was probably friendly enticement to Fintry to follow Bruce's recent example and share his secrets with the King. The two had shared secrets before, in the early days of Guisian conspiracy. James had granted Bruce his pardon for past offences on December 8th, for the information about the plot he had betrayed. How much more anxious was he to obtain Fintry's secrets considering that Bruce had defected because he had not obtained the trust he desired and that trust had gone to Fintry.

James's discernment and his intimate acquaintance with Fintry confirmed Bruce's betrayal. He had been close on his heels harrying him for several years, watching with his own eyes and through those of Maitland, his Chancellor, who had intrigued with Fintry and gained his secrets to betray them. For the King perhaps the most envious memory relating to Fintry was of the six thousand crowns of his mother's dowry fund which he saw in the laird's hands, when he could not question but only complain feebly to Fontenay of the villainy of it. Now, although it was not Mary Stewart's money that was involved but King Philip's, James was just as prone to consider it was in the wrong hands and being distributed, or hidden, for the wrong purposes. Only recently there had been that undignified strike because of the pay arrears of his guards. What more deserving case was there than a King who had the coffers stripped off his pack horses and flung into the guard room because he could not pay his servants? Remembering his mother's gold had been dispensed by Fintry to the undeserving cases, James was resolved to prevent a repetition of such 'villainy'. This set him on the road to Stirling while others looked to the less important quarry, George Ker, who was embarking for Spain.

Bowes reported that Fintry offered the King fifty thousand pounds for his life when it came to the final stage of the questioning and torture at the Tolbooth. If so, it confirmed to the King that he had the invasion gold and therefore discouraged any settlement for a paltry amount; it also confirmed that gold was the subject of the interrogation and the motive for the torture and that torture having failed, there was the final sanction—the headsman. The King held back for two days while the expeditionary force was under arms and waiting to set out for the north. He was ready at the last minute to exercise his royal prerogative of mercy—at the price of Fintry's secret. But Fintry walked down the High Street with his lips sealed and carried his secret to the next world. James had played his ace of spades but was no richer.

## 11  The death of a judge and a summons for Logan

THE GOLDEN string led through Fintry's life to Francis Bothwell, but in the shadow of Fintry's death it twisted back to link him with his kinsman, Judge Graham of Halyards, and then with a loop it took in Robert Logan, the baron of Fast Castle.

Judge Graham of Halyards had, under penalties, to preside over Fintry's house arrest in the winter of 1590–91, at the time when the King began to examine the witches for evidence against Bothwell in order to bring about his perpetual banishment. As to Fintry, the King's object was to circumscribe him increasingly for the better watching of his movements, in the hope that he would eventually break out of the circle and betray what he wanted to know.

There had been a curious correspondence between Judge Graham and Douglas, the Scottish ambassador in London, when Fintry was in France in the Armada year. The Judge had sent various matters to Douglas on behalf of Scottish merchants in connection with business and money matters, but this was different. It concerned letters which he was prepared to pass on to London for examination, but only if Douglas's nephew in Scotland conveyed them south personally, and if their safe return was guaranteed by the nephew's father, that is by the ambassador's brother, thus invoking the strong family honour of the time to reinforce an ordinary common or garden pledge. The nephew wrote to the ambassador in London in April 1588 saying that Halyards was still delaying about the letters until he, the writer, could come to London. 'Fintry's going to France', he added, 'has also stayed his resolutions.' (In the manuscript the name is not completely legible but the Hatfield Commissioners who have its custody give it as Fintry.) 'He is so certain,' the nephew continued, 'that he cannot tell in what way to end, but for what you willed me to offer him he will in no way accept of it.' It should be understood that James's ambassador, Douglas, had no official salary and made his living by trading secrets mainly to the to the English secret service, not a very good way to ensure his loyalty to his Sovereign and his country. His try-out price for Halyard's mysterious letters was disdained, they were important beyond ordinary values, in the eyes of a Judge of the Court of Sessions accustomed to handling weighty affairs. The following year the nephew again wrote to the ambassador at his residence in Lime Street about them and said that if he found the opportunity to travel he would bring the letters and 'move my father to give his obligation to my Lord of Halyards'. Unfortunately, the correspondence does not tell the story to the end, although it did look as if Halyards was so mistrustful and undecided that he would never let them go. But even the hint of them would surely be turned into a commodity and sold by Douglas to England to help pay the rent at Lime Street. It is extremely probable, therefore, that Halyard's links with Fintry over these mysterious letters had a place in Fintry's dossier and were something Bowes would be aware of when he hovered in the background at Fintry's interrogation and torture. There was also a black mark against Halyards in that he had sheltered the chief of his clan, Montrose, when the latter raised forces along with Huntly and Bothwell at the time of the affair of the Bridge of Dee.

These things may have led to Fintry being questioned under torture as to how far Halyards was his accomplice and how far he shared his secrets, and in the laird's agony something may have come out. At any rate, at the end of Fintry's first day of examination, Tuesday, 13th February 1593, the judge was assassinated. He had received that evening an order from the Palace to quit the town. The circumstances appear to have been ominous because between sixty to eighty of his friends and kinsmen rallied round and provided him with their protection on the way down to Leith. When they were going down Leith Wynd they looked round and saw a force not far behind, headed by the Earl of Lennox, the King's lieutenant, and Sir James Sandilands. This was the same Sandilands whom James, years later, set as a blood-hound on the trail of the schoolboy Gowries after their older brothers were murdered at Perth. Lennox and Sandilands were carrying clubs, according to the diarist Calderwood, and Graham's followers turned round to defend themselves and the judge. Shots were exchanged. Someone skilfully picked out the judge who fell wounded, and his followers and protectors were put to flight. Halyards was carried into a house. Later a French page entered the house and without molestation or restraint 'douped a whinger' into the wounded judge and finished him off.

The ordering of the quarry into the open, the menacing, club-in-hand pursuit, the discriminating shot and the determined dagger all added up to plain, planned murder. The royal direction for it, apparent from its agents, was a sable twin to the royal command for the execution of Fintry two days later. If Halyards shared Fintry's secret this was a self-defeating operation with regard to gaining access to it. But the calculations here were different; there were still torture sessions ahead to wring the secret out of Fintry and the shadow of the Maiden or Scottish guillotine to coerce him. If Halyards was Fintry's confidant and executor, the fear would be born in the King's mind that the judge might forestall them, even though they won Fintry's secret. The fact that Halyards was so heavily guarded seem to confirm this motive for it, or at least it confirms that there was a strong motive for his murder, of which he was acutely aware. The murder of Halyards disposes of the idea that Fintry died because he was the persistent offender and the undoubted leader of the Spanish faction and not because of his precious secret. This was already disproved in the process employed in Fintry's examination; after recovering from the drunken stupor induced by his friends—also a strong pointer—he confessed enough to have himself hanged. The King, however, was not satisfied and ordered him to be re-examined and threatened with the torments of the boot, according to Calderwood. Halyards was in no sense a leader of the Spanish plots, yet from among them all he was the only one struck down along with Fintry; his only possible significance lay in the secrets he might have shared with the leader. For such golden secrets both men died, Fintry because he would not yield the secret of the invasion gold and Halyards from fear that he would change the place of concealment, suddenly.

Even if we cannot know the precise grounds for the King's belief that the judge was the repository of Fintry's secret, the fact of his assassination on the day of Fintry's examination is significant and cannot be ignored. Nor can we ignore the other pointers; the two had been close together for months during Fintry's house arrest, they were involved together in the mysterious matter of the letters which were to go to London and which had a strong element of secrecy and, finally, Halyards was the man who would normally be Fintry's executor because of close kinship and his legal standing. By means of innocent-looking instructions concerning his worldly estate Fintry may have contrived to pass on the secrets of gold in his custody to his fellow conspirators or his overlords in the conspiracy. The communication might well be something that Halyards himself would make little of, because Fintry could speak naturally in the private and oblique language of the underground, as he did when he wrote from prison about George being better without an old 'gloyd' that might have stammered. A later conspirator, Lenin, called this Aesopian language, but a dead judge could make no communication for Fintry in Aesopian or any other language. That was how King James wanted it and it appears to be the only motive for the judge's murder.

This double seal on the secret placed Fintry's friends and followers in difficulties that were made evident by the signs of the search which began after his execution. The signs were not confined to the search plan of Logan and Napier alone. This we are approaching—the evidence of an inquest following Fintry's death. But before ranging so far we are compelled to halt at the other incident connected with Fintry's examination which for us is nearly as dramatic and perhaps more full of meaning than the death of the judge— the loop of the golden string which at this very time took in Robert Logan, Francis Bothwell and Fast Castle.

On 12th February 1593, the day on which Fintry's examination was to begin, Robert Logan, the master of Fast Castle, was summoned to appear before the Privy Council to answer upon 'his treasonable conspiring, consulting, trafficking and devising with Francis, sometime Earl of Bothwell'. It has already been remarked that Bothwell's crime, for which he was first imprisoned in Edinburgh Castle and then outlawed, was basically his continued intrigue with Fintry which disquieted the King while in Denmark and on his return. 'Hypocritical dissimulation,' Chancellor Maitland called it, and it was he who drove the process against both Bothwell and Fintry. Logan's summons on the same day had the same meaning as the questioning of Fintry.

The King and his Privy Councillors had enough on their plate on 12th February 1593 without raising extraneous issues with Logan or anybody else. James's examination of Ker was just over, he was in the middle of his military preparation for the march to the north to allay popular discontent concerning Huntly, he was about to let Angus slip from the Castle, he was planning how to assassinate Halyards and he was pressing Fintry. In this state of single-mindedness during these crowded days it is unthinkable that he would have allowed Logan to obtrude on the Privy Council agenda unless he was connected with the predominent purpose of the hour. An order was also out to the Edinburgh magistrates to bring in Logan's servants, Matthew Logan and William Craik, believed to be lurking about the town.

What were the common questions concerning scheming with Bothwell to be put to both Logan and Fintry? Fintry volunteered information on nearly everything without question. Names he had named, which did not much interest the King because he wished to protect these friends for his future intrigues with Spain. Details he supplied concerning the invaders, who were to arrive in the spring; they were to number thirty thousand and were to land at Kirkcudbright or within the Clyde, depending on wind and tide and weather. Money was to come first and was to be used for supplies for the invaders and to raise Scottish forces. This was where Fintry's answers ceased to be credible. The money, he declared, was to be sent after the 'blanks' reached Spain, which meant the signatories risked all before the Spaniards ventured a thing; it meant also, since Ker was leaving in January, that the gold was to be delivered recklessly and hurriedly at a time when the spies of Bowes and the Kirk abounded. It further meant that, even with a reckless hurried delivery, a few weeks at most were allowed to spend the gold on supplies, to spread it over the country to 'wage' soldiers and to arm them (quite apart from drilling them), to march them south from Angus and Forfar and Aberdeen and infiltrate them into Kirkcudbright. Never could an army have been recruited, supplied, armed and brought to the end of a long march in such record time.

Even if the King had received no contrary inside intelligence from the agent Bruce, even if it was unknown that negotiations concerning the invasion gold dated back several years, he could not have swallowed Fintry's story of this impossible last minute organisation of commissariat and treasury. The Spanish ship at Kirkcudbright could have brought in the gold when the invasion prospects were fairer, during his absence in Denmark, but the King's association of Logan and Bothwell with his interrogation of Fintry reflects what he really believed about the invasion treasury. His thoughts apparently dwelt on the time when Bothwell collaborated with both Bruce and Fintry for the seizure of the Port of Eyemouth, when, as Bruce reported, Bothwell had 'listed and maintained troops of men all summer'. In James's mind's eye was the broad highway between the Bell Rock and the Berwickshire cliffs that might have linked Fintry and Bothwell, when the latter was lurking among the bays and caves with his 'listed troops' for a whole summer, waiting for the Armada. This was the matter that could supply common ground for questioning Logan and his servants on the same day as Fintry. Had Fintry come down from the Tay to Fast Castle when Bothwell and his listed troops were in command there? Had 'foreigners and strangers' come in? (This question, incidentally was raised by the Privy Council some years later in another connection, and it had been raised by Queen Elizabeth when Logan was a minor.) Was the invasion gold a fact which had materialised in that place at that time, or in that place later on, instead of being a preposterous promise of something that was to arrive five minutes before the invaders?

Just as Fintry preferred meeting the headsman to giving an answer, so Logan preferred being declared an outlaw to making an appearance. The King could not stop to look for Logan, the outlaw, in view of his march to the north, and he would probably have had as little success as in the hunt for the more notorious outlaw, Bothwell, which had been going on for a while. When he came back from the north the latter had turned the tables and was looking for him, and very soon cornered him in his own palace of Holyrood, in his own bed chamber. Afterwards, when Bothwell was on the run again, Logan's half-brother, Home, was the Captain of the King's Guard and a prop of the Sovereign. Without difficulty, the outlaw Logan merged into the ranks of the King's loyal subjects, as so many proscribed persons did in an age of weak law enforcement.

If Logan had appeared before the Privy Council on the day of Fintry's examination, what could he have answered as to Fintry's dealings with Bothwell at Fast Castle or the coming and going of 'foreigners and strangers'? His own random search at the castle with Napier shows that he could have answered nothing precisely, but his letter to Walsingham the year before his 'master Bothwell' enlisted troops for Spain shows that he himself had opened the gates to Spanish conspiracy. He had gone to Huntly in the north with an introduction from the Master of Gray and discussed assistance for the Spanish invasion, and his report broke off at the stage where he was expecting the arrival of Huntly's agent, Ker, to enter into details. The least help he could offer would be to put Fast Castle at the disposal of the men who were to open the coast to the Spaniards and seize the nearby Border port of Eyemouth. While his stronghold was in their hands the invasion gold could have been delivered. King James seemed to have some reason to think so when he associated the questioning of Fintry with the questioning of Logan. Probably the King was sharing a shrewd idea of Bruce who had been mixed up in it all although not to the same extent as Fintry. Like the King, Logan had some such notion himself and so had John Napier or his friends, the Chisholms, who were not innocents in the matter of Spanish gold. So also had Bothwell—so had George Ker, Fintry's accomplice, whose life was spared, who escaped from Edinburgh Castle and went into exile, returning to the castle on the crag like a homing pigeon.

## 12 Spanish inquest on the lost gold

IT IS our modest hope that the 'contract of magic' of Napier and Logan has been growing in significance and has not become part of the litter blowing about on the historical landscape that we have thought it necessary to traverse. We wish it to be seen as laced to the secret that was sealed by the death of the underground leader, Fintry, and doubly-sealed by the death of his kinsman, Judge Graham. That secret concerned the invasion gold mentioned in every document and negotiation relating to the projected landings of Spanish forces in Scotland; it featured in Mary Stewart's letter on the landings, in the negotiations of Maxwell, Hamilton and Huntly with the Duke of Parma, in Father Crichton's letter about the 'blanks' and in James VI's invasion memo.

If we are not failing in our purpose, the Fast Castle search should now be recognised as part of an unsuspected reality. The searchers, not just Napier and Logan, but their circle, had real connections with the Spanish plots and Spanish gold. It was the grim fact of Fintry's torture and execution that made the invasion gold inaccessible, and provided he reasons for the search. Bruce's betrayal of Fintry was a jealous and contemptible reality; just as real was the curiosity and the cupidity that inspired King James to pursue Fintry's secret. He displayed a half-knowledge of it in his invasion memo, and this was enhanced by the inside information from Bruce which he rewarded with a pardon. By dashing off to Fintry's Stirling prison at Christmas, and by presiding over the last scenes in the Tolbooth dungeon, he betrayed his determination to possess the whole secret.

It may be objected that, allowing for the truth of all these things, only conjectures have been made concerning the actual existence in Scotland of a special invasion fund and that without direct evidence of the delivery of this large sum of money it must remain hypothetical. If it were not hypothetical for us, if it had not been hypothetical for the searchers, there would have been no secret about it, no betrayal, no torture, no seals of death and no search. The hypothetical reality of the gold underlies all the rest, like the invisible foundations of a bridge resting on the bedrock of the river. It is the reality of realities.

John Napier of Merchiston 1550–1617 (from an engraving by R. Cooper).

James VI of Scotland (from an engraving by C. de Passé).

Sir David Graham, 6th of Fintry (after Zucchero).

Still, our picture would not be completely satisfying without some signs of concern on the part of the Spanish authorities over the loss of the gold and some evidence of their attempts to recover it. These are not absent either, although if this kind of evidence were not available it would not imply that there had been no concern and no recovery attempt and no gold. Naturally, the treasurers of King Philip would not cause a notice advertising the loss of one hundred and fifty thousand golden crowns to be nailed to the door of the Edinburgh Tolbooth, with the offer of a reward to the finder. Despite necessary secrecy, however, there are unmistakable signs of a Spanish inquiry into the lost fortune.

We have mentioned the Kirk's alarm in the summer of 1594 at the arrival of Jesuits and the return of the agents of the 'blanks' plot. In general this may be taken as the beginning of the inquest both in to the lost gold and Fintry's death. The details reinforce this impression. The Napier and Logan contract, linked in time and in persons as it was with the return of the Jesuits and the 'blanks' plotters, may itself be seen as part of the inquest, or a by-product of it. We have already suggested that the information brought back from Spain by these people may have prompted the Fast Castle search and that the initiative in the contract for the search may have come from Napier as it was drawn up in his hand. Supporting this belief is the fact that George Ker, the 'blanks' courier was back. Ker was groomed for the job and had it passed on to him by Sir James Chisholm, which meant that, Napier, therefore, at this time, could have gained whatever knowledge was brought over from Spain about the landing of the gold.

That Father Gordon, who left after the 'blanks' plot, returned so soon was also a pointer to the inquiry. Soon after Gordon's return Huntly was in touch with Bothwell, almost certainly on the subject of resuming his military support for the Spanish faction. But since Bothwell had worked closely with the informer Bruce and had made himself a protector of Fintry, there was also reason and opportunity for Father Gordon to pursue inquiries in the direction of Bothwell and Logan and Fast Castle. According to Forbes-Leith in his work on the Scottish Catholics of the sixteenth century, Father Crichton, the organiser of the 'blanks' plot on the Spanish side is said to have returned with Gordon. From a look at the sources this does not seem certain, but what is just as significant, or more so, is that Father Tyrie came back then. Tyrie was in Spain with Crichton awaiting the arrival of the 'blanks' and was to help King Philip or Parma in filling in the proclamations and the like, but he was also Fintry's close collaborator, and had been during the whole period of the negotiation for the invasion gold, and it was on account of this that he fell foul of the eventual informer, Bruce. Tyrie, especially, would know what he was looking for and would know where to look, as far as anyone could know; his return to Scotland in 1594 is a very strong pointer to the Spanish inquest on the lost gold.

The Kirk made a strong protest at the presence of Tyrie and Ker in the country and demanded energetic steps from the King for their apprehension. The outraged ministers took it upon themselves to deal with Lord Home, who was accused of harbouring a whole company of Jesuits and Spanish agents at Home Castle. Home had reluctantly been brought to sign the Protestant Confession, and was by now the Captain of the King's Guard, which made his backsliding all the more scandalous and dangerous in the ministers' eyes. He was called before the Moderator and the serried ranks of the Brethren to answer questions. He denied knowing anyone called Cowie and protested he had not spoken with anyone who came off the Spanish barque grounded at Montrose. He granted that Father McQuhirrie had been at the castle, but only for half an hour and he had left no letters or commission. Tyrie had been in his service but removed out of it, and so on. At the end of the grilling, he dutifully vowed he would try to apprehend McQuhirrie at next sight of him as well as other Jesuits, seminary priests and papist traffickers.

The significance of the congregation of so many dark characters in the Borders was not that they were assisting in supporting morale or creating an organisation for a military demonstration, as were Father Gordon and his friends who had arrived at Aberdeen. They had a specific mission of another kind, the clearing up of the 'blanks' affair with respect to the treachery and collapse and with respect to the funds that were to forward it. Home Castle, which had harboured them, was linked in conspiracy with Fast Castle. Elizabeth and her soldiers, at the time of the North of England uprising, had treated the two places as interchangeable and expected the fleeing rebels to be at one place if not at the other. This, no doubt, applied also to the visiting Jesuits and Spanish agents, Tyrie, McQuhirrie, Ker, Cowie and others unnamed who were in the neighbourhood in the summer of 1594. Lord Home's half-brother, Logan, would make them no less welcome than Home and probably had more to discuss with them, judging from his sudden interest to employ Napier's skills for a castle search at the very time these visitors had been around. Cowie's name does not come up in any other connection. The spies had apparently reported to the ministers that he had been seen with the rest. These spies no doubt were, as always, servants of Ambassador Bowes, who never failed to supply the ministers with information. This otherwise unknown Cowie may have been a trusted seaman who had helped in the delivery of the invasion gold when Fintry was the receiver. Home swore he had not been at his castle, but he may have been at Logan's, which was more difficult to keep a watch on.

The following spring, in 1595, another Jesuit arrived secretly and when apprehended confessed that Spanish gold was his business; not to deliver it, however, but to administer rebuke for the melting away and misuse of what had been delivered in the past. His mission, in fact, had all the marks of a continuation of the Fintry inquest. This man was Father Morton, and he came with messages for Huntly's Jesuit uncle Gordon from Cardinal Cajetano and, significantly, for Fathers Crichton and Tyrie. He arrived at Leith, but a smart fellow passenger had already penetrated his disguise, and when he stepped ashore the Leith minister, David Lindsay, had him arrested. (God's constables were apparently on regular duty at all the ports.) Of course the envoy began the customary mastication of letters as soon as a hand touched his shoulder, but he was not allowed to complete the meal.

By his own request, apparently, he was taken to the King who with his harder experience of examining witches, and invasion couriers and treasurers found Father Morton a very simple and pliable subject. The whole story was extracted from him without resorting to the Christian advice of the ministers to bring in the boot and the iron wedges. His brief which he described to the King was to reprove the Catholic lords for squandering the treasure sent in the past and dispensing it to courtiers and heretics. There were to be no more subventions, he declared, until they explained themselves before the Councillors of the King of Spain in the Low Countries. From this it emerged at least that an inquiry was to be conducted into the gold that had gone into Scotland and that it was to be before Philip's Councillors of the Netherlands, not a minor administrative matter. Morton had arrived, apparently, to summon Huntly and the others to this inquiry and the summons was reinforced by the authority of Cardinal Cajetano, who had responsibility at the Vatican for Scottish affairs, and by Fathers Crichton and Tyrie who had been Philip's advisers in the 'blanks' affair. If the Jesuit Morton had any interest in gold still hidden he naturally would not imperil the hope of its recovery by mentioning it. King James would be the last person to enter into discussion with on such a subject. Yet they could not have gone far into discussing the gold of the past, and James would not miss the opportunity to discuss it, without bringing up the names of Bruce and Fintry, the golden boys of Philip and Parma. It is unlikely that the priest would give anything away other than what would help to lead the King on to further questioning and, from the direction and the depth of the King's questions Morton probably gained more than he surrendered. The fact that he landed in Leith, when his destination was Aberdeenshire, indicates that Father Morton was probing in the area of the inquiry which had drawn Ker, Tyrie and others back the previous summer; his encounter with he King may have been contrived as part of that inquiry.

Huntly was on the point of going into temporary exile when Father Morton turned up. He returned within a year secretly and without licence. He, even less judiciously than Morton, chose to land at Eyemouth, exposing himself to the danger of recognition at the ferries and on the long road north. It appeared he had some business to transact in the Eyemouth neighbourhood to justify his risk. Fast Castle was only a few miles away, and it may have been necessary to call there after discussing the squandered—or too well hidden—gold with the King of Spain's Councillors for the Low Countries.

There is no record of how Huntly fared with his Spanish Majesty's Councillors, but there is an account of the dusty answer his agent, Walter Lindsay, received in Spain in the same year, 1596. The authorities there emphasised to this young gentleman that large sums of gold had been sent to Scotland and had never fructified. The failure was apparently linked with Robert Bruce, who was under suspicion. This established that it was not a matter of gold wasted on heretics and courtiers as Father Morton had indicated to King James, nor was it a matter of gold that was delivered at Aberdeen or Montrose in 1594, since Bruce was certainly not connected with trust on these occasions. The large sums of gold that had not fructified then were not misspent and they had arrived while Fintry was alive. As to the suspicion attaching to Bruce, his own letter showed that he had not received the trust for gold to buy the government and raise an army by the time the Armada had passed, although he sought that trust. His defection in the summer of 1592 to

Bowes and King James shows that he still had not got it; if he had received and embezzled one hundred and fifty thousand crowns by then he would have had more pleasant things to do than tell tales to Bowes or King James. The suspicion attaching to Bruce, of which young Lindsay was informed, must have related to the betrayal of the gold's custodian, Fintry. Two or three years later he was put on trial at St Omer and his accusers included those who were principals with Fintry—Ker, Tyrie and Crichton.

Successively then in the years 1594, 1595 and 1596 there were signs of a gold mystery and scandal in relation to the Spanish faction in Scotland which Spanish authorities sought to clear up. The return to the scene of their conspiracies of Ker, Tyrie and others in the summer of 1594 was the first positive sign of the investigastion, which was followed up by Father Morton's mission in 1595. In 1596 developments involved Huntly on some business at Eyemouth, near Fast Castle, although without licence to be in Scotland, and also involved young Lindsay's discouragement at the Spanish Court because the mystery of the vanished gold in Scotland had not yet been resolved. There were signs in the last year or two of the century that it remained an open question. Ker was back again, landing as near as the skipper of the Burntisland boat could take him to Fast Castle, and Logan was dealing with another Jesuit inquirer, Father Andrew Clark. Finally, by 1600 a new attempt to solve the mystery was under way, a new search was being planned for Fast Castle. The partnership, however, was changed; instead of Logan and Napier, this time it was Logan and the young Earl of Gowrie. Yet if we grant that young Gowrie had perhaps been probing the castle and the cliffs before, in his youthful alliance with Bothwell, then the later partnership would not be entirely new, and for the young earl it would be the resumption of an earlier adventure and exploration.

# 13  The King's inner doubt and compulsion

THE SPANISH subventions for factions in Scotland virtually ceased in 1594, the year that showed signs of an investigation into the vanished gold. If money still came into Scotland during that year, at Aberdeen and elsewhere, it was probably from expectation that the lost gold would be recovered and that Huntly's faction would establish military dominance. Neither expectation was fulfilled. The King's campaign, under pressure of the Kirk and the English Court, gathered in an autumn harvest of submissions from the Catholic north. The honours had gone to Huntly at Glenlivet against Argyle, who held the King's commission. It was the only real battle of the campaign and, as before, Huntly withdrew before the royal standard. The King's advance into his principality was not, however, quite as before. Huntly had written Angus predicting another 'gowk's storm', but instead real gunpowder was used to blow up his castle at Strathbogie which had been fourteen years in building; there were also some real hangings and a large crop of real fines. Lennox was left in command to enforce the latter supported by a Council of barons and Protestant ministers, and he had power to effectuate the banishment of the leaders.

Francis Bothwell, the ally of Huntly retired into exile first, early in 1595 after the scattering of his Catholic friends. Had he chosen to go when Gowrie went and avoided involvement in Huntly's defeat, he might have been called back some day as a Protestant lord and friend of the Kirk, or at least there would have been friends to beckon him. For a little while he had retreated into Caithness, and then was in Orkney indulging, or planning to indulge, in some light piracy, like his ill-fated uncle before him. Perhaps he remembered the miserable, mouldering fate of his uncle and changed course in time, for, by June 1595, he was in Paris and corresponding with his and Logan's friend, Archibald Douglas, now only the shadow of an ambassador.

Huntly and Errol followed in Bothwell's wake, taking ship from Aberdeen in April, but Huntly came back without licence the following year, landing at Eyemouth as remarked. He arrived home in Aberdeenshire determined to restore his position, which was not so difficult since both his estate and Errol's had been made secure for them through their families and there had been no forfeiture, as in the case of Bothwell. The Countess of Huntly was Lennox's sister and Lennox had arranged the conditions of Huntly's departure. Now the Countess, Huntly's wife, began to play her part; she was the Queen's favourite and enjoyed a 'plurality of her kisses' as Nicolson, the English envoy, quaintly said. The very obvious moves for Huntly's restoration, and his illicit return, raised a storm in the Kirk, which the King thought timely, having got rid of Bothwell and other embarrassments. He proceeded to stage the showdown with the ministers and their supporters, the burgesses and lesser barons, which must have been in his mind for years. Following something of a riot and the invasion of his Council chamber, he withdrew the Court to Linlithgow, ordered the justiciary there too, and began to rally Highland brigands and Border rogues, making a show of turning his capital city over to plunder and the torch. The soil was to be sown with salt after desolation was complete. The threat was effective in bringing the burgesses, the crafts and the Kirk to submission; episcopal shackles were forged for the Kirk's organisation, and curbs put on its interference in judicial and State affairs.

Deserted by the feudal lords and lacking enough support in the burghs the Kirk leaders were bereft of power to resist. The devout Earl of Angus was the last great lord they had been able to consort with, according to one of them but he, alas, had been cut off by witchcraft. Francis Bothwell had been the King's 'particular enemy' and a 'sanctified plague' promoted by God—what he might do next only God knew. At the hour of the King's fury, the stalwart minister Bruce had addressed a letter to Lord John Hamilton to procure his intercession, but for all his pains he merely succeeded in sending Hamilton on the road to Linlithgow to turn the letter over to James, who accused the minister of conspiring to put the Heir to the Throne in front of the Sovereign. There was no sword of Gideon to defend the Brethren. The spirit of the ministers, however, was not entirely broken and the King left them with their power to tyrannise and terrorise at the expense of the general citizenry and his recalcitrant nobles. They might continue to send clerical detectives and informers into private houses to sit at table with the family. It was a means of compelling conformity and creating the unitary State and was also an exceedingly cheap system of police surveillance, as it was run at the expense of the victims. After his victory over the Kirk,

James negotiated with the banished Catholic earls for their official return on condition of submitting to this surveillance and accepting the Protestant confession.

To Huntly the King wrote the letter in which he declared he must love himself and his own estate first. 'Deceive not yourself to think that by lingering of time your wife and your allies shall ever get you better conditions', he said. 'And think not', he added 'that I will suffer any professing a contrary religion to dwell in this land.' It was safer not to give a name to the acceptable or the contrary religion since it was still unsettled what religion he might have to profess to wear the Double Crown, but by now he was fairly determined that he and his subjects must all go to heaven, or hell, the same way. Huntly, Errol and Angus complied and were received into the Kirk at an impressive ceremony in Aberdeen in June 1597. It was a bargain day in absolutions. Huntly, in exchange for his second-time signature to the Protestant confessions, was forgiven the Earl of Moray's murder as well as all his idolatries, treasons, calumnies and spoils. The next day, after a proclamation at Aberdeen Cross, the mulititude cheered and drank the health of the penitents then tossed away their glasses in abandon.

The whole scene was now changed. In the north the Catholic bastions were down. In the south the strategic Border points and coasts were under the King's command. The once dangerous alliance of Bothwell, Maxwell and Claud Hamilton had vanished and left scarcely a wrack behind. The Kirk, too, was tamed, as well as the Catholic plotters; the leaders within the State were either crypto-Catholic administrators who were tepid about the mass, or Protestant lords who were indifferent to the Kirk. Perhaps the bias of the government personnel was towards Rome and the English ambassador might justifiably describe the Council of eight, the Octavians, who reigned for a while as hollow papists.

The King's principal secretary, Elphinstone, was a Catholic, so was Seton, President of the College of Justice and Hamilton, the Lord Advocate; Lord Home, Captain of the Royal Guard was a most reluctant Protestant. Lord Burghley received a catalogue of the Scottish nobility for study in London in 1592; he placed figures over names of influential persons described as papists and brought the total to a dozen in an incomplete list. There was no basic change in the ruling personnel by the end of the century, but with most the aggression or conspiracy of the Armada days had become muted. An amorphism in religion had set in within ruling circles, Catholic lords being at pains to conform and Protestant lords declining the honour of leading the Kirk. This was caused by the pull of the wealth of the Indies behind King Philip and the rival attraction of the merchant wealth of the city of London behind Queen Elizabeth. The King was in an advantageous position to exploit both and the governing class was becoming more closely knit behind him; the profits of the Reformation, in terms of land and revenue, had been assimilated. As the century drew to a close, and Elizabeth's days were clearly numbered, an expectancy arose of new benefits under the Double Crown, benefits at secondhand from the new commercial and floating wealth of the world.

In this situation with the priviledged class less divided, the King seemed to have realised his ambition of making his dealings with Spain a matter of his own secret diplomacy. At any rate, he made final moves to liberate himself from the perils and vagaries of the Spanish faction, which ealier he had been compelled both to encourage and to restrain. In 1596, his unofficial envoy at the Spanish court, Poury Ogilvie, expressed the new situation in a demand that King Philip would deal no more with the Scottish Catholic earls but only with the King. Ogilvie's mission was formally repudiated by James but this demand alone confirmed that it was in fact a mission from the Scottish Crown.

Not all of this advance in kingcraft is to be ascribed to the genius, perverse or otherwise, of James Stewart. As an infant he was a mere pretext for power on the part of the regents and aspiring regents and an instrument for his mother's dethronement and downfall. He remained so until his youth, when his cousin Esmé Stewart (also known as D'Aubigny, who later became Earl of Lennox) overthrew and extinguished the Regent Morton, but only to make James an instrument of his own ambition and a pawn of Guise. The elder Gowrie threatened to destroy rather than liberate him. The Master of Gray freed him to a degree by teaching him to balance England against the Catholic powers. Chancellor Maitland, on the other hand, tutored him under chancy conditions to balance Spain and the Spanish faction against England; the same Maitland inspired the policy that split the Spanish faction geographically and separated Bothwell and Maxwell on the Borders from the Catholic camp in the north, destroying the one and undermining the other.

Finally, the crypto-Catholics in the south helped the King to discipline and subdue the Catholic earls of the north, while simultaneously the indifferent Protestant lords enabled him to tame the

Kirk. By no means was the end result an individual performance, although the compulsion to carry it out was his own. It derived from his uncertainty concerning the Single Crown, which in turn grew out of inner doubt concerning his paternity.

When the scholar, George Buchanan, was on his death-bed his last act was to raise a mirror to the world's doubt. His friend James Melville and others had left the sage's bedside to inquire concerning the progress of his history at the printer's workshop. The work was being set up for the press, and they found the printer had stopped near the end of the seventeenth book of the chronicle, at the description of the burial of Riccio where it stated that after the Queen of Scots returned from directing her vengeance against the assassins of David the first thing she did was to cause his body to be removed from its interment before the door of the neighbouring church. It was placed in the royal tomb which contained the remains of the late King, her father, and his children. 'What stronger confession of adultery could she make?' the historian asked. The printer thought it was dangerous and might stop the whole work. His friends came back and told Buchanan, stressing that the King would be offended and 'stey all the wark'. 'Tell me if I have told the truth?' the dying Buchanan asked.

'I think so,' said the informant.

'Then,' said the scholar, 'I will bide his feud and all his kin's. Pray to God for me and let him direct all.' Buchanan ended his Book XVIII laconically and sceptically with a single sentence, 'Not long after the Queen retired to Edinburgh Castle as the time of her delivery drew near; and on the 19th of June, a little after nine o' clock in the morning, she brought forth a son, who was afterwards called James VI.' The phrase 'called James VI' said everything. The King's boyhood tutor, Buchanan, held to his doubt about his royal charge on his death bed; under such a man's influence it is not surprising that a lifelong uncertainty was bred in James Stewart's mind.

The King was a youth, and in the hands of Gowrie at the time Buchanan's reflection on his title first appeared in print. Gowrie and his associate Colville came near to acting on the doubt by plotting with Walsingham and the Hamiltons. But more than fifteen years later, with his greater destiny at stake, James let no such reflections pass. He was indeed so touchy on the score that he attempted to extend censorship beyond his own realm; his Secretary, Elphinstone, wrote to the English government demanding that the poet Spenser should be severely punished for casting a shadow on the

Queen of Scots under the character of Duessa in the *Faerie Queene*. On the other hand, Elphinstone's justification of the King's title to the English Crown was to be voiced abroad. Monsieur Jesse, a French literary hack, was employed to accomplish this as a side line to his duties as historiographer of the King of Scots, a post created as part of the propaganda for the Double Crown. Another Frenchman, Damon, also worked in the propaganda department, and so did an Irish scholar named Walter Quinn who wrote a treatise on the succession in Latin. The King himself collaborated with an Englishman, Dickens, in replying to the book on the succession published by Father Parsons, the English Catholic leader, under the pseudonym of Doleman.

The King might be happy enough with his case in the general debate on the succession, but the sharp protest against Spenser's reflection on his mother revealed his awareness that, within the open genealogical debate, was the inner doubt about who had sired him. His grateful acceptance of a contribution on his legitimacy by Colville, the former Bothwellite and tool of Gowrie, was a confession of his pathetic need to be shielded against this vulnerability. Colville was credited with an earlier book or pamphlet written to proclaim his bastardy; it was degradation to accept aid from this quarter, but no dubious champion and no pamphlet could dissolve his inner doubt and insecurity. From this stemmed his obsession which went beyond ordinary ambition. The Double Crown with all its power and grandeur was needed, not only for vanity's sake, but to prevent the Single Crown from falling off his head some day, and to still a lifetime's uncertainty. With justice, the Jesuit McQuhirrie could say that James was ready to take the Crown of England from the hand of the devil himself, to the wreck of both Protestants and Catholics.

There was no joy in store for anyone who might walk between the devil and the King when his hand was outstretched for the dream of his nights and days. Someone did walk between—the student of Padua.

## 14 The student of Padua and the monstrous visage

THE EARL of Gowrie studied at Padua University for five years and then leisurely journeyed home taking in Geneva, Paris and London. He had left Scotland in mid-August, 1594, when he was in his seventeenth year, and was back in Edinburgh by May, 1600. His secret plan to visit Fast Castle was disclosed to Robert Logan after he had had time to settle down privately in Perthshire, after his court attendance and other formalities of his return had been completed. This leads to the culminating point of our Fast Castle treasure inquiry. All that remains after this is to look at the strange story which brought his interest in Fast Castle to light, when both he and Robert Logan were dead. Because we are near the final conclusions we cannot afford to miss anything at all with a bearing on the projected Fast Castle visit or the tragedy which prevented that visit. For that reason we pause at Paris, where Gowrie paused and where the webs of rival international conspiracies were being spun.

In Paris, the young Earl became linked to a chain of events that went back to 1596, when Huntly and Errol were temporarily in exile. During that year they combined forces with the permanent exile, Bothwell, to prevent King James reaping benefits at the Spanish Court from their defeat. Indeed the King's shadowy envoy and kite-flyer Poury Ogilvie, set out that year to take advantage of the benefits in Europe rising from King James's strengthened position. He carried with him what purported to be memorials concerning a treaty between King James and King Philip. To counter Ogilvie, the Catholic earls and Bothwell employed the Jesuit Dr John Cecil as their agent. Cecil shadowed Ogilvie on his road to Rome and beguiled him there while watching his intrigues like a hawk, and then took him from Rome to Toledo. Here, while Ogilvie was secretly negotiating with the Spanish authorities, Cecil was at trouble to draft a counter-statement to the King's memorials which he presented along with a denunciation of the envoy. He had the satisfaction of leaving Ogilvie behind in a Spanish gaol.

The sequel to the memorials was as important as the mission. The document, which justified the King's dealing with his Catholic subjects, insisted that Spain's future negotiations should be with the King only and not with his Catholic noblemen, as in the past. Dr Cecil's counter-blast was frankly aimed at continuing the recognition of the Scottish Catholic lords and persuading the Spanish to have no truck with the King. He concentrated on destroying the claim that the King had cherished his Catholic subjects, and dismissed contemptuously his pretence that he lived only for the day when he would avenge his mother's death.

Strangely, King James found a defender in the Jesuit ranks—no other person than Father Crichton, the invasion expert. Crichton produced a tract against Cecil's paper with the help of an English student named More, and his apology for the King of Scots began to circulate in 1598. He represented that the King had never raised his hand in anger against any Catholic, he had only acted to save them from a worse fate at the hands of the Kirk mob, and that when embarrassed and driven to do so by rash and unlawful acts and conspiracies on the part of some of his Catholic subjects. This was rich considering that the unlawful acts and conspiracies had been lovingly conceived and brought into the world by Crichton himself, a thing Dr Cecil did not lose sight of in his rejoinder. While he was about it, Crichton accused Cecil of being an English intelligencer, which he was; but then Ogilvie who travelled with the King's memorials was a double agent. The King was a double dealer in presenting memorials for Philip's benefit and officially repudiating them for the sake of Elizabeth. Crichton himself, when in the Tower, had supplied Walsingham with more information than was good for the health of his friends, according to Mary Stewart's agent Morgan, who was another two-timer. Everyone in the conspiracy trade was two-faced or paid tribute in the common coin of intelligence at some time or another.

The Crichton pamphlet of apology for the Scots King reflected a cleavage among the Jesuits and lay Catholic exiles that was already annoying the Spanish authorities. In the year before Crichton's pamphlet appeared the King of Spain's adviser, the Duke of Feria, communicated with his sovereign on the subject from Barcelona. 'Your Majesty will have seen my opinion as to the removal of dissension among the English,' he wrote. 'The evil is increasing and the only remedy that has ever occurred to me is to remove the principle agitators from Flanders, all of whom are supported by your Majesty's bounty. The object in all this is evidently to further the interest of the Scottish king. . . . Hence it will be well to remove the chiefs of the party, Charles Paget, William Tresham and Ralph Ligon. . . . It is a matter of no less importance that your Majesty should command the General of the Society of Jesus to avail himself of some opportunity for removing Father Crichton.' The Duke of Feria went on to say that Crichton was an avowed advocate of the King of Scots and had spoken to him frequently on the King's affairs with passionate feeling. In his place as Jesuit superior in Flanders he proposed the appointment of Father Gordon, 'a quiet and dispassionate person divested of prepossession in favour of his own sovereign'.

Crichton was removed and Father Gordon took his place. An effective leadership was now being exercised also by Father Parsons, the principal agent of Spain among English Catholics. The death of Cardinal Allen, without realising his dream of English overlordship, had increased Parsons' authority. The changes prescribed by the Duke of Feria explained to Philip, their object was 'to further the in-opposing Parsons, Paget and Tresham, were driven to the doors of the English embassy in Paris to offer themselves as spies in the service of Elizabeth. But they had interests other than Elizabeth's: as the Duke of Feria explained to Philip, their object was 'to further the interests of the Scottish king'.

Naturally, the change was reflected in the actions of Father Gordon, Huntly's uncle. Soon afterwards he set out on a new mission to Scotland. He found things greatly changed in the north east since his nephew had signed the Protestant Confession at the Old Kirk in Aberdeen, an event celebrated by wine bibbing and glass smashing at the Cross. Many had been undermined by Huntly's example, he lamented, his nephew was in fear because of the heavy penalties, he might suffer for harbouring him, and the priest himself saw enough to realise that power did not reside in the north any more. He, therefore, obeyed the King's order to depart for Huntly's sake, and planned to return to the country, but this time to the capital and at his own risk. He realised that power now resided with the crypto-Catholics at court, the men who had helped to defeat the earls in the north but who had also helped to get them easy terms of exile and had interceded to bring their exile to an end. Accordingly, he took the bold course of sailing openly into Leith and going straight to Holyrood by night to seek an interview with the King without any backstairs manoeuvres. His open show avoided the appearance of conspiracy and enabled him to make contact with the King and the ruling set. He was ordered abroad again, nothing worse, and significantly was allowed by King James to live with his friends at Seton house until the time fixed for his leisurely departure. It was ample time for his mission and that house, traditionally the hatchery of Catholic plots, was not the worst place in he world for Gordon's purpose.

In considering the plot that was hatched on this occasion it must always be borne in mind that Gordon, the new superior of the Jesuit organisation in Flanders, owed his promotion to the sharpening of King Philip's policy against King James. The Seton plot on this occasion, therefore, could bode no good for James. It had the gloss, however, of being something for his benefit since it involved the King's approval for a secret mission of Lord Home to Rome to further his campaign for the English Crown in that quarter. At the same time, by rumours and spies' reports of Home's mission, it was aimed to create alarm in the English Court and make Elizabeth more amenable to James Stewart's demands. Within this mission of Home, however, was the real kernel of the plot: Home was to make contact on behalf of his Seton House friends and the Holyrood crypto-Catholics with circles abroad working for the Infanta of Spain and her claim to the English succession. In short, Home's mission was a double-crossing one or, on the kindest appraisal, it was to buy an option for the Scottish crypto-Catholics.

Home appeared in Paris in May 1599. Neville, the English ambassador there, reported his arrival to Robert Cecil, who had succeeded his father, Lord Burghley, as Elizabeth's chief Minister. The Scottish double agent, Colville, had told Neville that Home was to proceed to Rome to the Pope on a mission for James who, according to Colville, was declining in his Protestant faith and beginning to entertain secret intelligence with the Catholic princes. Ambassador Neville urged Cecil to keep a private eye on the Rome negotiations, adding that it would be a pity for the King to be lost if a small matter could retain him.

All of the English ambassador's despatches from Paris at this time contained an oblique and peculiarly insistent pleading for the Scottish King. He may never have been recognised as King James's agent while drawing his pay as Queen Elizabeth's ambassador, but this he most assuredly was. There would come a time when Ambassador Neville would be discovered at a secret meeting on Candelmas day at Drury House, London, with the Earl of Essex, the Earl of Southampton and Sir Charles Danvers, and later he would escape with confinement in the Tower, while the others went to the scaffold. As for Neville's anxious concern in Paris for the Scottish King, the fact that James had made a deal with Essex and his friends in his bid for the Double Crown explains all.

The month after Home's arrival in Paris, Ambassador Neville sent word to London that the Catholic exiles, Paget and Tresham, had come to the embassy to offer to spy for England. (He meant they had come to offer to spy for Scotland or the Scots King and get their pardon and pay from England. The Duke of Feria's naming of this pair as James's servants, along with Father Crichton, must be remembered.) Very diffidently, the ambassador recommended to his chief that the two should be employed experimentally; declaring himself unworthy to advise Minister Cecil, Ambassador Neville nevertheless proceeded to do so. He recommended that all priests and recusants apprehended in England should be severely examined (otherwise tortured) to find out how far they were involved in Father Parsons' campaign of support for the Infanta of Spain. On a grander scale, he counselled that in the peace negotiations with Spain a clause should be inserted involving the abandoning by the Infanta of any claim to the English Crown, similar to that extracted from the Scottish Queen at the beginning of Elizabeth's reign. It was almost as if James Stewart was at the back of Ambassador Neville dictating his despatches and fiddling with the thumb screws intended to teach the English priests a lesson if they dared to support the Infanta instead of James Stewart.

The purport of the things he recommended was made quite clear by Neville; he said it would 'give satisfaction to some who had taken hot alarm and who have precipitated themselves into dangerous councils both for themselves and us. I mean f 150, the King of Scotland.' He explained a further valiant effort to make Elizabeth's flesh creep in September by conveying a report of Paget, the Catholic informer, that great efforts were being used to win f 150, the King of Scotland, to join c 100, the King of Spain, against a 100, the Queen of England. 'If there be not some course to prevent it, it will surely draw that way in the end', he warned. An account of the Master of Gray's activities followed in October. Gray apparently had been at the embassy several times declaring he was not bound to any prince unless he received good cause—which he had found in the Netherlands apparently, since Neville reported he had seen a letter written by Gray in which he confided that he had had very private access to the Infanta and the Archduke and 'much inward communication with Bothwell'.

In January, 1600, Neville was reporting again about Lord Home. 'The Lord Home', he wrote, 'who was gone out of this town towards Italy is returned again and, as I learn, has been in Brussells. I was advertised that he was reconciled [by Parsons' mediation] with the Earl Bothwell. I did not much credit it but this journey of his to Brussells, where Bothwell is, makes it more probable, besides the confirmation of it I received lately by a Scottish nobleman here.' He then went on to give his news the usual alarmist slant. There was a mystery in it, he said, and it was not done without ƒ 150, the Scottish King, being privy, 'for there was no greater with him than the Lord Home and his uncle Sir George Home'. This time his news was more calculated to make King James's flesh creep, than Elizabeth's; not only was James not privy to the Bothwell and Home reconciliation but when Home returned James barred him from court for 'trysting with Bothwell'. The uniting of these two, Bothwell and Lord Home, had been his greatest peril and it had been part of his life's work to divide them. The Scottish nobleman who had confirmed the Bothwell and Home reconciliation for Neville was Gowrie apparently, who had by now arrived in Paris and was the only person answering to the description of Scottish nobleman then frequenting the embassy.

This was the Spanish plot that was taking shape when Gowrie turned up at Paris. Father Gordon had brought Lord Home from Scotland; Father Parsons had brought Bothwell from Spain and Bothwell and Home were reconciled at Brussels by Father Parsons' mediation. The Master of Gray was called to Brussels for audience with the Infanta and the Archduke. He also had 'deep communication' with Bothwell. Then Gowrie turned up and, conversant with it all, began to have similar 'deep communication' with the English ambassador, whom he accepted as Elizabeth's trusted servant, unconscious that he was the obsequious servant of that rising sun, James Stewart. Robert Bruce, the Kirk leader, in the meantime appeared in Paris also, to confer with Gowrie who was conferring with the English ambassador, and with Bothwell and Home.

It hardly looked like a Spanish plot; but it was a Spanish plot of 1600, not 1568. The conquest and invasion of England belonged to the past; the current struggle was for the succession. The drawing together of this circle was not even inspired by the aim or hope of persuading any one of these persons to work for the claim of the Infanta of Spain, the limited aim was to restrain the competitor and aggressive rival James Stewart within his own realm and end his attraction as a candidate in England's eyes by making him a very limited monarch, who would have little say in determining Scottish policies or Scotland's friends when he was immured within his palace in London four hundred miles away. Then, with all his impoverished favourites and uncouthness, he would be no bargain at all for the English. They would have this ungainly fellow on the throne, but with an uncertain Scottish government their insular security would still have an open end at the Scottish Border. Apart from how this might favour the Infanta's claim if England's rivalry remained unresolved, Spain had a vested interest in a separate Scotland.

The extraordinary thing was that Fathers Parsons and Gordon, prompted by Philip and encouraged by the Infanta, were seeking to build some kind of bridge between the Scottish Catholics and the Scottish Kirk and English Court. Bothwell and the Master of Gray, who had sided with Spain before, were enlisted as bridge builders, but Bothwell in exile was impotent without the hope of his return through reconciliation with Home and others to whom there had been major shifts of power in Scotland, and the Master of Gray, although free to return to Scotland, was a faded opportunist without even a potential following like Bothwell. Home, representing the crypto-Catholics, suffered from their handicap of facing two ways, and according to his half-brother Logan, he lacked the decision either to help his friends or to hurt his enemies. Gowrie had to be the pivot and the leader of this enterprise if it was to work at all.

The first question seems to be whether it was even credible; it appears less incredible if we examine the contrasting intrigues and alignments of the King. While Spain was trying to build an alliance that reached as far as the Kirk, James was seeking to enlist friends in the just as improbable citadel of the Vatican. He had already found a base among the Catholic exiles who were in rebellion against Father Parsons' pro-Spanish policy: Father Crichton had turned pamphleteer for his sake, and to further his cause Paget and Tresham turned informers. Among the English Catholics at home he had a base too, represented by a gentleman called Ashfield, who came up to Holyrood to discuss the terms for English Catholic support. The Governor of Berwick, Lord Willoughby, who had allowed him to pass through, learned what he was up to from Ambassador Bowes and thereupon sent his cousin Guevara and three assistants into Scotland to bring the plotter back. They took Ashfield for a walk along Leith sands, plied him with drinks when he was tired, then bundled him into a coach and made for the Border. Meanwhile, their accomplices had burgled the man's lodgings and sent his papers, which proved the extent of James's dealings with the English Catholics, on to Berwick. The King stormed and raged at Willoughby and Elizabeth, but when the day for receiving his regular pension from the English Queen came round his protests became muted. When money is offered you must give up shaking your fist to open your palm.

There were the crypto-Catholics in his Privy Council too. Altogether James was not without his Catholic friends just as he had his Protestant friends in important places at that time: Essex at the English Court and Neville in the English embassy at Paris. But the Vatican? This was a fortress he had not yet scaled. Or had he? Home's mission to Rome seemed a bit hollow, lacking the reality of his meeting with Bothwell in Brussels, for which he was banished from Court on his return. But about the time Home was 'trysting with Bothwell' the French ambassador, Monsieur de Bethune, came to Edinburgh to renew the ancient league with Scotland. On this occasion Beaton, the Catholic Archbishop of Glasgow residing in Paris, advised King James on the opportunities for representation at the Vatican. Since Monsieur de Bethune was going to Rome soon after his Edinburgh visit, to be France's permanent ambassador there, he would have an opportunity of advancing James's interests if in the meantime the King opened up correspondence with the Pope. So Beaton persuaded, insisting that Pope Clement was jealous of the 'grandeur of Spain' and was well disposed towards James's title—so were many other princes in Europe, Beaton declared.

The subject of the letter from the King to the Pope was to be a petition for a cardinal's hat for the Scottish-born Bishop of Vaison so that he could look after James's claim to the English Crown. The King wrote an appeal on these lines to Cardinal Cajetano, the Duke of Savoy, the Duke of Florence and other princes and cardinals. But the small matter of the form of address to His Holiness caused the ink to congeal on his quill; eventually Secretary Elphinstone drafted the letter to the Pope, *Beatissime* and all, and it went to Rome bearing the royal signature. Years later, when James was in London and in a corner Elphinstone was cajoled and coerced into confessing that he had got the signature by a trick—and was ruined.

These wide-ranging manoeuvres on James's part for the succession gained him solid ground in many directions. But the accompanying policy of deliberately trying to make Elizabeth's flesh creep by exaggerating the intrigues and their peril had the opposite effect; the reports and rumours were accompanied by other sinister whispers that James did not intend to await the natural death of the English Queen. The whole situation tended to the fostering of the peace moves between England and Spain made the Queen's attitude towards James even more wintry.

The effect was also to produce a warm and cordial reception for Gowrie when he arrived in London. He had departed from Paris with a flattering introduction from Ambassador Neville, who said Gowrie was one of whom 'exceeding good use' could be made by England. He attested that he knew him very well and had 'enjoyed good communication with him'—too good, for Gowrie's health and safety. But the ambassador could not disguise his feelings for Home, who had applied for a passport at the same time, and he kept him waiting several days after his farewells with Gowrie, presumably to prevent them travelling together, and disparaged him in his London despatch. His secret despatch to Edinburgh appears to have been the source of King James's information that Home had been 'trysting with Bothwell' in Brussels. The information conveyed about Gowrie to Holyrood was apparently much more lethal.

During Gowrie's two months' stay in London he was received with distinction by the Queen who is reported to have held 'great conference' with him on the state of Scotland, and to have appointed a guard for the safety of his person. He conferred also with her chief Minister, Sir Robert Cecil. He spent enough time with Lord Willoughby for it to be remarked on, and this was a hint that the collaboration was to continue. (Lord Willoughby was Governor of the Border town of Berwick.) While Gowrie was still in London and at Court, a despatch arrived from Holyrood sent by the English agent Nicholson referring to the ranting fits King James turned on especially for Nicholson's benefit. The agent said the King indulged in expressions of the utmost discontent and anger on the subject of the intended peace between England and Spain, he was particularly indignant because Elizabeth had resisted every amicable application of his on the point of his title, yet in the atmosphere of the Spanish peace talks the names of the Lady Arabella Stewart and the Infanta were continually cropping up and, consequently, James was vowing to look to his just rights and provide for his future. About this time, Elizabeth's officers at Hull seized a consignment of muskets intended for the Scots King; these were regarded as part of his threatened preparation to assert his just rights, and confiscated. Perhaps the fit of royal anger on this occasion had been brought on by a secret report from Neville or the spy Colville in Paris about the continued development of the Spanish-inspired plot of Bothwell, Gowrie and the rest, which was being beautifully timed to coincide with the Spanish peace offensive in England.

On his long trail north, Gowrie had plenty of inner occupation to offset any tedium of the road. He had been named by the dubious Neville as the man for England. The honour of leading the party of the English court was not so much achieved as being thrust upon him and at a time when the relations between King James and England were abominable. By the ministers, or the toughest core of them, he was at a time of lowering trouble being invited to lead the party of the Kirk. No one had possessed the courage or selflessness among the lords to fill the role since the time of the good Earl of Angus twelve years earlier. Bothwell had filled it only erratically and Lord John Hamilton and other promising candidates had adroitly sidestepped it at the critical moment. As if that were not enough, he was involved again with Bothwell whose 'unquiet spirit' would not rest until some adventure was attempted to achieve his return from exile and his restoration. Perhaps if he had realised fully the changes that had come about in his six years of absence in favour of the King's power he would never have listened to minister Bruce, Francis Bothwell, Sir Robert Cecil or any of them.

Everyone was so tentative. The shadowy meetings in Brussels, the Paris talks at the English embassy and with minister Bruce, and the secret discussions in London had yet to advance to a precarious reality. Home's reconciliation with Bothwell had yet to be tried, and it remained to be seen if he would detach any of the other crypto-Catholics from their prospering loyalty to the King. Whether Huntly and his friends in the north would re-assert themselves and whether minister Bruce would rally the failing courage of the Kirk were also things to be tried. The chief trial of all was in the mind and soul of the returned student of Padua: whether he went forward or faltered might determine everything.

If, like Shakespeare's Brutus, he was appalled by the monstrous visage of conspiracy then, like Brutus, he had not recoiled or retreated, not at first encounter nor now, when he was entering Scotland. The hidden loyalties, that had sustained his father and grandfather in their enterprises and that had restored his family estates after forfeiture, were being invoked in some way as they were periodically among the mysteriously close-knit feudal families of Scotland. As well as this was a hint of a hidden strength of his own; later, after he was killed, the remark was attributed to him that if a man had a design his strength lay in revealing it to no one. Perhaps he had a secret weapon that was exclusively his own; and perhaps it was the Stewart papers more revealing than any yet exposed, locked away in a silver casket.

There was another power that might have fortified him, the power that was changing the whole world—yellow glittering, precious gold. The Spanish inspiration of these moves against James was undoubted, and Spanish support was to be expected for all the expensive operations any plot, and this one in particular, involved. Bribes for courtiers, money to win back lost allies and furnish their strength, money for the invasion by Bothwell and his friends from Spain to enable the exile to rally and rule the Borders again—all this was implicit—Bothwell's return and restoration was an absolutely essential ingredient. The King caught whiffs of the danger in rumours and in threats from Englishmen, and these were duly made a subject of protest to Elizabeth.

Spain had stopped paying out money for the invasion of England in 1594. It was by then a lost cause and there had been much wasted gold. But for the invasion of Scotland by Bothwell to halt the dynastic adventures of King James and prevent the assimilation of Scotland in the English State, there was room for a Spanish change of policy and heart. It was not for nothing that Bothwell sat down and drew up a list for the Spanish authorities of the friends who would welcome his invasion. Spanish state affairs at this time were bordering on insolvency, but there was the old invasion gold which to all appearances had been delivered and was anxiously sought after Fintry's execution. This, the Bothwell invasion, was an occasion for a serious attempt at its recovery.

Father Morton testified that the Catholic earls were to help Philip's councillors in the Low Countries with their inquiries, which had been continuing even as late as the year prior to Gowrie's return from Padua. George Ker, Fintry's accomplice, had been back at Fast Castle then and Father Andrew Clark had had some confidential business with Robert Logan still more recently. At the time of the first signs of the Fintry inquest Fast Castle had been signposted as the location of the lost gold (the Napier and Logan search pointed a finger in that direction), and at the time of the later signs of inquiry Fast Castle was still signposted. With Gowrie back it was to be dramatically signposted again, in correspondence and in secret meetings with Robert Logan.

This surely, was the other quiet power that Gowrie possessed, the secret, as far as it was known or had been pieced together, concerning the lost invasion gold. Going by his actions soon after his return, Gowrie had been entrusted with valuable information to lead to the gold's recovery. Bothwell, Ker and the rest, who hoped to return to Scotland through the conspiracy, had helped with information and so had the Spanish authorities, if their fathering of the project counted for anything. Perhaps Gowrie was left to collect additional information from Fintry's kinsmen, the Grahams. There are signs of this, but it was not surprising, in view of its background, that the new style Spanish plot and the new Spanish or Bothwellite invasion plan should be mixed up with a gold hunt. There was nothing incongruous in it, nor was it odd for it to be part of the assignment and trust of the leader of the conspiracy, Gowrie. It was a serious trust and central to their schemes—besides, Gowrie had been Bothwell's comrade in arms and Bothwell had been Fintry's protector. The sorcerer's apprentice was returning to the search of Fast Castle.

## *15 Fast Castle and four men in a boat*

A CAVALCADE of friends escorted Gowrie on his return to the capital and crowds shouted their welcome as the company rode up the street. When told of it the King, according to Caldwell, said in great anger, 'There were more with his father when he was convoyed to the scaffold.'

Carey, in a letter to Cecil, mentioned a taunt of the King's that the ministers had not turned out for the procession, a taunt thrown off in conversation with the earl along with snide remarks about his reception at Elizabeth's Court. Gowrie, however, was pictured leaning over the back of the King's chair during the delivery of some of these barbs, while the King ate his breakfast; there was not enough bitterness to affect the King's appetite or disturb the Earl's ease. The pedant King and the young erudite Earl enjoyed their joint egotistical excursions into the fabulous world of learning, and their fencing over matters political and diplomatic passed off harmlessly.

It appeared that in his ironies relative to the English and French courts and the ministers, the King's purpose was to convey to Gowrie that he knew what he was up to. When, in matters gynecological, James invited Gowrie to say what might bring on a woman's miscarriage, the query was probably prompted simply by the Queen's current condition. Gowrie said fright or sudden terror was the most likely occasion; James met this with an outburst of mocking laughter, declaring he should never have been there in that case, in view of the slaughter of Seigneur Davie in his mother's presence. This rejoinder was supposed by Calderwood and later commentators to represent a stab at the Gowrie family conscience, because of the guilty part played by both the Earl's father and grandfather in the affair, but the Gowries had no contrition about Riccio and it was as much a stab at Darnley, his own reputed sire. If James was deliberately ribald towards these ghosts who were around when he was in the womb, if he made play especially with Seigneur Davie, his suspected sire, it was again an oblique intimation to Gowrie that he knew what he was up to, and was ready for him.

Although the King did not vent his dark suspicions and resentment openly on Gowrie, he took it out on Nicholson again. For the

144

second time within a month he expressed his feelings in a violent interview with the English envoy: he repeated his protest against Elizabeth's haughtiness on the subject of a Spanish peace and the discriminatory kindness shown to the Infanta at his expense, and alleged that some Englishman had bragged that Bothwell was to be let loose upon him once more. On the matter of the seized muskets he was all indignation; on his honour he declared that the muskets had been intended for the use of his household, and he considered it shameful for the Queen to act as if they were to be turned against herself.

In June, the month after Gowrie's return, a convention of the estates was held to give effect to the schemes for money and arms the King had already brought forward at a meeting in December, when he suggested the alternatives of putting a levy on every head of cattle or selecting a thousand human heads whose owners would have the privilege of dividing equally between them the raising of the money he required. The estates were curiously cool and offputting with regard to all his schemes and by June both the cattle and the humans were still faltering. Only the privileged circle of the great nobles had fallen utterly under the spell of the distant Crown— like James, the crypto-Catholic leaders of State and indifferent Protestant lords shared his covetous fascination, but not the nation. The exception in the case of the nobility proved to be Gowrie. He stood up in the June convention and opposed the taxes the King demanded, heading the barons and the burgessess, the majority of the nation as far as it was represented. The assembly was arrested by Gowrie's speech and the courtier, David Murray, who was standing by supplied the commentary, according to Calderwood. 'Yonder is an unhappy man,' he said. 'His enemies are but seeking an occasion for his death, and now he has given it.'

According to Nicholson's report to Cecil, the King positively raged. He turned on the barons and the burghers, after compliments to the nobility, and warned them that he would remember this day and that he could pull them down as easily as he had built them up. The Laird of Wemyss on behalf of the lesser breed refused to be cowed; he declared the Throne was surrounded by flatterers and liars. The matter was put in perspective by the one other high born dissentient, apart from Gowrie, Lord President Seton. Concerning the King's plea for an army to make sure of his title at the Queen's death, he said it was utter folly to attempt to seize that ancient Crown by conquest. Who could be so mad as believe, he asked, that the poor country of Scotland could raise an army for the conquest of England, and said that it was notorious that there were various towns both in England and the Low Countries each of which could raise more money than the whole of Scotland together. Seton, of course, understood quite well that James wanted his pygmy army not to conquer England but to incite England's potential enemies in Europe and rally his Catholic friends in Elizabeth's realm, the followers of Paget and Tresham and Sir Edmund Ashfield. An army for incitement and blackmail and intimidation, not an army for the battlefield, was the compass of James Stewart's heroic vision, a stage army to blow trumpets and beat drums and sustain the illusion of his inevitable advance on London.

At this June convention Gowrie and Seton were two top people who turned the opposite way from James's gaze. Was it a sign that the Brussels bloc of the Kirk and a re-born Spanish faction was beginning to take shape? Significant also was the firm stand taken by Lord President Seton against the King in a case that concerned Bruce, the minister, who went to Paris to hurry Gowrie home. The previous year the King had deprived Bruce of his stipend after a long and sustained conflict between them. Bruce had supported Bothwell against the King and appealed to Lord John Hamilton for help. He had, according to James endeavoured to put this nearest man to the throne 'forenent' him and even after the King's use of a heavy hand against the Kirk and the Edinburgh burgesses, Bruce had continued his defiances. It was very much in character that, when his stipend was cut, he promptly went to law and won. The King appealed to the Court of Session, and appeared before their lordships to command rather than argue, but without any effect whatever. 'My liege', said Lord President Seton, 'it is my part to speak first in this court of which your Highness has made me the head. You are our King; we your subjects. But this is a matter of law in which we are sworn to do justice.' He then declared that as honest men their lordships would either vote according to conscience or resign and not vote at all. Lord Newbattle backed him up: he said it had been spoken in the city both to the King's slander and theirs that they dared not do justice to all classes but had to judge as the King commanded. It was a foul imputation to which that day the lie would be given for they would now deliver a unanimous verdict against the Crown.

The King did not relish this hearty way of clearing him of slander and foul imputation at all. He flung out of court muttering revenge and raging marvellously, according to the unfailing witness, Nicholson, in one of his letters to London. But there was not so much purity of Justice as all that in the College, there was a strong hint that their lordships enjoyed themselves in throwing out the King's appeal and their pleasure in it could have had something to do with the memory of the murder of Judge Graham of Halyards, a member of the College, by the King's party. Lord Newbattle had particular cause to remember the circumstances since it was his brother George Ker who was a principal with Fintry in the 'blanks' plot and came near to sharing the fate of Fintry and Halyards. As to Lord President Seton at that moment, perhaps he found a degree of affinity with the minister, Bruce, in the Appeal Court, as he did with Gowrie at the meeting of the Three Estates, despite religious differences.

The Brussels bloc, however, was slow in building; Home had not declared himself or shown his hand in any way since his return, nor were there any signs that Father Gordon was successfully stirring up his nephew Huntly and friends in the north. The declaration of Gowrie and Seton and the negative decision of the convention were certainly a setback for James. Nicholson wrote to Cecil saying it had produced universal satisfaction in the country; but it was the lairds, burghers and ministers who were universally satisfied, it had produced no serious shifts or fissures in power at the top, as yet.

Gowrie withdrew to his Perth estates. After this challenge to the King's policy in Scotland there were things he might help forward in England. A fatal blow at James's hopes there would shatter that strange and wonderful harmony at Holyrood to smithereens, since it was all built on his prospect of the second Crown. By retiring quietly for a time Gowrie probably threatened the King more than by staying in the hurly-burly of the Court. Certainly, out of sight, he would worry the King more. The royal nerves were taut on account of Elizabeth's moves, and the moves of her ally in Scotland could not be allowed to go unwatched.

It was in the Canongate that there were further signs of Gowrie's activities. During July his brother Alexander, the nineteen-year-old Master of Ruthven, was keeping appointments with Robert Logan there, and so were at least two other persons, unnamed. One Logan wrote to, asking him to meet him and Ruthven in the Canongate 'Tuesday next', and saying that in regard to their plan they should come to Fast Castle. He said that he had concluded with Gowrie's brother, Ruthven, that it would be best to go there quietly in a boat, as the King's hunting would soon start and Ruthven had informed him that Gowrie thought this would be the best time to enterprise the matter. To the other unnamed associate Logan wrote recalling that when they last had met in the Canongate he said he had spoken with the Master of Ruthven about their 'conclusion', and since then he had received a letter from Gowrie himself to the same purpose, which had raised his heart ten stages. To this second unnamed associate Logan also mentioned the plan settled by young Ruthven and him to come to Fast Castle by boat; his correspondent was to come with Ruthven and Gowrie and only one other man, four in all, in a fishing boat and they would land as safely as at Leith shore. The castle would be quiet, but when half a mile from the shore they were to give a signal.

For the record of this correspondence we depend on Logan's Eyemouth notary, one named Sprott. The whole story of Fast Castle's four men in a boat depends on Sprott's testimony which emerged when he was under examination for guilty knowledge of treason. The letters he attributed to Logan he admitted to be copies or forgeries, but he went to the scaffold protesting that his story was true and that the letters were based on a genuine correspondence to which he had access. We can allow that Sprott's copies were garbled, from his lack of clear knowledge and understanding of what was going on, and slanted to suit his purpose of blackmailing Logan's heirs, but the essential truth of his testimony has to be conceded for one very good reason. The King's ministers in Scotland were in conflict over Sprott's story and the truth spilled out between them. One lot, because they or their friends were compromised, especially regarding the identity of the unnamed associates of the Gowries, sought to suppress the story, or to treat it as wholly fictional and fraudulent. The other side proceeded to doctor it, forcing Sprott to withdraw names and burying the whole question of the accomplices. The official attempt at suppression and the accomplishment of the doctoring put the seal of veracity on Sprott's testimony, and this is further confirmed by looking at the political circumstances surrounding Sprott's trial which will be examined later.

As well as writing to the unnamed accomplices, Logan wrote to Gowrie expressing his joy and thanks for the letter he had received from the Earl and saying that the Master of Ruthven, his brother, had imparted some of his intentions. As with the others, he described the arrangement he and Ruthven had made for them coming to Fast

Castle by boat, making it seem a matter of passing the time on the fair summer tide. But this time he talked also about concluding at Fast Castle their plan which had already been devised by Ruthven and himself. He added that he wished Gowrie would send Ruthven or come himself to Leith or Restalrig immediately to confer on matters over wine and confection. What was to be accomplished at Fast Castle, therefore, was not talk, which had to take place at Leith or Restalrig over wine; once at Fast Castle it was a matter of carrying out something already devised by Logan and Ruthven—the Fast Castle visit apparently involved action.

Other points from the copy letters of Sprott and his oral evidence fill in the picture. Logan expressed his disagreement with Gowrie about bringing his half-brother, Lord Home, into the affair and said he trusted Gowrie had received proof of his own constancy ere now. This evidently referred to dealings between them before Gowrie went to Padua and bears out what we have already suggested, that Gowrie had been at Fast Castle with Bothwell when they were comrades in arms. He went on to say, however, that he completely disagreed with making his brother a counsellor because he had not the resolution to aid his friend or harm his foe. In short Home, the partner in the conspiracy of Brussels, was not to be relied on in the opinion of his half-brother, Logan. (The lord of Fast Castle was equally concerned about Gowrie's tutor, Rhynd, being kept in ignorance.) As to the timing of the visit, he wanted it before harvest, which was, of course, a busy time in the fields of the Dow Law and Auldcambus farms round the castle.

There was a reference in the letters, a pointed and particular one, to some Paduan tale or adventure. Logan brought it up in his letter to Gowrie saying 'I will never forget the good sport your brother told me of a nobleman in Padua.' It kept on coming into his mind, he said, because of its connection with the purpose they had in hand, and he referred to it again in a letter to the unknown lord in which he begged him if he foregathered with young Ruthven, because he was somewhat 'consety', to be very wary of his 'reckless toys of Padua'. He added that it was one of the strangest tales he had ever heard in his life and resembled their own purpose.

What is to made of the 'reckless toys of Padua'? It strains the imagination to fit them into a conference of people at a lonely sea castle or even a plan to imprison someone in such a place. There was evidently the spice of danger connected with the 'reckless toys'. Apparently they were dealing with someone liable to 'go off' or 'blow up' if recklessly handled, in other words dangerous explosives. Confirming this in a way was Logan's use of the phrase 'eirdit quik', that is earthed or buried alive, when dilating on their project —he would rather be 'eirdit quik', he wrote, than have his halfbrother brought into the affair. It is not a fate one ordinarily contemplates, but the phrase might readily have dropped from his quill when the thought was running through his mind of being entombed by an explosion. Apparently he could not get the thought of the 'reckless toys of Padua' out of his mind. For the Gowries to be dabbling with explosive mixtures was not a remarkable thing since chemistry or alchemy absorbed the Earl at Padua, and Padua itself had fame in such matters. It may be added for good measure that the two young Gowries who escaped after their older brothers died, lived to be noted chemists or alchemists and one was credited with the discovery of the philosopher's stone! It seemed, then, that the four men in a boat who were to sail quietly to Fast Castle when the Court was distracted with the buck-hunt and the countryside was quiet before harvest, were to engage there not in mysterious conferences, which had already taken place, but in some active enterprise which involved reckless toys or dangerous explosives.

Next to the 'reckless toys of Padua' another puzzle in Logan's letters was the question of revenge and the identity of Grey Steil. In one letter Logan wrote that he doubted not that they would, with God's grace, bring the matter to an end, which would bring contentment to all who ever wished for revenge of the Machiavellian massacre of dearest friends. In another, he said that there was no one of a noble heart who would not be glad to see revenge of Grey Steil's death. The uncritical assumption has been left undisturbed that Grey Steil was the older Gowrie, the young Earl's father who was executed while King James was still a minor, but under his authority. This assumption was founded on the further absolutely baseless assumption that the Fast Castle visit of the young Gowries was connected with a plan to kill or imprison the King in revenge for their father's death. It is blithely averred by historians and Gowrie-commentators alike that the elder Gowrie was known as Grey Steil, without a single citation of any contemporary who ever referred to the Earl by that legendary title. Hume Brown, more cautiously, said that Logan called him Grey Steil, adding it was a name applied to more than one popular hero in Scotland, but there is nothing to sustain the assertion that Logan called him by that name. When referring to the revenge of Grey Steil's death Logan was not writing to

Gowrie, he was addressing himself to the unnamed accomplice. In discussing revenge with Gowrie he had referred to the Machiavellian massacre of dearest friends; this certainly had an inclusive reference to Gowrie's father because he had been persuadad to sign a letter confessing his guilt of treason on the pretence that it would secure him an audience with the King and his pardon. Machiavellian enough! It is reasonable to infer that when Logan referred to Grey Steil in his letter to the nameless one he was making a similar pointed and intimate appeal to the feelings of his correspondent; in other words the proper identification of Grey Steil could put us on the track of the identity of the unnamed correspondent.

Grey Steil was one of the limited number of printed romances in circulation in that day and had a pedigree in the form of legend and ballad. The tale relates, however, to the return of a younger exile and it scarcely fits our Gowrie's father. On the other hand there was Graham of Fintry whom James had sent to the block; his career as leader of the underground was an epic of persistent struggle against continuous persecution. He was warded on four or five occasions, ordered abroad twice, deprived of his movable property and the income from his estates and finally executed and forfeited; his underground career started after seven years of exile which began in his youth. Logan's memory of his exile and return was naturally vivid because Fintry came back with the Master of Gray, Logan's cousin, and was at first engaged in the underground service of the imprisoned Queen of Scots, whom Gray and Logan also served at that time. Logan's Grey Steil was, therefore, far more likely to be Fintry than any other man who had suffered death in that reign.

If Grey Steil was indeed Graham of Fintry the revenge motive against the King would certainly apply to anyone owning friendship or kinship with the martyr. The older Gowrie was sent to the block when James was still a minor and under the domination of Arran, but James sent Fintry to the block in his maturity with hate and in cold blood. To whose feelings of feud and revenge was Logan appealing? The letter was not addressed to Gowrie, but it could have meant something to a Graham. The Grahams had staged an armed battle with Sir James Sandilands and other retainers of the King in Leith Wynd at the time their kinsman Judge Halyards was picked on, and killed, and this caused a blood feud. Years later another battle was fought, this time in the Royal Mile, between the Grahams and Sandilands and his men. The Grahams could still be expected to feel strongly about the deaths of both Halyards and Fintry, and not only against Sandilands but also the King. The indications are that Logan addressed his appeal in terms of blood feud to the head of the Grahams, Montrose, who was now the King's Chancellor, and that his Grey Steil whose death called for revenge was none other than David Graham of Fintry; alternatively Logan's letter could have been for the Master of Montrose.

Logan also addressed his unnamed correspondent as Gowrie's special and best beloved, which in the case of Montrose might not be misapplied since they had been comrades in arms against the King and in association with Bothwell at Doune, only months before Gowrie left for Padua. This association would not make it inappropriate for Montrose to be drawn into a new Bothwell plot against the King on Gowrie's return. There was also a new family link; some time before Gowrie's return his sister Margaret had married the Master of Montrose—their son became the Marquis of Montrose famous during another fateful period in Stuart history.

There was also the link in terms of Fintry's secret—which was what all the shadows on Fast Castle walls was about. Apart from Fintry's underground associates, the likeliest person to have clues concerning the secret Fintry and Halyards had shared was the chief of their clan. The voyage to Fast Castle of the four men in a boat begins to wear the semblance of the pooled endeavour both of the family and the political executors of Fintry to wrest his secret from the grave.

Reverting to marriage links, it is curious if nothing else that the just mentioned sister of our treasure hunter, Gowrie, had a daughter who in time married the son of our treasure hunter, Napier. In other words, Napier was close enough to the Gowries for his offspring to marry theirs, at a time, of course, when the links of parents determined the choice of the young persons. This has some bearing on why Napier's 'contract of magic' survived. Napier, we suggested, preserved it, although a dangerous document, as an oblique commentary on the Gowrie tragedy. His son and heir would know what it was all about both from his father and from the Gowries. Like his father, he would pass it on as a veiled secret of the Stewarts and a cryptic commentary on the tragedy of the Gowries. There were political reasons why Napier's son, Archibald, should not be explicit any more than his father; he was made a peer under the Stewarts and associated himself in their defence along with his famous brother-in-law, the Marquis of Montrose.

But we have digressed; it is Montrose as candidate for the role of

Falkland Palace, Fife (from an engraving by Slezer).

The turret room at Gowrie House, an imaginative reconstruction (from an engraving by Jan Luyken).

one of Gowrie's unnamed accomplices that we are attempting to demonstrate. Was he one of the four men due on board the fishing boat for the Fast Castle voyage? There is one other clue. After the tragedy which we are about to describe, the King made an immediate move to seize the two schoolboy brothers of the Earl of Gowrie, and sent along Sandilands, who had presided over the killing of Halyards, to Dirleton Castle to achieve his purpose. The bereaved mother dealt calmly with him; she had just received news of the deaths of her two eldest sons and had hustled her two young sons over the Border, realising that she might never see them again either. In the devastating circumstances she maintained dignity and restraint of feeling, until Sandilands said it was intended to place her two youngest sons under the control and custody of Montrose. 'False traitor, thief!' she burst out passionately and bemoaned the peril of her boys falling into such hands. This is Calderwood's account. The Earl of Gowrie and Master of Ruthven had been betrayed and killed and it appears that Lady Gowrie regarded Montrose as their betrayer. She believed him to be a thief also, or a thief in intent, with regard to the prize which was the aim of their joint enterprise. This outburst has been ascribed to her recollection of the part Montrose played in the execution of her husband, but it was Arran mainly who was behind that, and since then Montrose had been in conspiracy with her and Bothwell against the King and had been in arms with her son against the Sovereign; also, of course, her daughter had not long since married the Master of Montrose. The cause of her outburst, therefore, must have been far more immediate. We suggest Montrose as an unnamed accomplice of Gowrie, with some assurance. Was he the Judas among the four men in the boat? Perhaps this also. If Montrose and Sandilands, despite their blood feud, were collaborating in carrying out the King's behests against the Gowries it smelled somewhat of betrayal.

As to revenge, either for the death of Grey Steil or the Machiavellian massacre of dearest friends, it is difficult to see how success in the treasure hunt could give the deep contentment of this kind that Logan hoped for. But there was a reference to other things in the correspondence; in a note to his messenger and confidant Laird Bower, Logan stated that he had received a new letter from Gowrie concerning the purpose that had been spoken of with the young Master of Ruthven, and also he perceived he might have 'advantage' of Dirleton Castle if Gowrie's 'other matter' took effect, as he hoped it would. Logan added that he had assured Gowrie's courier that he would send Bower over the water within three days with a full resolution of his will 'anent all purposes'. While he was on the subject, he declared to Bower that he cared not for all the land in Scotland if he got a grip on Dirleton, 'the pleasantes dwelling in Scotland'.

The 'other matter' and 'all purposes' need not have us confused if we remember that Gowrie had arrived back primed to lead a conspiracy of remarkable ramifications. It involved the minister Bruce who had been accused of wanting to transfer the Crown, Lord Willoughby who had recently carried out a daring kidnapping raid and Bothwell who had beseiged the royal palaces in the past: it involved, too, the crypto-Catholics with their secret leanings towards the Infanta. Bothwell had an invasion plan and a list of friends he hoped might help it. Willoughby had a sixteen-gun mystery ship that might serve any purpose. Gowrie had the sheathed political sword, the casket letters. In any of these facets of the Brussels plot, and others, Fast Castle could have played an invaluable role and Logan could have been of inestimable service. So large a part might Logan and Fast Castle have played that Dirleton Castle as a reward might not rate as excessive generosity; anciently the Logans had built up their estates by just such hidden services.

The immediate purpose that Gowrie had delegated to his 'consety' teenage brother, however, the purpose of bringing four men in a boat to Fast Castle, this was distinctly marked off from the 'other matter' or 'all purposes'. These remained within the guidance of the more mature Gowrie and were a separate part of his discussions and dealings with Logan, not covered in the latter's talks and arrangements with young Ruthven. We shall see in a moment that when the King came to pry and probe and press over the matter of a pois it was young Ruthven he summoned and badgered. The matter between Ruthven and Logan, Fast Castle and four men in a boat, was surely the treasure hunt all over again; its precedent was Napier's projected visit six summers earlier. It would be arbitrary to connect the two occasions if there were only the bare record of Logan's secret dealing with Napier in July 1594 and then his secret dealing with Ruthven in the Canongate in July 1600, both centring on Fast Castle. But when the magic word pois crops up on both occasions and the actors are in both cases linked to the same background of conspiracy and close to the secret of Fintry, the connection is inescapable. The golden string encircled both dates and also the four men in a boat with the 'contract of magic'.

Logan's last letter to the Gowries was sent off on the last day of

July, but there were other invitations being pressed on them, apparently connected with the hunt rather than with pleasure sailing. The Court moved at the beginning of August from Holyrood to Falkland Palace across the water. In the accounts of the Lord High Treasurer the last entries for July consist of payments made to the royal messengers for conveying 'clois letteris' from Edinburgh and Falkland to the Earl and Master of Gowrie respectively. Calderwood at the time recorded that while the Earl of Gowrie was at Strathbran the King sent him sundry letters supposed to contain an invitation to Falkland. Gowrie's calculation, therefore, that he would be free from the demands or the prying of the court during the August hunt at Falkland was being upset, apparently, by the King's importuning. Nevertheless, he continued to make plans for being on the south side of the Forth. On August 1st he sent Captain Ruthven from Atholl to tell his mother, who by then was at Dirleton Castle, that he was about to come. The next day the Earl moved from Atholl down to Gowrie House in Perth. Most of his men and all his provisions were at Dirleton, so Carey reported later from Berwick; it may have been business pending with the King that caused him to delay a few days in Perth. Very early on the morning of August 5th the Earl's brother, Alexander Ruthven, rode from Perth to Falkland. Governor Carey of Berwick had it that the King had sent for him; Alexander told his brother, so Carey declared, and the Earl had commanded him to go. At any rate, about seven in the morning Alexander, having completed the ten or twelve mile ride, arrived at the royal stables at Falkland. The green-coated huntsmen were ready to troop out and the King had his foot in the stirrup.

# 16 Nightmare in the afternoon

ONLY THE word pois was needed to bind the Gowrie project at Fast Castle to Napier's and to confirm that they had both the same object. This word was not lacking. Young Ruthven was compelled to make his visit to Falkland Palace just after the letters from Logan arranging the castle visit had been delivered. It will be remembered that it was with Ruthven that Logan devised the plan that involved the four men in a boat and the 'reckless toys of Padua'. At Falkland stables the young man approached James, bowing lower than the King's knee—a more humble courtesy than he usually made, James later observed. It was noticed he looked very downcast while the King patronised and laid a hand on the youth's shoulder. According to the King the subject of their talk was—a pois.

James broke it off and mounted his horse to join the hunt, leaving Ruthven standing at a breach in the park wall. He rode up a little hill above the wood where the dogs had picked up the scent of the buck and where he hesitated, then directed Naismith the surgeon, riding beside him, to return and bring Ruthven along. As a result of this afterthought the young man was conscripted for the chase which lasted from seven in the morning until eleven. The buck took them in a wide circle and sensing its inescapable doom returned to its own territory near the royal stables. After the kill, the King immediately took the road to Perth without returning to the Palace or even waiting for a fresh horse, which was sent on after him. He told Mar, Lennox and the rest of the huntsmen that he had to ride there to speak with the Earl of Gowrie.

Some rode on with him with their wearied horses. Lennox returned for his sword and a fresh mount and was soon at the King's side again. The King opened up further to him concerning his purpose. 'You cannot guess, man', he said, 'what errand I am riding for. I am to get a pois in Perth.' He then explained part of the talk he said he had had with young Ruthven, and asked Lennox what he thought of the young fellow, seeing he was his brother-in-law, and whether he had even noticed him to be the subject of any high apprehension; his own opinion was that he was not very settled in his wits. He insisted afterwards that throughout the whole of the hunt the young man had shown continual pensiveness and maintained a raised and uncouth stare. Rather in contradiction, he also later insisted that Ruthven had continually importuned him with his purpose and pressed him to hurry, and was the cause of him riding on without witnessing the ceremonial butchery of the buck or changing his horse. Lennox was warned that Ruthven wanted the pois matter to be kept a close secret. The King thereby inhibited the subject as a topic for chatter on the way. Lennox thought the pois story was unlikely but he expressed the opinion that Ruthven was a discreet and honest gentleman. The King's reference to Lennox's relationship with Ruthven was a matter later stressed. It was, however, rather tenuous—Lennox had married Ruthven's sister when Ruthven was a boy of ten; she had died a year after and Lennox had remarried since.

About one o'clock the huntsmen reached Perth. A mile from the town Ruthven pressed forward to announce their coming to his brother, the Earl of Gowrie, who welcomed the King at the Inch. The Earl had been sitting at his midday meal when the news came and his unpreparedness led to the King being kept waiting an hour for his dinner. During the wait the King, by his own account, attempted to discourse with Gowrie, but if his younger brother seemed not quite settled in his wits the Earl himself seemed to be completely out of his; according to James he got no direct answers but half words and imperfect sentences. During the dinner, too, the Earl was very pensive, as his brother had been all the way to Perth, and stood dejectedly at the end of the board where his Majesty sat. He neglected the rest of his guests shamefully, according to the royal account, so that the King had to take the situation in hand and teach him some lessons in hospitality.

What follows is still the King's story but paraphrased by Mr Patrick Galloway, the minister, in a sermon delivered at the Mercat Cross. It was a big occasion. The platform of the cross was hung with tapestry and the King was there to back up Mr Galloway with a harangue. Many of his nobles were there to support the King, but it would seem that Mr Galloway stole the show by delicious narration and by springing a dramatic surprise at the end.

'On Tuesday last,' quoth the good Patrick, 'Alexander Ruthven came to Falkland to his Majesty and found him at his pastime. And so he leads him from Falkirk to Perth, as a most innocent lamb to the slaughterhouse. There he gets his dinner, a cold dinner, yea, a very cold dinner— as they know who were there.

'After dinner Alexander Ruthven leads his Majesty up a turnpike and through a trance [a passage] the door whereof checked to with a lock, then through a gallery whose door also checked to, through a chamber and the door thereof checked to also and last of all brings him into a round, and the door thereof he locked also.

'In the which there was standing an armed man with a drawn dagger in his hand. Then Alexander covers his head and says: "I am sure your heart accuses you now. You were the death of my father; and here is a dagger to be avenged on you for that death." Judge, good people, what danger your David was in. An innocent lamb, he was closed in twixt two hungry lions thirsting for his blood, and four locks between him and his friends.

'What sort of delivery got he? It was wholly miraculous. I shall point out to you five or six things which you will all call and acknowledge to be miracles. First of all his Majesty standing between two armed men, he, at his entry, should have been astonished at the sight of an armed man to take his life. Yet on the contrary this man was so astonished that he might neither move foot nor hand. Was not this miraculous?

'Yet further when Alexander had taken him by the gorge and had held the dagger to his breast, so that there were scarce two inches between his death and his life, even then by his gracious, Christian and most loving words, he overcame the traitor. The words so moved the heart of the traitor that he began to enter into conditions with the king.

'And so he went forth to his brother, from whom he received commission to despatch him hastily. He then coming up again brings a pair of silk garters in his hand. After he had locked the door he says: "You must die, therefore lay your hands together that I may bind thee", to the intent, no doubt, that he, being bound, they might have strangled him and cast him in a cave or pit which they had prepared for that use. Now here is the third miracle. The King answers the traitor, "I was born a free prince, I shall never die bound." With this each grips the other's gorge till in wrestling the king overcomes and gets him under him. Now is not this miraculous. The Master of Gowrie, an able young man in comparison with the King, I am assured had strength double, yea threefold greater. And yet is overcome and cast under.

'Now yet another miracle. When they are thus wrestling up comes John Ramsay by the black turnpike and, at the King's command, gives the Master a death stroke.

'Now, yet a miracle. Into the chamber with the King gather four. My Lord Gowrie comes up and eight with him. At first he drives all four in a corner and never rests. But John Ramsay chanced to cry "Fy, cruel traitor, have you not done evil enough? You have got the King's life, must you have ours?" At which he drew a little back and, in back going he got the stroke whereof he died.'

158

Mr Galloway concluded his recitation of miracles at the Cross with his dramatic announcement that he had received that day a letter from the missing witness to the miracles, the quaking man with the dagger in the turret-round who was to have aided in the King's despatch.

It was truly yet another miracle and must at first have suggested to his listeners a resurrection from the dead. Only a few days before, the body of a man named Henry Younger was brought to Falkland Palace when Galloway was preaching by royal command. Younger was suspected of being the man with the dagger in the turret and was on his way to prove his alibi, but finding a party of armed searchers making their way towards him the thought evidently occurred to him that they might not be interested in his alibi and he ran for it. They hunted him down in a cornfield where they found him crouching low, and one Henry Bruce put a rapier through him, for which he was made a colonel. Galloway had spread out his arms above the human sacrifice and proclaimed to the King, 'Thank God! The traitor that should have slain you could not be taken quick, but there he lies dead.' However it was not a letter from the dead and not, therefore, a major miracle. There was a new candidate for the role of the quaking man. Galloway gave out his name as Andrew Henderson, chamberlain to Gowrie; anyone who knew his writing, he said, could come to him and see the letter. The minor miracle involved consisted in the fact that the wanted man was given out in proclamation as a 'black grim man', which was to be expected, but in the person of Henderson he had changed into a low set chap with ruddy complexion and a brown beard. Calderwood the Kirk chronicler said that Galloway did not convince many people partly because he was a flattering preacher and partly because others had been named before Henderson, namely Oliphant and Leslie as well as Younger who was slain. The circumstances that were most unlikely, Calderwood added caustically, were all turned by Galloway into miracles.

The King's chaplain, Galloway, felt indeed that he was swimming against the stream. This was very apparent when he repeated his performance at Glasgow, miracles and all, and again with the King on view. There he declared, 'God forgive them that say the King cannot be believed.' To eke out the Christian miracles that had saved the King he invoked, this time, testimony against the powers of darkness which had been involved. 'How can it be,' he asked, 'that such a nobleman as the Earl of Gowrie could have

159

fostered such a treason? If the earl had bidden still in Scotland he might perchance not have attempted such a treason. But when he went to Padua there he studied to necromancie. His own pedagogue, Mr William Rhind, testifies that he had those characters upon him that he loved so much that if he forgot to put them in his breekes he would run up and down like a madman.'

However it might be presented, August 5th 1600 was a day of deep tragedy for the house of Gowrie. By the evening of that summer day the corpses of the young Earl of Gowrie and his teenage brother, Alexander, were laid out together and the Perth baillies were called in and charged by the King to preserve them unburied until they understood further of the King's pleasure. One John Melville was given the unpleasant task of removing the organs of the deceased to comply with the King's will and his account to the Magistrates remained unhonoured for years. It was 'a wonderful pleasant and seasonable morning', according to the King, when young Ruthven appeared at the stables, but the green huntsmen were cowering under a low mantle of cloud and rain when they rode back late at night.

Eight thousand words in print were devoted by the King to describing what happened. The account bearing the title of 'A Discourse of the Unnatural and Vile Conspiracy' was scarcely less burlesque than Galloway's sermons. The man in armour with a dagger was made to appear even more ludicrous by James, who testified that he stood trembling and quaking rather like a condemned man than the executioner in such an enterprise.

The little round or turret room of Gowrie House seems to have been a preposterous place for a private murder session. It had one window looking out on the front court yard which was within summoning distance of both the front gate and the main entrance to the house; the other window opened on to the public street. It was the most publicly situated room of the whole house; with a score of guests wandering aimlessly around and public curiosity aroused by their presence it would have been impossible not to attract attention from this vantage point.

The severance of the King from his friends by four locked doors, which appealed so much to minister Galloway's fancy and the King's, was a laboured myth. The black turnpike led directly from the gallery chamber, where the turret room was, down to the courtyard, and this quick route to the outside world was available all the time; there was no point in Ruthven carefully locking four doors behind him if there was an easy exit at the end of their progress through the building. The King, in his story, reserved the exercise of calling for help until Ruthven's return, then he stuck his head out of the window and bawled. The only violence from Ruthven apparent to the startled witnesses below was a hand raised to the King's mouth to stem the shouts of treason and murder.

It was perhaps not surprising that the King's page, Ramsay, should be first up the turnpike after the King's call for help. He had been snooping round the gallery through which the King and Ruthven had passed, thus belying the tale of the four locked doors. Later he nosed out the turnpike leading directly to the gallery chamber on the other side of one locked door. The King's relations with his young minions and favourites bred a feline jealousy and the page's prying and exploratory movements carry a hint of this feeling in relation to the disappearance of the King with Ruthven, although it may, on the other hand, have been his assignment from the King. Ramsay had the hawk on his wrist when he dashed up the turnpike and he cast the bird and its lead away from him in the chamber to draw his hunting dagger. It accorded with the feline streak that he struck at Ruthven's neck and face, although the King instructed him to strike low because of a suspected mail doublet. Perhaps it was significant that the King was so collected in instructing his rescuer and then cool enough to put his foot on the hawk's leash. A big flapping bird in the room where murder was going on would certainly have been disconcerting, but a man who had just escaped death might have taken time to draw his breath and let the bird flap, or fly out of the window, if it was so inclined.

It was realised later that people put their own 'rash and lewd' construction on the events in the turret leading up to the tragedy, and this was why Mr Galloway presented his miracles so fervently. He had to labour all the more persistently because at first the entire body of Edinburgh ministers refused to accept the King's story. Only the threat of permanent banishment and loss of their livings brought them later to heel, all except one, the minister who had gone to Paris to haste Earl Gowrie home—Robert Bruce. The stubborn stand against the King by Bruce is arresting, for it turned into a deadly and protracted duel between the minister and the monarch. Only to mention it is enough to indicate that the affair had some deep political motivation, of which no one was more likely to be aware than the minister Bruce who had been with Gowrie in Paris.

The apologist for the King, the minister Galloway, allowed some dark suspicions of a political background to escape him at his Glasgow performance, where he said that there was no small number of people who had heard poisoned untruth. He referred then to Gowrie's high reputation, the mistrust in the King's story and also to whether Gowrie, if he had plotted, had backing. 'I doubt not but he had a back,' he ventured. 'The Lord discover it,' and he added, 'I have said before to your Majesty, if you seal not up the fountain thereof it is a manifest tempting of God; and I exhort your Majesty and Council to do it.' Apparently, when he turned to address the King with these remarks he received no encouraging glance. He therefore swiftly changed over and declared that Gowrie was a secret man and he believed none had foreknowledge of the treason save the earl, his brother and the devil that led them both.

Tht devil that led them both or, alternatively, that led King James appears to be the only being with the final answer. There are more doors and locks barring the route to the heart of the story than the King or Galloway counted on the way to the turret room; despite the many doors and locks, there may be that quick, dark, corkscrew stair leading to the solution or its clues as there was such a handy stair to the gallery chamber that enclosed the turret at Gowrie House. It is the pois that represents such a stair and is the short cut to the heart of the matter. The King claimed it was the reason for his ride to Perth. His treasure story is a preposterous one and is ascribed to Ruthven as his pretext for coming to Falkland, which is demonstrably false since Ruthven was summoned, but it is through its transparent falsehoods and their transparent motives that the truth is restored. The truth is that the King rushed to Gowrie House to break into a secret of hidden gold on the eve of the Gowrie search of Fast Castle.

# 17 *The man with a pot of gold*

IN THE King's story of the pois that took him to Gowrie House after the buck was killed we come face to face with a man with a pot of gold. Lennox was the only one to confirm that the King made any mention of this strange story on the road to Perth and he said he remarked that it was unlikely. According to the Master of Gray, who met Lennox later in England, Lennox confessed that he did not know whether the fatal conflict had been instigated by Gowrie or the King. He certainly could not know whether the story of the pois originated with Ruthven or the King since he was forbidden to check it with Ruthven. The story, as Lennox said he heard it, was that young Ruthven at the stables had told the King about 'a man with a pitcher full of gold coins of great sorts'. This pitcher of gold and the man were what the King was on his way to investigate; Ruthven was supposed to have locked up both.

The strange thing is that Lennox, in his evidence of what happened that day at Gowrie House, never recalled any moments of curiosity about the man and the pitcher. He seemed to have shown no interest at any stage in how the King was progressing in his investigation. When the King appeared to be lost and there was an argument about whether he had ridden away he went round searching with the rest; he never suggested that, since Ruthven was missing too, they must both be together looking for the man with the pot of gold. In short, he behaved as if he was as much in the dark as anyone else and had never been told the story of the treasure. Perhaps he never had.

The world soon knew the story, however, in the authorised version by King James. According to the King, Mr Alexander Ruthven, on his appearance at Falkland that morning, began to discourse about a chance encounter with a 'base-like fellow' in the fields outside Perth the evening before. The stranger had his cloak drawn up to his mouth and faltered in answering questions about himself. He behaved so suspiciously that Ruthven began to look at him more narrowly and saw there was something hidden under his cloak; he pulled aside the lapels and found a great wide pot under the man's arm full of coined gold in great pieces. He took the man back to

163

town with him and, without anyone's knowledge, bound him in a private room and locked many doors on him, leaving him alone, his pot with him. Then, at four in the morning he had set out for Falkland, to report the strange affair to the King whose first answer, according to his own immaculate word, was that he could not interfere. 'No man's treasure that is a free and lawful subject', he lectured Ruthven, 'can appertain to the King, except hid under the earth.' To Ruthven's reply that the fellow was going to hide it under the earth, he carefully expounded the distinction in law between a deed and the intention but, thinking it might be foreign gold brought in for distribution by Papists, he then told Ruthven, so ran his legend, that he would send a servant with a warrant to the Perth provost and baillies to receive the man and the money into custody. This, it was said, only occasioned greater effort by Ruthven to persuade him to come to Perth, on the grounds that he would get a poor account of the money if it was put in such hands. It was then, James said that he was forced to break off. The court were horsed, the game was found and the gentlemen were wondering at his delaying so long. He said he would give a resolute answer at the end of the hunt.

Deserting the King's account for a moment there is the evidence of Drummond of Inchaffray that he had saluted Ruthven on the way to the stables, he saw him in conference with the King for a quarter of an hour then, when the King left, Inchaffray invited Ruthven to breakfast, but the young man declined saying he had been ordered by his Majesty to wait upon him. There followed immediately an episode which is part of the King's story: the surgeon Naismith came down from the little hill above the wood to fetch Ruthven to tail along with the hunt.

The whole eight thousand words devoted by the King to describing what happened that day relies for credibility and veracity on the fifteen-minute talk at the stables with young Ruthven. Did he come unbidden with a tale of a man with a pot of gold devised to lure the King to his death at Gowrie House? True or false? The High Treasurer's cash book says with emphasis—*false!* The payment recorded there for a boy to bring Mr Ruthven a closed letter from the Palace points to a summons to this stable interview. This is emphasised by the inclusion within the same entry of the boy's expenses for delivering on the same errand a closed letter to Lord Inchaffray—and there, waiting for the interview to end, was Lord Inchaffray.

They had passed each other, Inchffray coming away from, and Ruthven going towards, the stables and the King. Neither had anything to do with the hunt and both lived miles away, Ruthven at Perth and Inchaffray at Crieff, or nearby. They had only nodded in the passing, neither finding it necessary to explain his presence to the other at the odd hour of seven in the morning. In spite of their wordlessness, Inchaffray waited around in order to go for breakfast with Ruthven. It was rather like two people of today meeting each other in the waiting room of an appointments board; one does not need to explain to the other what he is there for and can calculate how long he will have to wait for the other to join him for coffee. This wordless encounter of two men at a royal interview backed by the two letters that brought them there destroys utterly the King's account that Ruthven came unbidden and unfolded the deceptive cock-and-bull story of the man with the gold under his cloak.

Although the record in the cash book of the King's letter to Ruthven taken alone led Louis Barbé and others to the fair inference that it was this letter and nothing else that brought Ruthven to Falkland, these investigators missed the fact that the recipient of the other royal message despatched at the same time had appeared at Falkland simultaneously with Ruthven. They assumed, apparently, that Inchaffray's letter was connected with some quite different business. When two letters from the royal hand are sent out at the same time and the two men who receive them duly appear before the royal presence at the same strange hour, the matter is surely beyond all reasonable doubt: each of these persons has been commanded to wait upon the King. The behaviour of both Ruthven and Inchaffray at Falkland confirmed this. We see the pot of gold dissolving like a mirage and along with it the alleged plot to lure the King to his death in Perth.

On the other hand, if Ruthven did not invent this man with a pot of gold why did the King invent him? The answer is that a pois or treasure was the true explanation of his ride to Perth and he was obsessed with it; not being able to abandon the treasure motive that prompted him, he gave it this fantastic twist and from necessity fathered the whole thing on Ruthven. He had been questioning Inchaffray that morning as well on the real pois that the Gowries were after, and concerning which he had some inspired but inadequate knowledge. He may also have questioned others. Certainly there must have been discussion of it between him and his informants or informers. The pois, therefore, as the cause of his ride to

Perth was not a strict secret, nor was there reason for it to be if the Gowries were alive. If he gate-crashed into their treasure hunt or forced them to disclose full knowledge of it he could openly lay claim to the prize either as treasure trove or as the Papist gold of subversion. He had a perfect and open right to inquire. He was cock-a-whoop and seemed full of cheerful expectation. Ruthven, on the other hand, was abject, bowing lower than the King's knee, and the King left him for a time looking dejected and staring fixedly on the ground. The young man had probably agreed to disclose everything, subject to his brother's consent. The King, who had patronised him with his hand on his shoulder, seemed well enough pleased with the way things were going and could afford to remark on and rouse speculation about his victim's discomfiture. Was he in his right wits? He was in a mood to boast too, to Lennox. 'You'll never guess man, my errand—a pois.' This rings true enough. The false note is in the lip-service Lennox later paid in court to the man with the pot of gold, yet he showed during the events at Gowrie House that his mind was an utter vacuum with regard to that strange fellow, although he was supposed to be the cause for them all being there.

On the way to Gowrie House it was all right to boast and jest about the real pois and it did not matter if Inchaffray and others who had been questioned spoke of what was on foot. But on the way back it was different. There was the blood of the Gowries on the King's hands and on the hands of his huntsmen. He had shouted treason out of the turret window to incite and justify this blood letting and he was on his way to Falkland and Edinburgh to repeat the cry of treason to the whole world. If the story of the pois stood unchanged the world would answer back, 'there was no treason; there was plain murder for the motive of gold'. Next morning there was still confusion, the minister Bruce protested that a letter from Falkland despatched post-haste by Moysie, the notary, quarrelled with eye witness accounts, but the King soon had it sorted out and by the time he wrote his eight thousand words on the 'vile and unnatural conspiracy' everything had fallen into its place. The gold he sought had not been buried gold; it was being perambulated in a field in a pot under a man's cloak. A dialogue with Ruthven was furnished, too, which described how the King had lectured young Ruthven on the difference between buried gold which he could claim as treasure trove and gold in a pot under a man's arm to which he had no royal title. For full measure, he threw in his homily on the distinction between intention and deed in the matter of buried gold. It was all in James's pedantic style and the elaboration of the disclaimer confirmed the very point he sought to deny, that he went hell-bent to Perth to wrest the secret of the pois from the Gowries and killed them in the clash and frustration that ensued. In short, on the eve of the Gowrie's secret visit to Fast Castle the King's dash to Perth supplied the word pois in the sense that it had been used in the Logan and Napier agreement and linked the two occasions. The embellishments added by James aimed to clear him of a motive for murder.

The King, however, was not so free in the exercise of his imagination as we may have thought when writing his story. We know better in our Freudian century; the images we dredge up from the depths to satisfy our own or the world's conscience can betray us. The man with the pot of gold is preciously like the man with the water pot, that gentleman of the Zodiac called Aquarius, the heavenly water carrier or diviner. Indeed, it is plain to see that the man with the pot of gold is in the same kind of trade as Aquarius and is a hard working gold diviner, a discoverer of buried gold. The very image the King conjured up to prove that the treasure of his disinterested investigation was above ground was an image of his guilt; it indicated the opposite and pointed firmly to the bowels of the earth. The King, however, soon asserted his royal authority over this disloyal fellow by shutting him up in the turret room and changing him into a man in armour with a dagger; he completed the metamorphosis by reducing him in the end into a quaking, shaking jelly fish. Was not that a miracle, as the preacher Mr Galloway would have said?

The invasion of Gowrie House had produced in the Earl of Gowrie the same dejection and gloom that more or less close arrest on the way there had created in the mind of young Ruthven. 'What sorrow means this haste?' the Earl had said when the King and the green huntsmen were heralded. It was small wonder that he tried to help along a rumour during the afternoon that the King had ridden away, to clear his house of this murderous crew before they struck their blow.

The account of the tragic day is not balanced if we do not concede that the King himself was in danger at certain times, especially after the killings. The townsfolk were roused and even the muster of the Murrays for an innkeeper's wedding might not have been sufficient counterweight. Later the King said to the minister Bruce, 'if I had wanted their lives, I had causes enough. I needed not to hazard myself so.' This was as good as saying that he had regarded the Gowries as dangerous traitors on the day he rode to Gowrie and that he had deliberately hazarded his life, despite this knowledge, not, of course, for the sake of an illusory pot of gold the traitors had used as bait for their trap, but to strike at conspiracy on the wing in the hope that precious things would be released from its claws and drop to the ground—the gold secret and perhaps even the secret of the casket letters. The King had learned that even with sufficient causes for a man's death it did not always pay to hustle him to the block by judicial process. He and Arran had rushed the older Gowrie to the scaffold but it had not secured them the casket letters. Fintry had been turned over to the executioner quickly, too, without any result concerning his secret. It had been a case of waiting and watching with the younger Gowrie, therefore, and hazarding his own life when the moment of truth or revelation seemed to have arrived at last.

It was a seasonable moment for destroying the Gowrie plans and that of their accomplices. If there was gold to be got it prevented them reaching it; if the Stuart papers and secrets were about to be exposed, it prevented their exposure; if Willoughby's mystery ship had a mission, it destroyed that mission, just as it nipped Bothwell's invasion plan in the bud if that plan were ripening. But nothing fell to the ground from the claws of conspiracy, no inner secret, and the point of the sword could not extract it. Ruthven's withdrawl from the turret to consult again with his brother was the crucial moment. The King had already pressed Gowrie at dinner, as his settled gloom and abstraction had shown; he had pressed Ruthven at Falkland and was pressing him again in the turret retreat. Meanwhile the small group of assassins were skulking around; young Ramsay was hovering in the gallery outside the turret door, then measuring the steps of the black turnpike; the servant Wilson, Dr Herries with the club foot and Sir Thomas Erskine were not far out of sight of Ramsay, and the larger body of retainers was within call. Ruthven's return from his brother declaring it was of 'no avail' was the signal of doom. He was struck while on his knees craving royal indulgence and trying to stem the alarm and clamour of treason. When his brother's death followed minutes later all the scheming at Brussels and Paris and London was undone, and also the plans laid by Logan and Ruthven at their Canongate meetings. But the secrets the King had sought from the older Gowrie and Fintry still eluded him. There was, however, a distinction from previous killings: Fintry's death had been an unavoidable excess when it was policy to conciliate and not to kill; now killing was policy. Home, Huntly, Elphinstone, Montrose and the rest were being sternly warned, and so were all the subdued or crypto-Catholics and the Kirk, and even Elizabeth. As Father McQuhirrie had said, the King was ready to take the Double Crown from the hand of the devil himself and who ever came between was in deadly danger.

The special vengeance which followed against the Ruthvens marked the King's ugly mood and warning. Conversely, the special honours heaped then and years later on the group of assassins present at Gowrie House expressed the King's conviction that this was the turning point in his fortunes and he had won his last important battle. As to the Ruthvens, the iron boots were transported from the Tolbooth over to Falkland as their reward. The official cash book entry follows after the entries about the 'closed letters' to the Gowries and Inchaffray and supplies a grim commentary on the meaning of the letters. Perhaps in the hangings and torture of Gowrie dependants the spread of terror was not the sole aim, and the secret gold and the secret weapon were still being pursued. Immediate measures were taken also to guard against the future use of any hidden sword of the Gowries. Within twenty-four hours the King's bloodhound, Sir James Sandilands, was despatched to Dirleton with a force of horsemen to bring back Lady Gowrie's two surviving sons, but they had a short start and slipped over the Border. James eventually caught up with them when he moved to London; his first proclamation as King of England on April 1603 declared they had crept into the kingdom with malicious hearts against the King, were disguising themselves in secret places and contriving dangerous plots against the royal person. One of the two teenagers escaped abroad and was condemned to lifelong exile; the other was confined for nineteen years in the Tower. The extreme apprehension of the schoolboy Gowries expressed in the King's first English proclamation advertises that the hidden Stewart papers had not been recovered in the raid on Gowrie House. It was not the friendless schoolboys themselves whom King James dreaded on ascending the throne of England, but the deadly inheritance that might have been passed on to them.

In surveying the Gowrie tragedy only one writer seems to have come close to the possible connection linking the casket with the tragedy. John Hill Burton, the historian, remarked that it was tantalising to find two such mysterious affairs coming close together yet never meeting so as to give assistance to each other. He observed that the letters were in possession of Gowrie's father, then no more was heard of them, but he added it was possible they were in Gowrie House at the time of the tragedy. This was unlikely, but the possibility that the casket was reposing in some cupboard or hiding place at Gowrie House when King James was ordering a search of the dead men's pockets conjures up yet another picture concerning the deeds of that day. In the final degradation it is likely that the dead men not only had their pockets turned out but also had their home ransacked. Night was falling when the King's party set out for Falkland; the killers were there longer than it took to rifle the dead men's pockets. The two mysteries not only met but the one (the casket) was surely part motive for the other (the killings). The pois sent King James precipitately on his way to Gowrie House that day and caused him to hazard his life in the events that ensued. But, as he said to the minister Bruce, he had 'other causes' if he wished to take their lives, and possession of the casket was surely one of these 'causes'. Indeed, James had as many fears of the Gowries as there were facets in the conspiracy growing up between Gowrie and his friends. All these fears and 'causes' had been behind the sword and dagger thrusts outside the turret room and in the black turnpike stair of Gowrie House.

# 18  An authentic treasure, curse and all

IF AN authentic secret treasure must have the hallmark of a curse, the pois of Fast Castle cannot be faulted. Fintry and Judge Graham died violently in protecting its secret; the Gowries were killed on the eve of their search; Francis Bothwell lived the half life of an exile in Spain; Robert Logan escaped safely into the grave, but the curse vaulted after him and his bones uplifted for trial at the High Court. Only James Stewart escaped. James Stewart—yes—but not the Stewarts. The curse leapt nimbly into the royal cradles and grew up with the princes; Henry, the heir apparent, died prematurely, and Charles lost his head. The old royalist, the Earl of Crawford, writing more than half a century after that latter event connected it with the Gowries. He averred that the 'malicious calumnies' of the ministers Bruce, Rollock and Melville concerning the Gowrie tragedy were clandestinely propagated and served as a pretext for rebellion and, especially, that the seditious meetings of 1637, 1638 and 1639 were so inspired. Of course, this sedition and rebellion in Scotland combined with the English revolution to push James Stewart's son to the scaffold, where the ghosts of the Gowries were waiting to welcome him along with the gremlin guardians of the Fast Castle pois. We have left out John Napier from the consequences, or the gremlins did—but he was not a wizard for nothing.

The curse apart, we return to murder at Gowrie House to underline the treasure's reality and sum up the evidence. Outside the turret room King James commanded Ramsay to 'strike low' because Ruthven was wearing a secret mail doublet. (This reflected the doubts with which Ruthven had answered the King's summons.) The King was gripping Ruthven's head under his arm and the young man was on his knees. Ramsay chose to strike high, at his face and neck, and James must have released his hold. It was at that moment that he put his foot on the hawk's leash which Ramsay had thrown out of his hand when he drew his dagger. The gesture shows there was no anxiety about Ruthven's fight or resistance and displays also an extremely cold-blooded attitude towards the unresisting victim's fate. To cap it James seized the wounded and apparently staggering man and threw him down the steep turnpike.

The club-footed Dr Herries and the servant Wilson found him lying bleeding at the foot of the dark stair and struck him again, and finished him.

It would have come to an end anyway. The brothers were already dead men in the eyes of the King, who had his 'causes', but he had not planned to be the executioner or to 'hazard' himself; this we can believe from his general character. The impulse arose out of the pois. The dash to Perth was precipitated by some leaked information about the Fast Castle search, and the situation causing Ruthven's death arose out of the King's frustration at the path being blocked to his further knowledge, apparently due to the stubborn resistance of the elder brother, Gowrie. Ruthven had come back from him with a negative message which set off the King's incitement and cries of treason. 'I had not the wyte of it' were the last words the young man was heard to say by his killers ('it was not my fault'). He was still excusing himself and vainly conciliating, not yet fully realising that death, which he was trying to hold at bay had come. Perhaps we are all a little incredulous when death comes.

If it had been the King's mission to settle accounts for his larger 'causes', the plotting with Bothwell and Willoughby and the like, he would have focussed on Gowrie himself. Instead he focussed on Ruthven. He summoned him to Falkland, he conscripted him into the chase, he pressed and coerced him at the stables as well as in the removed turret room and, finally, he helped with his own hands to overpower and kill him, giving both the incitement and the command for his death. This all arose out of the King's confessed object of investigating a pois with which Ruthven was mixed up, and happened at the time Ruthven was thoroughly mixed up with Fast Castle and Robert Logan. It was he who had met Logan in the Canongate, not his brother, and together they had devised the scheme for the four men to come to the castle in the boat and the plan that was to be followed when they got there. Killing Ruthven in trying to force the pois secret out of him, was the grim historical fact King James imparted to the second major search project aimed at the treasure of Fast Castle. His later distortion of the picture of the pois needs no further notice; the man with the pot of gold belonged to his deceitful dream world and was of the same texture as the mailed man with the dagger in the turret room who took to quaking. But the truth he sought when he presided over the death of Ruthven was the same truth he pursued when he drove Fintry through the tunnel of torture to the block—he thirsted for the knowledge of the invasion gold. Our credo concerning the Fast Castle treasure has therefore two major and massive buttresses. One is the projected search by the philosopher and mathematician, John Napier, backed by his surviving search document and reinforced by his and Logan's known connections with the Spanish gold smugglers and conspirators. The other is the projected search by the Gowries after the Earl's return from Padua, backed by the same connections. The contractual details in the latter case are supplied in Logan's letters, instead of a 'contract of magic', and the King supplied the missing word *pois* and put a point to it by murdering Ruthven. The wall of our credo has not only these two major buttresses, but it is shored up all along its length by the story of the Spanish conspiracies. At the same time, the reality of the hidden gold was confirmed by the execution of the underground leader Fintry and the assassination of his kinsman Judge Graham; and reconfirmed by the King's repeated attempts to break into the secret.

Early on we rejected Mark Napier's theory that the treasure at the castle was a blind to lure John Napier to the place and to extract the military secret of his drawing board for the benefit of Bothwell's plots. Better acquaintnace with everyone concerned and with the political realities should have made that speculation seem even more arbitrary and artificial than it did at first. In the case of the plan to bring four men in a boat to the castle, the Gowries and their unnamed friends, there is a similar speclation that has no shred of evidence or support at all. It implies that the King was to be one of the four men in the boat and the object was to provision the castle and hold him a prisoner there. (This was after he had been lured to Gowrie House by Ruthven appearing unbidden at Falkland.) Since Ruthven did not arrive unbidden the speculation has its throat cut at the earliest possible moment, which saves it lingering on. What James could have done for his captors at the castle, other than help them to consume their meat and drink, it is difficult to imagine. There is a superficial attempt to compare such a kidnapping with that which was carried out by Gowrie's father at Ruthven Castle, known historically as the Raid of Ruthven when a thousand armed men stood by and the backing was composed of the powerful feudal alliance or 'band' including Mar, Glamis, Angus and Lindsay with promises from others to stand in, and when the militant Kirk, which was not yet even partially tamed, was also bound into the conspiracy with hoops of steel and there was a prearranged recognition of the new government by the English Court which inspired and backed the venture. To compare all this with an alleged attempt to seize the King aided only by a single quaking footman in a glory-hole is to slide from history to farce.

If the young Earl was following in his father's footsteps at all it was in tentative emulation of the older Gowrie's second plot, when he sought this time not to kidnap the King again but to prejudice his right to the Crown and replace him by the Hamiltons, who had been sent up to Berwick by Elizabeth. The young Earl's links established with Lord Willoughby, Governor of Berwick, while both were in London hinted at such a move; the hint was strengthened by the secret dealings which Robert Logan began to enter into with both Willoughby and Guevara, the kidnappers of Ashfield, who had daringly plucked away James's Catholic friend from under his very nose. This implied the emergence again of the casket letters; the aim of their use on this occasion would have been not so much to prejudice James's hold on the Scottish Crown as to tip the scales against him in the claim for the Crown of England. That in itself would automatically have undermined the absolutism he had been building up in Scotland and would have split the unanimity of his lords.

We have tried to keep the Fast Castle treasure clear, apart from these other things, by stressing that there were several strands in the dealings beween Gowrie and Logan as the correspondence revealed. The treasure hunt was Ruthven's department, and related to the schemes he worked out with Logan in the Canongate. As to the casket letters and Lord Willoughby's ship, in case they still seem to eclipse the pois, we will say a last word about these mysteries. They did not eclipse or exclude the search for the pois, the complexity was in the nature of things.

It seems certain that young Gowrie was in possession of the casket. We would rule out the suggestion of an earlier chapter that it might be the prize that beckoned the treasure hunters, but we will not rule out that Fast Castle could have been its place of concealment when the older Gowrie was plotting with the Hamiltons through his own agent, Colville, in Berwick. It could still have been its place of concealment when he died, as Arran's search warrant at Fast Castle implied. There or thereabouts it could have remained, with young Gowrie falling heir to the secret of the combination of the safe—that he was armed with this political weapon all the external events seem to proclaim. He was certainly a premier nobleman of Scotland, he had grown into manhood abroad and after six years' absence was isolated, yet he was courted by the Infanta of Spain and by Elizabeth when both were fretted by James Stewart's dynastic aggression. Elizabeth feared for her life, and the Infanta and her sponsor, Philip, feared for the Spanish prospects in the succession. Bothwell and the Master of Gray, who reinstated the Gowries to their estates, would not fail to acquaint their Spanish patrons about the Stewart papers which the Gowries had held and still held and which were prejudicial to James's claim. This was a strong reason for Gowrie becoming a centre of attention at Brussels and Paris on his way home from Padua.

When he arrived in London his welcome exceeded both his rank and the measure of political influence this returning student could be expected to wield. In his audiences with Elizabeth could she have forgotten that years before, through her ambassador Bowes, she had tried to buy the Queen of Scots' letters, whether forged or genuine, from his father? The reason was then that young James Stewart was becoming obstreperous; now he was a dark menace. The diplomatic talks in London would scarcely have been complete without the letters coming up again as a subject for discussion, a subject that in all probability was remitted for future development between Gowrie and Lord Willoughby, when they established regular relations with each other through Robert Logan. At the time of the young Earl's murder the secret still remained hidden, as it did when his father died. From all the dealings of the young Earl and his father with Fast Castle, from the castle's proximity to Berwick where the secret would have been revealed, from the fact that this weapon of the Queen's letters once before lay at Fast Castle before being sent to York—from all that, the conclusion to be drawn is that Fast Castle could have been the repository for the casket, and may still be so today. (There we can rest, except to add that a psychic consultant who has volunteered to help in the present Fast Castle search does not see a picture of the casket within the castle frame. A small chapel on the island of Fidra offshore from the Gowries' castle of Dirleton is given the honour of being the repository by our psychic friend.)

The mystery ship of Lord Willoughby did not sail conspicuously into the centre of the picture after Gowrie's return, but it was intended to have a role and hovered in the background. It is said to have been seen, or something resembling it was seen, in the Forth at the time of the tragedy, when the Gowries' friends waited for them in vain. Gowrie elder during his plots had found use for a ship, moored at the quay of Dundee, perhaps his son's childhood memories and the romantic ideas of a young man added the ship as trapping to the plot. Yet, if the plot was a tripod resting on Berwick, the Scottish coast and France or Flanders, communication was important and a ship that carried sixteen guns could not be interfered with lightly. Also, a ship that could convey a hundred men as well as bear its sixteen guns might bring Bothwell back to set the heather on fire in the Borders. Without the active opposition of the Homes, Bothwell would soon rally a large and loyal following again, even with few or no Spanish legionaries to aid him. Politically and militarily a ship landing Bothwell and a hundred men was more realistic than an armed footman in the pantry or study. Incidentally, the overtures of the exiled Earl to the Spanish government at this time have been completely misconstrued as an attempt to revive the old Spanish invasion plans which had as their object the establishment of a bridgehead in Scotland for the invasion of England. Now Spain's interest in Scotland as well as Bothwell's was exclusively directed against King James, to undermine his power and his English succession claims. Spanish landings in Scotland, therefore, or Bothwell's landings with Spanish aid, would have an entirely different meaning; if they were to take place at all they would not be directed against England, but would enjoy England's aid, the aid of Lord Willoughby.

The mystery ship, alas, was not fated to play a part in this new-style invasion plot; it was another casualty of the daggers at Gowrie House. Robert Logan and Lord Willoughby had to meet to consider an alternative use for this ambitious vessel. (It will be remembered that in the beginning of 1599, when Gowrie was still at Padua, Lord Willoughby in Berwick received from Elizabeth's minister Cecil an inquiry as to what manner of man this Robert Logan of Restalrig was. Willoughby sent back a report that was frank, but not totally unfriendly, 'a vain, loose man, a favourer of thieves reputed, yet of good clan and a good fellow'. It was a view from the outside; by 1601 Willoughby could have given a much less distant report.) One day in early summer that year he and his cousin John Guevara repaired to Robert Jackson's house in Bridge Street, Berwick to meet Logan and his son Matthew, the Eyemouth notary Sprott and Logan's man, Laird Bower. They met as established friends and, so far as Logan and Willoughby were concerned, as partners to be. The partnership centred in the ship, which after the death of Gowrie had become a white elephant. By March 1601, Willoughby tried to get it off his hands to his government 'at a reasonable price'. He described it as a vessel of one hundred and forty tons to carry a hundred men and armed with sixteen pieces of artillery, and said that he had bought it to cope with the Dunkirkers, that it had been in action against a pirate which had carried an English prize into the Forth. Altogether an unlikely prospectus. He frankly confessed he could not maintain it out of his own purse—which must have been obvious on the day before it was commissioned. It was an unfortunate time to try to sell. Minister Sir Robert Cecil and Lord Admiral Howard were just then beginning their secret dealings with King James, like Essex and Ambassador Neville before them. They were in no mood to bail Willoughby out of any enterprise he had entered into against James on account of his fervour for Elizabeth's cause. Logan and Willoughby had met, therefore, to form a partnership to bear the burden of the ship between them. They planned some enterprise that was to take the ship to the Indies, the Canaries and through the Straits, but the main use they had in view for their one-time promising mystery ship was to maintain it jointly against the approaching day of wrath when they might have to employ it for a quick getaway.

Providence, however, furnished Willoughby with an alternative escape route and he never had to answer to King James I of England for that impudent kidnapping affair on Leith Sands or any murky part in Gowrie's plans. He took a 'great cold' in his ship when it was lying at the mouth of the haven in June 1601, an unseasonable cold it seemed, and died. The partnership at sea of Logan and Willoughby was stillborn.

These transactions all reflected how complex Gowrie's plot had been. Another facet was in the stand taken by the tough minister, Robert Bruce, who rallied a revolt of the Edinburgh ministers against the King's story of the 'vile and unnatural conspiracy' the very first day after the Gowrie killings. Under intimidation the other preachers retreated and left Bruce standing alone. After several spirited dialogues with the King, during which Bruce remained unrepentant he was banished. When waiting for his ship for Dieppe he put up, where? At Logan's place—Restalrig. Bruce was allowed back after a year to resume the debate with the King—James found some fascination in these dialogues. The fact was he did not know the real depth of the plot which had threatened him. By drawing Bruce out on the grounds for the minister disbelieving his account of the tragedy, he hoped to gain insight into the truth that sustained his opponent. The minister had agreed to persuade the people against their lewd conclusions and uncharitable constructions concerning the King's quarrel with the young man in the little private turret room. What then? 'You might have had some secret cause,' Bruce replied deeply but non-commitally. Rejecting a series of articles laid down for his reinstatement to royal favour, Bruce was asked with what did he find fault.

'I cannot remember all,' he replied 'but one thing I remember. You would have me resolve according to your book, and who can do that?'

'There is never a false word in that book', the King declared warmly.

'Yes, Sir, there are sundry', said Bruce, calling his Sovereign a liar cheerfully.

'Well, then, we shall put that clause out of the articles', came back the King just as cheerfully. A small matter such as his truthful and solemn account of the 'vile conspiracy' could not be allowed to hinder progress and peace.

If it was unprofitable for James to demonstrate bloodily at the minister's expense that he was an absolute monarch—he demonstrated elsewhere. A town officer called Archibald Cornwall was presiding over a roup of poinded goods at the Edinburgh Mercat Cross. He picked up a brod or painted panel with the King's likeness on it and hung it on a nail he drove into the gibbet; he was reported arrested, tried and hanged and the gibbet that was adorned with the royal portrait was burned. Nobody wanted to put a foot out of place after the fate of poor Cornwall and the magistrates denied Bruce any lodging in Edinburgh when he was at Holyrood for one of his dialogues. Bruce again went to Restalrig to live until he returned home to his permanent house or village arrest. Between these two, minister Bruce and Logan of Restalrig, there was a private understanding of the truth behind the Gowrie mystery and of the 'secret cause' that moved James Stewart to stain his hands with Ruthven's blood.

The very complex but nascent plot extended, then, to the Kirk, to Bothwell in Spain and the Spanish Government, to the English Court and the Governor's house at Berwick and, tenuously, to some crypto-Catholics in the Privy Council. Among its trappings was the Governor's mystery ship, among its weapons the casket with its letters, among its needs gold, among its inheritance the dead underground leader's secret of money hidden at Fast Castle. With all these complexities a plan to search for this hidden money was not incongruous. Also, if all the mysteries met at Fast Castle it was not remarkable, it was that kind of place. If Gowrie's several purposes were confided in Robert Logan, this was not strange either, he was that kind of a man. A destined conspirator, as we have described him, he probably owed his position of background influence and trust to the relation in which he stood to a hidden organisation of his day. In King James's confidence was another similar man who carried out his private and dubious commissions—Sir James Sandilands, who with his gang set on Judge Graham and was posted to Dirleton with a body of horse to seize the schoolboy Gowries. Sandilands' family had held the chief office in the order of the Templars and St John up to the Reformation, and since then he had quietly annexed the Order's property.

Whatever impelling curiosity the King had concerning the depths of Gowrie's dealings, he was not concerned with pulling the entrails out of the plot and displaying them on the iron pins and high points throughout the Kingdom, he was interested only in cutting off and displaying its head. His baleful glance at the preacher Galloway on the Glasgow platform had discouraged that worthy man from developing the theme of Gowrie's backers. As a deliberate policy he was dedicated to encouraging a general betrayal of Gowrie and making a triumphant show of his authority over this one man and his family with the backing, if possible, of the entire nobility and the nation. It was savage and sufficient encouragement for the rest, even for Elizabeth, who took it in that sense when she wrote the letter which faintly congratulated him on his escape, although at once her tone changed into a warning against those who prematurely wished to celebrate her death. For James to triumph over a solitary conspirator maximised his own power and minimised the strength of the opposition to him. He could not afford, as candidate for the English Crown, to uncover deep-laid plots within his Kingdom and expose great schisms within the State. The open end to England's security which his kingship promised to close would then have appeared to gape in spite of him. It was only as an absolute monarch capable of ruling Scotland from London with a clerk of his Council, as he later boasted, that he would be acceptable to London merchants and English county land-magnates, and as such he was eventually installed although they needed a revolution within forty years to destroy the brand of absolution he brought with him.

The one word *pois*, we said, was all that was needed to bind the four men in the boat, the Gowries and their friends, to the treasure searchers Napier and Logan. The King supplied the word on the day of the Gowrie tragedy, August 5th 1600, but we may bind the two search projects at Fast Castle yet more tightly together, if we go back to that morning. Inchaffray, as we saw, received a sealed or closed letter from the King by the same messenger as Ruthven and appeared with him at Falkland stables before the hunt. It should be mentioned that about midday he was riding home towards Crieff when overtaken by the hunters on their way to Gowrie House, and he made out that on the spur of the moment he joined them. He was there when the King stuck his head out of the turret window to yell treason. Who was Lord Inchaffray? We suggested he may have been the fourth man with a reserved seat in the boat; his link with Montrose, his brother-in-law, seemed to qualify him because Montrose was implicated by Lady Gowrie's distressed cries of 'Traitor' and 'Thief'.

The connection is not as slender as that, however, for he clearly had something to do with the matter the King was probing with Ruthven. Andrew Lang questioned why Ruthven was at Falkland at seven in the morning if he had not come to lure the King. Why was Inchaffray there, before seven, although he had nothing to do with luring the King? They had both been summoned to further the King's urgent probe into the pois, which he confessed was the subject of the talk at the stables. The information that predisposed the King to think that Inchaffray could help his inquiries is sealed to us, but we do know that Inchaffray was down on Bothwell's list of friends, along with Logan, Gowrie and others—the list of the friends who would help his invasion. There are other things we know, also, that connect him, not only with the Gowrie and Bothwell conspiracy at large, but in particular with Ruthven and Logan's plan to bring four men in a boat to Fast Castle.

At the start of our inquiry we established Logan's relationship with the Spanish faction. Napier's interest in the Fast Castle secret did not seem so clear until we established his relationship with the plotting Chisholms, the Spanish gold smugglers. Believable or not, the same intimate connection existed in the case of Lord Drummond of Inchaffray; while Napier was married to the youngest of Sir James Chisholm's daughters, Agnes, Inchaffray was married to the eldest, Jean. If this still seems too fortuitous to confirm any Fast Castle connection, let one other name be mentioned, that released by the Eyemouth notary, Sprott, when under examination concerning what took between the Gowries and Logan on the eve of the tragedy. He declared that the Laird of Kinfawnes was one of the unnamed accomplices, but later, under pressure, withdrew the name and said no more about it; and neither did his relieved examiners. If Sprott accused Kinfawnes entirely at random, it is a staggering coincidence that his stab should have landed just where it did—Kinfawnes, like the other two men mixed up with Fast Castle, like Inchaffray and Napier, was also married to one of the Chisholm sisters.

The links of these men with the plotting Chisholms were more than marital. We shall see in a moment that Inchaffray belonged to this set before his marriage and there is a happy little picture that shows how closely all these people were knit. After marriage Inchaffray had a double link with the Chisholms; Napier too had a double connection with them. Marriage at the time, moreover, was very much the servant of political and feudal alliance. The three in-laws of the Chisholms were linked to an important power group which had its strength both at Holyrood and at the Bishop's Court in Vaison. The Bishop of Vaison was brother-in-law to these three —Napier, Kinfawnes and Inchaffray. We must look again at the two pictures portraying the projected Fast Castle searches, of 1594 and 1600: the naked tower of the castle on the beetling crag is constant in both; in the foreground in the one case is the philosopher, Napier, with Logan; in the other Logan is seen with the two young Gowries and their two unidentified accomplices. But in both pictures there is that scarcely noticed huddle of cloaked figures in the corner shadow, and in both pictures the figures in umbra are the same—they are the men of Vaison.

We are, therefore, not dependent solely on the magic word *pois* spoken by the King to bring the two Fast Castle searchers together, the Napier and the Gowrie plans. Napier's connection with the search in 1594 and the involvement of Inchaffray and Kinfawnes with the Gowrie enterprise in 1600 reveal that both searches were inspired and mounted by the Chisholms or the Vaison Court. This is not something to marvel at since Vaison in France was some sort of clearing house for Spanish funds consigned for use in Scotland. At the same time, the Chisholms, who smuggled in crowns and pistolets around the year of the Armada, were obviously persons who enjoyed the trust of the Spanish treasury, as had Fintry and the agent Bruce before he defected. We may recall that the agent Bruce referred to the unfavourable opinions concerning King James expressed to Parma by William Chisholm, the Bishop of Vaison. From this we can see that the Chisholms had the ear of Parma as well as the trust of the Spanish treasury. They were the people who would naturally have the duty to direct a search for missing gold.

The point, which we hope will be taken, is that if both searches were mounted and inspired by the Spanish authorities acting through the Vaison group and employing Napier in the one instance and Gowrie in the other, then at last Napier's contract with which we began this inquiry will be seen as a serious historical document. At last we have got the message. We can almost hear the old wizard, Napier, drawing a deep, deep sigh. His was surely a message to be read in its context, as every communication should be. Insofar as it has not been read before in its context but always read with an indulgent smile, then it can mean that the invasion gold is still there. It was there, apparently, when Napier died in 1617.

To return to the context of the message, the relations between the Chisholms and their in-laws are mirrored in a letter written by John Chisholm to the Bishop of Vaison not long before the 'blanks' affair. Indeed it was a letter being carried by the courier, George Ker when nemesis and Mr Knox, the Paisley minister, overtook him before he sailed away. It retailed that Huntly was still in the north, that Fintry was still in prison, young Merchiston (that is Napier) and his wife were well, so was the Bishop's other sister Lady Kinfawnes and Inchaffray was still unmarried. All were there: Napier who later signed the treasure contract with Logan, Inchaffray who was in time summoned with Ruthven for early morning questioning at Falkland, and Kinfawnes whose name was given by notary Sprott as one of the shadowy accomplices of Gowrie—they were all bracketed with Fintry and Huntly. A death and a wedding were mentioned in the gossip. The Bishop's sister, Margaret, that is Napier's sister-in-law, was being married. 'There were many noblemen thereat'; after naming some of them, including Inchaffray, the writer mentioned the bridegroom as an afterthought, the Laird of Muschat, 'we cannot count him but one of our own' John Chisholm reported approvingly. This seemed to be a membership condition with regard to marriage into the Chisholms, being 'one of our own'. In relation to the Vaison circle, that phrase 'our own' was a stone slab that covered a deep well. In the eyes of the renowned Protestant preacher Andrew Melville, Lord Inchaffray was one of the devil's own. At a meeting of the Lords of the Articles in May 1594, they were discussing the bringing of the rebellious Catholic lords of the north to Justice. The stern and craggy Andrew addressing the lords on behalf of the Kirk said there were some there as guilty as those they were pretending to try. There was a laugh from the corner where the lay abbots Edward Bruce and Inchaffray were seated, and from the King Melville's denunication drew a query as to who was suspected.

'One laughing there', he answered.

'Do you mean me?' asked Edward Bruce.

'If you confess yourself guilty, I will not purge you,' the minister replied, 'but I meant Inchffray there, beside you.'

The King, however, picked up Bruce's 'Do you mean me?' query and quipped, 'that is a Judas question—"Is it I Maister?"'

The laugh became general and the accusation against Inchaffray was lost in it. Yet, when the Lords reached their finding, while there was a majority for forfeiting Huntly and his friends, there was a minority headed by Montrose and Inchaffray against. This was consistent with Montrose and Inchaffray filling the bill of the unnamed accomplices of Gowrie, when he was later building a bridge between the Kirk and the one-time Spanish faction; it was consistent with Inchaffray being involved with young Ruthven in the projected visit to Fast Castle, which the King interrupted by his summons to both Ruthven and Inchaffray to appear at Falkland.

Gowrie's conspiracy, we saw, grew out of Lord Home's deceptive mission to Rome on the King's behalf, which ended with Home 'trysting with Bothwell'. The Vaison group at this stage contrived a more serious, and perhaps a more deceptive, mission to Rome. King James was persuaded to sign petitions to the Pope and cardinals and Catholic princes to secure a cardinal's hat for the Bishop of Vaison, John Napier's brother-in-law, and Inchaffray's. The avowed object was to advance King James's claims to the English Crown in the quarter of the Vatican. The chief agents in the move were Sir Edward Drummond, Supreme Judge of the Bishop's court of Vaison and cousin to the Bishop, and Elphinstone the King's Secretary at Holyrood, another cousin of the Bishop. Sir Edward Drummond came to Holyrood and drafted the letter to the Pope, and Elphinstone got the King's signature for it.

In London, years later, King James looked back on this doubtful service and saw it as a black trick designed to lead him not to the steps of the English Throne but to the pit. Retaliation followed swiftly and he caused Secretary Elphinstone to be ruined. It is significant that his anger over the Vaison cardinal's hat affair followed on immediately after the revelations from notary Sprott's trial and examination which brought in Kinfawnes, a Vaison in-law, and also involved a suppressed letter of Gowrie's that doubtless compromised others. His belated retaliation confirmed how far the Chisholms and their cousins and in-laws had been involved with the Gowries, and also how far they were mixed up with the Gowries in the search for the pois. In 1600 James had been fearful to inquire too far, but by 1608, on firmer ground, he could crane his neck to look down into the abyss. It disturbed him. His retaliation against the Bishop of Vaison's cousin, Elphinstone, is the real curtain to the Gowrie affair and, in a sense, to the story of the Fast Castle pois.

# 19 Logan's end. Truth and the doomed notary

NOT LONG after the deaths of the Gowries, Robert Logan conferred with the other person who knew some of the truth about the Gowrie plot, Lord Willoughby. At first the laird fell into a melanocholy state, according to his notary, Sprott. He disappeared for some days and then, about a fortnight later, on the Sunday, he was with his henchman and crony, Laird Bower, at the Kirk in Coldingham, and the next day Bower dined with him at Gunsgreen House. There Logan discoursed gloomily about the scaffold. When three months had gone by, however, he stopped rehearsing his scaffold speech and felt safe enough to go to Berwick and visit Lord Willoughby, the Governor.

Willoughby, it seems, was apprehensive about any letters relating to the Gowrie affair which Logan might have lying about. Logan came back and had Laird Bower search for his main letter sent to the Earl; the procedure had been that Bower brought back all letters delivered after they had been read. There is a hint of the minister Bruce's influence here, for when Bruce sent a letter to Lord John Hamilton at the time of the Edinburgh riot of 1596, he had his messenger bring it back after it was read; this rather made matters worse for him because Hamilon forthwith carried a copy to the King that was more compromising than the original. The notary Sprott helped Bower to look for the particular letter which Gowrie had read and sent back. According to his confession, Sprott found it and kept it long enough to copy it. The search for this letter was not really a tidying up operation, since it was not until two years later that Logan burnt letters from young Ruthven and Father Andrew Clark, according to Sprott. The search was probably to allay Willoughby's fears. The other dealings with Willoughby, concerning a share in his great ship, followed the succeeding summer. The reserve plans for a quick getaway in the ship with Logan may not have greatly encouraged Willoughby, for he had reason to fear that King James whom he had crossed both openly and secretly would soon be his new master. Willoughby's sudden death on his own mystery ship from a unseasonable 'cold' left a question mark.

Perhaps Logan had his protectors. His retention of compromising letters, hidden in Laird Bower's house for safety, might compromise him but they could also have provided for his safety by compromising others. In any case, his protectors appeared to be exacting a price. His half-brother, Lord Home, was willing to co-operate in his desire, for an unspoken reason, to sell his lands. A deed was drawn up, therefore, to convey the lands of Fenton to Home, but apart from any gift or concession implicit in the price, Lady Home wanted Logan to leave two thousand marks out of the security and take her word for them; she would not allow Home to sign the deed otherwise. When Logan demurred she darkly remarked to him that since coming to town she knew he had been in some dealing with Gowrie that would have got him Dirleton. This took place at Edinburgh early in 1602, and Logan told Sprott it sounded a knell in his heart. He warned the notary to keep out of her way to avoid her questions, and said he would rather be 'eirdit quick' than that she or Home should know the truth of the matter. His 'buried alive' phrase had cropped up again prompted by this unpleasant reminder of the Gowrie project at Fast Castle.

Home's uncle, Sir George Home who became the Earl of Dunbar, followed Lady Home's example in seeking to exploit Logan's necessities and difficulties. By 1605 he had acquired Logan's house at Gunsgreen and the lands of Flemington, but fifteen thousand marks of the purchase price were left unsettled. Elphinstone, the King's Secretary who became Lord Balmerino, about the same time acquired Restalrig House and its lands and teinds, and left eighteen thousand marks unsettled. When Logan made a pilgrimage to London in 1605, the year in which these transactions took place, he was hopeful of collecting his balances, but his expectations were cruelly disappointed. He wrote back to Bower saying it was hard to trust any man. Those he took to be his friends, he declared, had defied him and told him that if the King heard what had moved him to put away his lands he would not be playing the companion in London very long. He went on to France. Bower believed that he was going from there to Spain to meet Father Clark and Bothwell. His journey to London brought him no joy.

Fast Castle was amongst the first of his possessions to go, when it went to Douglas of Pitendreich in 1602, but this appeared to be merely a cover for its transfer to the Earl of Dunbar. Although the Earl duly acquired it from Douglas, it still required Logan's acquiescence. Reproached by his wife for parting with the castle—she at first blamed Bower for it—he replied unrepentantly that if he had all the lands between the Orient and the Occident he would sell them or give them away. In his state of peril and mood of uncertanty he could have no thought now of further plans to solve the 'old mystery' at the castle. Out of the old plans had sprung his quarrel with Napier, the deaths of the Young Gowries, the abrupt end of Willoughby, the forlorn absence of Bothwell, the blackmailing threat of Lady Home and the whole menace of the future. Enough was enough. It was time to leave Fast Castle and its cursed pois to the demon guardians or to the ghost of Fintry. On his return from France he settled into the sociable and drowthy environment of the Canongate, but the plague, too, joined the fellowship, and he died of it in the summer of 1606. Landless he left the world, but by no means penniless.

The 'old mystery' had not quite done with him, however, nor he with it. Three years later they came to the churchyard in South Leith and dug up his bones to cart them to the High Court. There the dempster, David Lindsay, pronounced over them a conviction for treason and a sentence of forfeiture. 'And this I give for doom,' David Lindsay intoned, after declaring 'the name, memory and dignity of the said umquhil Robert Logan of Restalrig to be extinct and abolished, his arms cancelled, riven and deleted and his posterity excluded from his offices, honours and goods moveable and immoveable in all time coming.' The curse of the treasure had pursued the laird beyond the grave.

This all came about because of the notary, George Sprott of Eyemouth, who had handled some of Logan's affairs and gained an insight into some of his secrets through his trusted agent, Laird Bower. Bower could not read and fell back on Sprott to identify important papers for him. Sprott, besides, profited by conversations in which he took part and conversations overheard. The hungry notary, who was frequently near Logan's board and was grateful when the laird gave him extra money for 'corn for his children', lapsed into a still leaner time when Logan was gone. After a while he took to making copies of Logan's letters to the Gowries, and he sold them to debtors of the Logan estate who used them to discourage Logan's heirs from pressing for the sums still owed; Lady Home's blackmailing example was followed by some lesser people as well as by Dunbar and Balmerino.

In 1713, when the Earl of Crawford published his treatise on the Gowrie and Logan conspiracies at the age of eighty-three he said he came on the record of Sprott's accidental evidence while he was

Keeper of the Crown Manuscripts for Charles II. The record showed that the Earl of Dunbar had been walking in his garden with a country gentleman who told him about this Sprott; the gentleman had been lately in Sprott's company and had learned from him hitherto unknown facts about the Gowrie conspiracy. The Earl of Dunbar promptly informed the Lord Advocate, Hamilton, who sent the official, Watty Doig, to seize the notary and bring him to Edinburgh for examination. But the charming tale of Dunbar learning about Logan's complicity in the Gowrie plot while strolling with a country friend in his garden was altogether too innocent. We have already noticed the record of the fifteen thousand marks Dunbar owed Logan for Gunsgreen and the lands of Flemington—the debt showed up at Logan's death in his testament and inventory. Later, the evidence of Sprott revealed that both Elphinstone and Dunbar defied Logan to collect the debts under threat of informing the King of his reason for selling his lands. Doomed and badgered by the Lords, Sprott must have enjoyed a little bitter pleasure in verging on this evidence of the blackmailing debtors in London, without spelling out their names. Dunbar had a personal interest to seek out someone like the notary to bring to light Logan's complicity with Gowrie, even if he had feared to betray the laird in his lifetime, and Sprott was conveniently found to be trading in the evidence he wanted. Perhaps some well disposed connection of Dunbar had tempted Sprott into such trade or, if it was a happy accident for Dunbar, it was the sort he was on the look out for because it not only suited his own purpose by liquidating his large debt to the Logan estate, which it did in the end, but it promised to do a turn for his master, King James, in London. King James had by now banished several ministers including the redoubtable Melvilles, Andrew and James, as well as Robert Bruce, and half a dozen others; it was an appropriate time to strike another blow at disbelief in the King's story concerning the Gowries which these men kept alive.

If there were motives for opening up the Gowrie story again there were also motives for keeping it closed, motives which influenced high-placed people in Scotland. They had escaped investigation at the time because the King had not thought it polite to inquire too deeply into Gowrie's associates. These conflicting motives influenced the course of the examination of Sprott and its results, but one thing was certain. From the time the prison gates closed on Sprott after his arrest by Watty Doig, there was only one way out for him and that was the way to the scaffold; if he was not to be hanged for guilty foreknowledge of treason he was to be hanged for forgery.

His examination fell into two parts. He was seized in mid-April and from then until 5th July the Privy Council, headed by the King's Secretary of State for Scotland, Elphinstone, by then Lord Balmerino, had him questioned painlessly and then twice questioned under torture of the boot. Sprott testified at the start to the genuineness of the letters bearing Logan's name and addressed, as Calderwood said, to 'certain persons whose names could not be known because the letters were not directed on the back.' He also confessed to guilty foreknowledge of treasonable dealings between Logan and the Gowries. 'When he was booted,' Calderwood went on, 'he protested all was false he had written or said and he willed his hearers to give him no credit thereafter if he spoke or wrote otherwise.' This was strange. The torture did not make him confess more; it moved him to withdraw what he had already confessed and declare it was all falsehood and forgery. The matter is still more strange if we believe the Kirk historian, Calderwood, who averred that 'Secretar Elphinstone was earnest to bring this purpose about.' Calderwood added that Elphinstone got little thanks for his effort later. According to Calderwood, then, the Lords of the Privy Council tortured Sprott in order to make him deny his confession and to discredit the stories he had been spreading about the extension of the Gowrie conspiracy to Fast Castle. Up until 5th July, they apparently wanted to hang him as a forger of mischievous letters and bury with him the compromising letters from Logan to unnamed noblemen who had been Gowrie's accomplices.

The Earl of Dunbar did not desire it that way. He wished to strike a new blow for the King at the doubters and delinquents in the Kirk. He also wished to wipe out his debt to the Logan estate. To throw out the Fast Castle conspiracy because someone was being compromised or made suspect was to throw out the baby with the bath water. Coming up from London to Edinburgh he took Sprott out of the Tolbooth dungeon, or laigh house, treated him kindly and cured his legs which had been cruelly bruised by the iron boot and wedges. This kindness after cruelty, as it does in our day, produced a canine gratitude. Sprott became Dunbar's slave even although he was conducting him to the grave, and reverted to his original testimony of a Logan and Fast Castle extension to the Gowrie conspiracy. Although he admitted that the letters and papers he was discovered with were mostly copies and forgeries, he insisted that this supplement to the conspiracy was true. From 5th July to his execution on 12th August Sprott collaborated unstintingly with his Privy Council examiners under the new direction of Dunbar. He reinstated the conspiracy in a dress suited to the taste of gentlemen whom he had previously upset. He believed he was sheltered now, anyway, from some of those who had come and threatened him, so he said, if he made revelations. The record of his examination, from 5th July, was kept by Lord Hamilton, the King's advocate, and was handed down by him to his descendants, the Earls of Haddington. Suspiciously, no record was handed down of the earlier examination from April to July; there is only an anonymous summary in manuscript from which the Kirk historian, Calderwood, borrowed.

The distinctive feature of the new examination was that it veered away from the unnamed correspondents of Logan and accomplices of Gowrie. The three letters involved were copies or forgeries certainly, but Sprott's general plea that all his copies or forgeries were based on genuine originals was said not to apply to them. Sprott obligingly testified now that these letters were 'imagined by me'. At the same time, he withdrew his deposition of the earlier examination in which he mentioned that the Laird of Kinfawnes and Scrymgeour, the Constable of Dundee, were involved in correspondence with Logan. This withdrawal was made on 6th August when the examination was drawing to an end. The drawback was that Sprott claimed he had erected these 'imagined' letters only on the brief note that Gowrie sent to Logan at the beginning, the one asking him to come west 'not only for that errand but for some other thing'. The few lines were not much of a foundation for his imagination. It is true Sprott said he had read also Gowrie's second letter to Logan which contained so much serious matter that it produced a long conversation between Bower and Logan; Bower was doubtful if Logan should imperil himself for the sake of the reward of Dirleton Castle which Gowrie promised. Sprott both read this Gowrie letter and overheard the conversation it produced, but his examiners put only the conversation on record and they did not choose to record any part of this serious letter which Sprott had read. It apparently brought in the unnamed accomplices again, perhaps even named them or hinted clearly at their identity. After the three letters to the unknown were dropped and Gowrie's important second letter was suppressed by the examiners, there remained little else of a documentary kind except this brief uninformative note from Gowrie, or rather Sprott's recollection of it, and so it remained on 9th August when the examination was closed. Sprott was told he would meet the Lords no more and he must prepare to die.

There followed a consultation with the prisoner, however, that was entirely off the record and which led to an additional examination of Sprott the following day, 10th August. Patrick Galloway 'the flattering preacher' opened with a prayer and then Sprott was immediately asked where the letter from Logan to Gowrie was 'whereon all the others were forged'. Sprott now gave from memory the main letter from Logan to Gowrie that came to be used as the picture of the Fast Castle extension of the Gowrie conspiracy and said that the letter itself was in his kist at home. It was found and, centuries later, pronounced a forgery like the other papers. But Sprott no doubt meant his copy; he explained he had read part of it surreptitiously when Logan was in the middle of writing it at Fast Castle and that it was the letter Logan had ordered Bower to look for when he came back from Lord Willoughby three months after the black day of the Gowries. He had found it for Bower and copied it—for himself.

This then was the evolution of the examination of Sprott which began as a discovery of letters and the extraction of a confession from notary Sprott of Eyemouth concerning the extension of the Gowrie affair to Fast Castle, and showed that Robert Logan was concerned with Gowrie but so were certain unnamed accomplices. At this stage Elphinstone, who directed the examination, employed torture to force a statement from Sprott that all was falsehood and forgery. The aim was to have Sprott disposed of as a malicious swindler and his stories quietly smothered. Then Dunbar took over. He discredited only the letters to the unknown accomplices, cleared Kinfawnes and Scrymgeour and left a residue of conspiracy adhering to Logan. At the close of the examination, however, he found himself a little short on conspiracy and had resort again to Sprott in an off-the-record session in which he obtained from him the knowledge of a lengthy letter from Logan to Gowrie. The formal examination was then re-opened to allow Sprott to give the substance of this letter as testimony and to intimate where the original or his copy was to be found. This made up for the suppression of the three letters to the unknown conspirators and for the lack of the important second letter from Gowrie to Logan, also suppressed; it supplied the substance of the indictment against Sprott for his guilty foreknowledge which sent him to the gallows. The indication throughout is that while the Lords of the Privy Council were playing down the role of the unknown accomplices, Sprott was playing up their role and was sparing of information about Logan. He collaborated only in the last minute with the production of Logan's lengthy letter; as well as supplying the substance of his own indictment it gave the Lords the 'model' on which it could be alleged the letters to the unknown accomplices were fabricated. The alternative for Sprott to this last-minute collaboration would have been a return to the torture chamber.

They set up the scaffold, Calderwood said, hard against the Cross so that Dunbar and other noblemen could have a good view from Sir John Arnot's lodging. Spottiswood, the Bishop of Glasgow, said to the 'flattering preacher' Galloway a little before the execution, 'I am afraid this man will make us all ashamed.'

'Let alone,' replied Galloway, 'I shall warrant him.'

Calderwood believed that Galloway had prepared most of Sprott's repentance speech for him. The Kirk chronicler also gave a reason for Dunbar's presence. 'The people wondered,' he said, 'wherefore Dunbar should attend on the execution of so mean a man, and surmised it was only to give a sign when his speech should be interrupted and when he was to be cast over the ladder.' It appeared that the stage managers of Sprott's examination, trial and execution had insured themselves down to the last detail.

Andrew Lang, the apologist for the King's story concerning the Gowries, rather naturally swallowed the careful dressing up of Sprott's testimony, especially the contrivance of the Lords to present the three letters to the unknown conspirators as Sprott's invention based on Logan's long letter. Lang gave it as a personal opinion that the substance of Logan's main letter to Gowrie was genuine, and said that he based his opinion on internal or literary evidence, he did not think, for instance, that Sprott could have invented the 'reckless toys of Padua'. We have surely more to go on than internal evidence for the truth of this and all the letters and for Sprott's story in all its essentials.

There is the external evidence of the lengths to which the Lords of the Privy Council went to discredit the three letters to the unknown conspirators. Their fear of the truth led them first to attempt to suppress and discredit everything, then they concurred with Dunbar in persuading Sprott to say that he had 'imagined' the three letters and had wrongfully denounced Kinfawnes and Scrymgeour. Finally, they re-opened the examination at the eleventh hour to make the case stand squarely against Logan alone, and adopted precautions on the scaffold to ensure it would stay that way.

The truth of Sprott's story is established externally by the massive effort to suppress the unwanted part of it, the three letters to the unknown conspirators, the second letter of Gowrie to Logan and the like. If the truth in the three letters is thus established by their dishonest suppression, then the truth of the whole of Sprott's story stands. The rest of it, Logan's letters and Sprott's testimony of conversations, is simply repetition and a natural extension of the facts that the three letters contained. As far as internal evidence goes, the most striking aspect is that the whole story does not contain a jot of evidence about a plot to kill or kidnap the King, a false tale invented by Sprott on the strength of the King's story of the Gowrie plot could not have been so utterly lacking any details to bear out the King's story. If the Fast Castle addendum to the Gowrie affair failed to supply new evidence of the designs of a few men against the King's life, it revealed that the intrigue had been much deeper than the charade which James had popularised in his coloured description of the 'Unnatural and Vile Conspiracy'. The object of the Privy Council in handling Sprott had been to board over the pit, just as James had been content to have it papered over in 1600.

## 20 The Secretary is ruined and the curtain falls

BY 1608 King James was no longer content to leave the lower depths of the Gowrie affair undisturbed. The spurious unity in Scotland had helped him to impress the English in 1600, and had served appearances in the campaign for the Second Crown. Now he demanded real conformity, not a deceitful semblance of it. He was beguiling the Kirk into acceptance of his bishops in return for greater licence to persecute and suppress the Catholic minority. By the nature of things, those who had been under most suspicion during the Gowrie affair were the greatest underground menace to his new schemes for remote control. It was necessary to make some examples again, to encourage the others, just as had been done in the case of the Gowries.

The two chosen victims were the Chancellor, Alexander Seton, now Earl of Dunfermline, and James Elphinstone, the President of the Council, now Lord Balmerino. The main blow fell on Balmerino, but Seton received his warning first. He was accused of encouraging the Kirk leaders to hold an unauthorised General Assembly at Aberdeen to prevent these Kirk parliaments from dying of disuse. Spottiswood, the King's new Archbishop of Glasgow, was his accuser. The King denounced the Aberdeen meeting as an illegal conventicle and Forbes, who had presided as Moderator, was imprisoned with five others while Dunbar was sent up from London to prosecute the prisoners. At about the same time Spottiswood accused Seton, and the King ordered an inquiry against Seton for egging on the minister Forbes. The inquiry collapsed through lack of evidence but it was a dark sign of disfavour.

Elphinstone, or Balmerino, put it on record that the new bishops in the Kirk laid a plot against him because they considered him the chief enemy of their authority. This all reflected the new power division that had opened up in Edinburgh. On the one hand there was Dunbar, formerly Sir George Home, whom the King had made his Great Commissioner in affairs of both Kirk and State and who was reinforced by Scottish Lords like Mar in London and Montrose in Scotland and by Spottiswood and the new bishops. Seton and

Elphinstone were on the other side of the fence; crypto-Catholics though they were, they were linked in sympathy with the old leaders of the Kirk, not the new 'flattering preachers' or bishops, and well they might be the friends of the old Kirk leaders because the new bishops were being set up not only to enslave the Kirk, but they and their assistants were appointed and paid to serve as full time persecutors of the Catholics.

The group of crypto-Catholic rulers of Scotland had thus split up. They had formed a compact core of authority, especially after January 1599 when Elphinstone had become the King's Secretary at the same time as their collaborator Montrose became Chancellor. Ostensibly they had served the King in building up his divine right and in taming both the Catholic earls in the north and the Kirk in the south. They appeared to have set the King's feet firmly on the road to his southern kingdom. As well as realising James's statecraft at home they were, it seemed, the ideal instrument for his diplomacy abroad, strengthening his hand at the French court and the Vatican, crossing Spain's path and ensuring a direction from Rome to the large body of English Catholics in his favour. This was the secret of the euphoria he felt in their presence.

Nevertheless, there had been a dark hint even at this time that because of double inducements and double loyalties they might steer him towards the pit, rather than to glory. There was Neville's report from the English embassy at Paris that Lord Home, his ambassador at large, had met Father Parsons, main English agent of the Infanta and by him had been reconciled with Bothwell, James's greatest enemy. A mystery, thought Neville, since none were greater with King James than Lord Home and his uncle Sir George. The young Earl of Gowrie had been beguiled by Lord Home's reconciliation with Bothwell, but Home's half brother, Robert Logan, had not been so captivated. The later blackmailing Logan suffered at the hands of Home's wife and at the more exalted hands of uncle George, the Earl of Dunbar, justified his preference for being 'buried alive' rather than suffer such tender mercies. Still, there had been others to nourish young Gowrie's hopes of a secret opposition within the King's Privy Council. Montrose surely had been one of the others, but Montrose as well as Home had failed Gowrie, hence the Countess of Gowrie's outcry against him as a traitor the night after the Gowrie slaughter.

Dunbar and Montrose, if they were drawn temporarily with others to the Infanta's way, returned to the King quickly. It was their wholehearted abandonment or desertion of the secret course that marked them off from their fellow-peers, Seton and Elphinstone, and they gathered others with them. The split was reflected in the examination of George Sprott the notary; those who guiltily knew of the deeper levels of the Gowrie plans menaced Sprott in his cell to stay silent or helped the process which produced the retraction of his confessions. Dunbar deceitfully persuaded them that Sprott's confession could be employed to erect a case against the dead Logan alone, especially did he persuade Elphinstone who stood to gain remission of eighteen thousand marks owed to Logan's estate; how much he might lose, Elphinstone did not ponder long enough. Dunbar proceeded to build up the case against Robert Logan, and quietly and simultaneously built up the case against others, against Elphinstone in particular.

From the sequel it was clear that what had been suppressed in the record of Sprott's examination concerning Gowrie's second letter and what had been smothered with regard to Kinfawnes and the unknown correspondents, had not been held back by Dunbar from the King. A line from Kinfawnes did not need to be extended very far to reach the Chisholms and the Court of Vaison, and by the same route it easily reached Elphinstone, cousin of the Bishop Vaison.

The King and Dunbar, however, did not choose to pick on Elphinstone for any tenuous connection with Gowrie that Sprott's examination may have revealed. Probably what damned him as much as anything was his wholehearted attempt to prevent the reopening of the Gowrie affair and to reject Sprott's tale out of hand; as Calderwood, the contemporary commentator said, he got no thanks for that. For James, however, the serious thing was the dark doubt it all cast on Elphinstone's earlier role; in this connection only one thing could spring to mind—the letter to the Pope. The preceding year, 1607, Cardinal Bellarmine, writing as Matthaeus Tortus, had taunted James with this letter which sought a cardinal's hat for William Chisholm, the Scottish born Bishop of Vaison, so that James's interests might be represented at the Vatican, especially in the matter of the English succession. Bellarmine referred to the same solicitation he, and also Cardinal Cajetano and Cardinal Aldobrandinus, had received from James. The suit or solicitation for the cardinal's hat made on behalf of Elphinstone's cousin, Chisholm, was drawn up and written by Elphinstone's other cousin, Sir Edward Drummond and it was Elphinstone who secured the King's signature to it and put it on the diplomatic bag of M. de Bethune so that it would safely reach the Archbishop of Glasgow in Paris and thence pass to Rome. Unquestionably James at the time had accepted all this as part of the good offices of Elphinstone and the Chisholms on his behalf. It was of a piece with his negotiations with Ashfield, the English Catholic agent, and Paget and Tresham, the English Catholic exiles. The recommendation to send such a letter, moreover, had not come from any suspect source, but was favoured by James's own ambassador in Paris, Beaton, and had been linked with the discussions with M. de Bethune, who came from the French court on a diplomatic mission to Holyrood prior to taking up residence at the Vatican as French ambassador there.

Now, however, the proposed good offices of the Bishop of Vaison at the Vatican appeared in a different light. If the Chisholms and Elphinstone had been conspiring with Gowrie, Willoughby, Bothwell and Father Parsons to ruin his prospects for the English succession then the letter begging for the Cardinal's hat had been part of their deep plot, probably the first step in it. Their object had not been to advance his cause but to undermine it and favour the Infanta's; spies had, in fact, reported these overtures to the Pope to Elizabeth. Elphinstone had denied them and drawn in Sir Edward Drummond to repudiate the delivery of any letter, but relations with the English court had degenerated and become abominable the following year.

In 1608, the King looked back on it in black anger. Elphinstone remained oblivious of his danger for a time, probably through reliance on the discretion of Dunbar. Then, in October following Sprott's execution, which was in August, he was summoned to court. When he reached St Alban's he was informed of the King's complaint against him and on Sunday before church he faced the King privately in a withdrawing chamber at Royston and answered questions about the letter to the Pope. The fault he confessed was that he had caused to be added the customary style of address to his Holiness, and the style of subscription without the King's knowledge, but in obtaining the King's signature he had made it clear that the document contained the suit for a Scottish cardinal. At the interview at Royston the King had not seemed displeased. He caused Elphinstone, however, to repeat his statement in front of a witness, Sir Alexander Hay, and then the royal attitude changed and the royal countenance darkened.

In London on the following Wednesday Elphinstone was directed to put his statement down in writing for the King. Sir Alexander

Hay brought him a note containing the command and Elphinstone now began to regret he had gone so far. He wrote to the King saying that he could not remember, craved leave to return home to consult his papers and asked to be allowed to bring Sir Edward Drummond from France. Instead, the King committed him to the Council of England to be examined on points concerning the letter to the Pope as the King 'remembered' them. Before the Council Elphinstone failed to synchronise his memory with the King's. Dunbar then sent Lord Burlie to him: Burlie was Elphinstone's friend. The advice he brought was for Elphinstone to remember everything the way the King remembered it, his life and estate would then be safe, although his honours and offices would be at the King's pleasure. Elphinstone accordingly put himself in Dunbar's hands or, as he said, 'entered into a more particular friendship' with him. The particular friendship involved, on Elphinstone's side, an offer of 'the park and palace of Holyroodhouse and if he desired Restalrig, he should have it for the price I bought it.' This was a confession of the bare-faced robbery of Logan in which both men had engaged; the price of Restalrig had not yet been half paid by Elphinstone, but even at the price it could rank as a bribe. Burlie came back with the message that Dunbar was pleased and would take Elphinstone under his protection while Elphinstone for his part rested content in Dunbar's power to 'calm all storms'. Before the process ended, however, he had signed a confession of treason in respect to obtaining falsely the King's signature for the letter to the Pope and was arraigned before the Council of England. In the great council chamber, crowded by the nobility of both Scotland and England, he had to listen to a catalogue of the horrible consequences of his act detailed grimly by Lord Salisbury, the English Chancellor. He had, it was proclaimed, gravely prejudiced James at the Court of Elizabeth, imperilled him with insurrection in Scotland and falsely roused Catholic expectations, thereby leading to printed slanders against the King and dangerous conspiracies, including the gunpowder plot. The King hid behind the arras in the chamber and heard Elphinstone confess his guilt in abject terms partly framed by Dunbar. The culprit was formally deprived of his membership of the King's council and remitted to Scotland for trial, where his estates were declared forfeit despite the assurances of Dunbar.

He was sent back to Scotland a prisoner and when he came to Newcastle he conveyed a message to James Melville, one of the ministers' leaders who was living in judicial exile in that town.

Elphinstone's message to Melville declared that he was thus harshly treated for standing for the freedom of his country and for being considered an obstruction to the power of the King's bishops. The fates and paths of these two opposite men crossed. One was the nephew and stern shadow of the wrathful Protestant prophet, Andrew Melville, who had seized the King's sleeve and reminded him that in Christ's kingdom he was but God's silly vassal. The other was the Court's chief crypto-Catholic conspirator, a brother to Father George who managed the Scots College in Rome and a cousin of the would-be Cardinal of Vaison. Their fate illustrated what Father McQuhirrie had said, that James Stuart was ready to ruin both Catholic and Protestant to attain the Crown of England. The Jesuit should have added that once the King's ambition was attained he would continue the ruin of both for his greater glory—his compulsion was to lay the foundations of revolution in both his kingdoms.

The next year, 1609, the process of forfeiture of the Logan estates was carried through accompanied by the grisly ceremony of displaying the bones of the laird at the High Court. Logan's long letter was produced as an exhibit this time; Sprott's examination had been based on his recalling of it. The three letters to the unknown conspirators were also produced and witnesses were called to testify that they were in Logan's hand; all have since been declared forgeries by handwriting experts. This, of course, confirms Sprott's confession that he used his knowledge for blackmailing purposes and it does not invalidate his insistence that his Gowrie recollections were true. As far as the three letters were concerned, their genuineness in substance is proven, as we have said, by Elphinstone's labour to suppress them and by the contrived withdrawal of Sprott's evidence against Kinfawnes, the suppression of the main letter from Gowrie and the like.

By now Elphinstone's fall had come about and Dunbar was able to drive the process alone, even though, it was reported, he had difficulty in carrying the process against Logan through the College of Justice and was compelled to apply pressure and persuasion, for which he was commended in London. The resistance was probably not on account of Logan's family. There had been no resistance to the process against poor Sprott. It was sensed that the evidence of the letters to the unknown accomplices of Gowrie carried a future threat of the Gowrie conspiracy being reopened and Dunbar laboured with their lordships of the bench to allow this warning or threat to stand. This, apart from the filching of Logan's fortune, was the main significance of the posthumous trail.

At the same time as Elphinstone's fall, restraints were imposed on Seton, who had allied himself with Gowrie in the convention to oppose the King in his dynastic adventure, and had sided with the minister Bruce against the King in the Court of Appeal. He had been accused of egging on Forbes, the minister, to convene the Kirk parliament or General Assembly when the King wished it to lapse into disuse. By serving as Provost of Edinburgh he was suspect of leading the burgesses of the capital city against the King and his bishops; the burgesses of Edinburgh, therefore, were ordered on their peril to remove the provost of their choice. The King's dictatorial decree was made acceptable by the democratic motive to which he ascribed it; in his letter to the Edinburgh Council he declared they must elect as their head one of their own neighbours and traffickers for the better preserving of their liberties, or they would answer to him for it. 'By God,' he said in effect 'I'll make you accept your liberty, if I have to throw you into the dungeons to enjoy it.' To pacify the King, Calderwood reported, they elected Sir John Arnot as their provost, a creature of the King's creature Dunbar.

If what was seen on the surface as the Gowrie conspiracy was, in fact, an incipient revolution in Scotland against James's absolutism fabricated to gain him a more resplendent crown and convert his native land into a backwater vassal State, then the fall of Elphinstone and the restraint of Seton marked the completion of the implicit counter-revolution which the killing of the Gowries had begun. In the course of the repression the Kirk's defenders and the crypto-Catholic conspirators, who had not united sufficiently in resistance, were sufficiently united in the dust of defeat. There remained framed within the posthmous indictment of Robert Logan the three letters to Gowrie's unknown accomplices; they were the royal advertisement that, if need be, more heads would be made to roll.

It is not surprising that when the rebellion against the Crown and the bishops, the rebellion of the Covenant, did ultimately break out, King James's tuppence-coloured tale of the Gowrie plot was among the first of the royal shibboleths to be scornfully cast away. As the old royalist Earl of Cromarty lamented later, the Gowrie story in the version of the ministers had been 'clandestinely propagated' and had become 'a handle for rebellion'. The political depth of the Gowrie affair is so to be judged. To the satisfaction of

the occupant of the royal box the curtain fell again on the dishonour
of the Gowries at the date of Logan's posthumous trail in 1609, but
within thirty years the curtain rose again on scenes of sedition and
rebellion and the King's story of the 'un-natural and vile conspiracy'
was trodden in the mud.

## 21 The pois remains

THE CONFLICT between Elphinstone and Dunbar that arose over the prosecution of Sprott had political undertones, as we have shown, since it involved resistance to Dunbar and the King within the Privy Council over the divergent aims and procedure in Sprott's examination and also in resistance within the College of Justice to the process against Logan, and expressed itself in the Edinburgh Town Council in the accompanying disagreement with the King over their Provost. But there was another element in it of a more private kind. We hope we do not appear to be straining after a false emphasis on our predominant theme, but the inner matter was the Fast Castle pois. After all, it was because of Sprott's Fast Castle story that the fissure at the top opened up.

We must bear in mind that Dunbar had prised Fast Castle from Logan as protection money, but he still had to prise open the castle's secret—for himself, or perhaps for the King. Elphinstone, on the other hand, was acting to protect the unnamed accomplices of Gowrie involved in the Fast Castle search plan framed by the ill-fated Ruthven with Logan, and it was also part of this service to the Vaison circle to protect the still undiscovered invasion gold. In this he had powerful backers and prompters. For the pointer to this we fall back on the English ambassador in Spain; according to his despatches a significant Scotsman came out of Spain on a special mission at the very time Sprott's slow examination was being conducted or protracted in the Tolbooth dungeon by Elphinstone and the Privy Council. Sprott was arrested in April and was not out of their hands until July; in June George Ker left Spain for Scotland after drawing fourteen hundred ducats from the Spanish treasury. Ker was the courier in the 'blanks' plot who escaped from Edinburgh Castle. He had received his assignment from the Chisholms, the gold smugglers, and was so much concerned with invasion gold that he was back in Scotland during the first evidence of a Spanish inquest in 1594 when Logan and Napier drew up their search contract, and was back at Fast Castle conferring secretly with Logan four years later. On both these occasions, as a fugitive he was putting himself at risk, and now he was exposing himself to great risk again. Ker had little interest in protecting Gowrie's accomplices for he had been too long out of the country to care, but he had a large pension from the Spanish government and was bound to their service. They in turn were unlikely to invest fourteen hundred ducats in any humanitarian object, but they had an interest in the lost invasion gold that had been a continuous subject of inquiry. The object of Ker's mission at this precise time, therefore, seems pretty clear; like Elphinstone, the Spanish government and Ker were concerned to see that Fast Castle's secret was not prised open during the examination of Sprott. Confirming this intervention of Spain there is not only the record of Ker's mission, but there is also the complaint of Sprott concerning the mysterious persons who were admitted to his dungeon to threaten him to keep quiet. This unofficial persuasion was a bonus on top of the pressure of the Privy Council and the lokman, the official torturer.

Arriving from London early in July, George Home, otherwise Dunbar, saw the damage that was being done to his work and took over. The chronicler Calderwood virtually attributed Elphinstone's downfall to his interference with the aims of Dunbar's process against Sprott. As soon as the proceedings began against Elphinstone himself Dunbar, with the reputed power to 'calm all storms', offered the unfortunate man his protection. The two had 'protected' Logan and together stripped him of his lands and now the one began to submit to the 'protection' of the other. In his letter of gratitude Elphinstone informed Dunbar that he could have 'the park and palace of Holyrood' and also, if he so desired, Restalrig for what he gave for it, that is at a thief's price. It appeared, however, that Dunbar wanted a different reward, the secret of the Fast Castle pois from the Vaison circle, but Elphinstone, a cousin of the Chisholms, did not or could not meet his demand. He was consequently forfeited for his part in the old Vaison affair of the cardinal's hat, but the more recent Vaison affair of the attempted suppression of the Fast Castle story entered into it, as Calderwood believed.

How far Dunbar probed towards the Fast Castle secret at this time it is impossible to say. His blackmailing lever supplied by Sprott against named accomplices of Gowrie was almost certainly employed, for he saw to it, that their names remained in the record of Sprott's examination although there was, significantly, no record preserved of Sprott's examination by Elphinstone and the Privy Council. From Kinfawnes, Inchaffray and others at this stage he could gain no more than they had known about the secret at the time the Gowries died, and the part the Gowries knew he could not reach. For that and the more serious silence of Fintry the credit was due to King James.

It is also impossible to say how far Dunbar was at this time inspired and instructed by the King in this third attempt to reach the secret of the invasion gold, the examination of Fintry in the Tolbooth dungeon being the first and the dash to Perth and examination of Ruthven in the turret room being the second attempt. There is the pointer that it was at this time another Ker or Carr gained ascendancy at the English court as a young minion and favourite and had his unblushing honours heaped thickly upon him. The ambassador in Spain, Cornwallis, left a note on the link between this Carr, under his title of Rochester, and his kinsman, George Ker, in Spain. Perhaps both Kers were in business dealing in the commodity of the Fast Castle secret at the same time, one serving the King of Spain and the other serving King James.

If the King was behind Dunbar in this later Fast Castle search and inquiry, then he just missed having intelligence from a much older hand than his new minion, Carr—from Francis Bothwell. James's ambassador, Cornwallis, kept his master Lord Salisbury regularly supplied with flashes of news concerning Bothwell's life in exile appertaining chiefly to his misfortunes. Either before or after a calamity which curbed his Don Juanesque career, he had to face a lawsuit for the price of a Spanish lady's maidenhead, as Cornwallis put it. At another time he fell under official suspicion of sorcery on account of his fortune telling and because he practised in the locating of stolen property by some species of divining. (Perhaps he was keeping his hand in for a return to Fast Castle.) Then he had to fly to sanctuary for throwing a subject of King Philip out of a window along with his sword and dagger; rather unfairly, his mistress of the moment was seized and thrown into prison for his offence. With it all he was tiring of the life, especially since the dream of his return to Scotland at the head of an invading force had collapsed with the end of the Gowries, for in an undated despatch in 1608 Cornwallis reported that the Earl had communicated with him offering to disclose to King James a means to gain five hundred thousand ducats a year from Scotland without burden to any man in return for his pardon and repatriation. Cornwallis had put him off by replying that he dared not touch the golden apple without permission because he concluded it was a feather from the wing of one of Bothwell's chimeras or 'an excuse to talk about an unrelated matter'. Yet it may have been an excuse to talk about a related matter; the same reports about Fast Castle that drew Ker to Scotland may have stimulated Bothwell to trade whatever knowledge he had to the King. The golden apple he offered may not have been quite the one he chose to describe in an open letter, but it could have been the apple the King once sought ardently—when he rode to Perth.

From all the signs we can regard the period that took in the trials of Sprott, Logan and Elphinstone as another chapter in the Fast Castle probe and search. The curtain came down on the pois in 1609 more or less finally. Thereafter there is only a suggestion of faint attempts to part it and slight rustles of its folds. For one thing, the Earl of Dunbar did not live to prosecute the search much further, his death took place in 1611, two years after Logan's posthumous trial. It may be significant that, soon after, his daughter conveyed Fast Castle to the Edinburgh merchant and burgess, James Arnot, the son of the Lord Provost foisted on the city by the King after he commanded the City Council to remove their respected provost, Seton, the leading Catholic of his day, who was denounced for inciting the Kirk to defy the King. Dunbar had been the patron of the older Arnot, but if the son inherited any part of Fast Castle's secret from his father or his father's patron, he appears to have made little of it and within a few years the castle was back in the hands of the Homes. Napier died in 1617 and we choose to regard his passing on of the 'contract of magic' as an intimation that the Fast Castle mystery remained at that date unsolved. Bothwell died and his son was restored to his exiled father's estates, but if he in time inherited any part of the Fast Castle secret it does not seem to have profited him either; he was a prodigal son of a reckless father and before his days were over had sold and expended most of the old monks' lands of Coldingham that by good fortune came his way.

By the middle of the century the castle was in the hands of Sir Patrick Hepburn when the then Earl of Home had an impulse to take violent possession of it, for which unlawful act he was fined £20,000 Scots. This is the last clear manifestation of the rage for possession of the castle. Near the end of that century it was acquired by Sir John Hall and remained with him and his descendants for a good deal longer than a century. All the time it appeared to be unprized and gradually tumbled down into the sea, or it may in part have been pushed into the sea from the vague knowledge that it harboured a precious secret from which it was wiser to avert the curious gaze. It was better to make it a wilderness. Nearly all of it lay below the waves when the present owners, of the family of Usher, acquired Wolf's Crag as an appendage to the surrounding valuable farmlands, in the present twentieth century.

The golden string has twisted and turned, looped and circled and been snarled by intrigue and knotted by death. In the end it appears to have led nowhere and been cast away and left to moulder in the earth. Yet the winding of the golden ball has, we hope, invested the Fast Castle pois with a reality it lacked before. We also hope the winding has disclosed a story of the sort mentioned in our prologue, involving the King and the Court, drama and death and the fate of the nation.

\* \* \*

Apart from historical research and the digging at the castle we sought to disperse the mists by approaching the descendants of some of the main actors in our story. This strengthened the conviction that once the principal efforts to uncover the treasure had been frustrated, by the terror engendered through the Gowrie affair and the acute conflict arising from Sprott's disclosures, a continuing fear subdued the rage of search. Thereafter the uncertain and fragmented knowledge was quickly dissipated and lost, and, but for Napier's manuscript, no hint of the affair would have survived. By way of a related instance of the triumph of oblivion, we have the testimony of the old Earl of Cromarty that the women relatives of Gowrie were the strongest supporters of minister Bruce's scepticism concerning the King's Gowrie House tale. Of course they possessed secret knowledge which gave the lie to James Stewart's imagination, but where is there any trace of that secret knowledge now? Where there are powerful political reasons to forget, even kith and kin do not privately inherit the truth and dangerous secrets are soon dropped by the way.

By the early nineteenth century, Napier's descendant and biographer had no family tradition to draw on concerning any meaning of the Fast Castle contract and had to fall back entirely on speculation. The present writer communicated with the present Lord Napier and Ettrick who was most kind and helpful. From him we learned that the original of the manuscript had passed out of the family's hands, probably near to the turn of the present century, and as to any family commentary on it, the only thing was the marginal note on a mid-nineteenth century abstract of the document which simply said, 'contract of magic'. We discovered that the manuscript had passed from Napier family care into the hands of Professor Glasier of Trinity College who was a Napier collector. On his death certain Napier originals were bequeathed to Cambridge libraries but not, sadly, the 'contract of magic' and friendly Cambridge librarians have not been able to discover its present home so far. Its importance for Fast Castle research is that it may contain some cipher, which would be in character with Napier and in keeping with his time, a hidden intimation that a facsimile does not reproduce.

Miss Logan is a direct descendant of Robert Logan and her secluded Murrayfield house in Edinburgh is loyally named Restalrig. At the time of interview with this dear old lady she was past her ninety-first birthday. Seated with her feet up on the couch she called attention to the framed manuscript on the mantelpiece which bore the description 'Reversal of Attainder' and represented a softening of the sentence of doom pronounced on the name and memory of Robert Logan by the dempster. In the little gallery there were studies in oils of the inevitable scene, Wolf's Crag, by nineteenth-century painters, inspired, of course, by Scott. But again it was the same— no private tradition or handed down secret and insight. A minor tradition, not quite related, was mentioned by Miss Logan; whenever any of the family was due to go, she said, a picture fell. She had clearly made no attempt to restrict the number of pictures in her home on account of this, probably because she did not consider herself clever enough to cheat Death; she remarked cheerfully that it saved one from being taken unawares. A thought occurred later, but it was outside the house and too late to inquire—was it perhaps, always a picture of Fast Castle that fell?

From everything so far, the personal inquiries, the digging at the castle and the search of the records, there has been one certain result—the David of conviction has slain the Goliath of doubt—we are convinced the Fast Castle pois was an important fact and is still there, preserved over the centuries by judicious oblivion. Terror, conflict and menace subdued and defeated the rival searchers nearly four centuries ago. Besides, there was the curse. The grinning skulls on the iron pins and the rattling of a dead man's bones in a box in the High Court bore testimony to its evil potency, as did the poor notary's ascent of the ladder perched on the scaffold. In a more impressionable age could these things have lacked a discouraging and inhibiting influence? Finally, there was the nature and manner of the concealment. The people who hid the invasion gold were inheritors of traditions of secret organisation. We need only cast a glance back at the links Logan and Bothwell sought with the spymaster Walsingham, the links Walsingham possessed at Cairo with the Sultan and at Malta with the Grand Master of the Knights of St John or, more pertinently, we can regard the example of the Court of Vaison. These examples reveal the deep roots and the far spreading tendrils of sixteenth-century conspiracy; such conspirators would have little to learn in the matter of transporting and hiding gold. The place they selected, the region of Wolf's Crag, had likewise a tradition behind it of secrecy and conspiracy and probably possessed inscrutable hiding places that had been made or discovered centuries before. To outwit all this cunning was no one's easy pastime four centuries ago or since and represents a further and final assurance that the Fast Castle treasure was never whisked away. It leaves only the simple question: *Can it be penetrated now?*

# Epilogue: 1971
## Lately through the tavern door

HEAD CHESTERS* IS backed by the Lammermoors, faced by the North Sea and haunted by smugglers' ghosts. It was once a post-house on the Great North Road and from its six hundred feet vantage it looks down the fields to the old coastguard cottages that crown the sea-braes above Redheugh shore. The coastguards moved to a more sociable site long ago, but the monument of white cottages they have left behind makes a pleasing picture with the passing ships, and recalls days when they had to carry the war into the smugglers' camp. Those contraband days are recalled also in *The Memoirs of Paul Swanston* written by Alexander Somerville, the hero of the Reform agitation of 1832. Somerville painted the inn as a place of revelry of the smugglers and also the place where they were surprised by the press gang and the army, so that they hurriedly stowed away their arms in the landlord's secret hiding places.

For reasons best known to themselves the ghosts of Head Chesters are most restless at about five o'clock on a Sunday morning. Then they start dragging heavy objects across the floor of the long attic which has its small spy window on the coast set within the gable end. The sounds could not pass for anything so dainty as gulls cavorting on the roof, even if they had clogs on. However, the muscular ghosts have lately suffered from neglect and may have left in a huff. All attention has been transferred to the ghosts of Fast Castle, to the point that the stable and beer cellar have been converted into headquarters for the castle searchers. The castle headland is only two miles away, if you are a gull, and can be seen from headquarters doorway at dawn, daylight or dusk and under the moon as well; only black-bat night and North Sea fog block the view of it.

It is within view of Fast Castle headland that we set down this afterword. If the word falters we can get up and commune with the subject of our reflections at the open tavern door. There is always a brooding mystery in the Wolf's Crag direction, but we are not taken in by it any more. It is an ordinary cosmic mystery that likes to hang around any lonely headland and the historic mysteries within the Crag's shadows are not so broody now. The path across the moor has grown into a friendly way and we are certain that in the end even the deepest of the castle's secrets will stop saying that it does not want to know us.

*Now on the A.1107; see footnote on p. 2

That is a matter of the relations between the castle and ourselves; between ourselves and the reader we must show modesty and express progress and hopes in restrained terms. We can say that progress in the research has been encouraging and stimulating, considering the minimal material we had at the initial moment of curiosity. And without the research the search would have been blind. What we have done of importance—it is important if the achievement is conceded—has been to join hitherto disconnected events into an unsuspected story that illuminates a puzzling phrase of Scottish history. We have connected the well known pois that produced the fatal quarrel at Gowrie House with the apparently merely amusing pois of John Napier's contract. Both of these we have joined to the Armada plots and succession intrigues and to the struggle in Scotland against the divine right of Jacobus Rex Scotorum.

Since the pointer was towards invasion gold we had to look for a cause for the searchers groping in the dark. We found it in the betrayal of the underground leader, David Graham of Fintry, by his envious subordinate, Robert Bruce, and in the subsequent hurried execution of Fintry and the assassination of his kinsman, Judge Graham. We have employed a double knot to bind the Gowrie mystery and the Napier contract, not solely the word pois and the links they shared with Fast Castle. The other knot was supplied by the Vaison circle of conspirators who directed the steps of both Gowrie and Napier towards Fast Castle; they had a hidden hand in the smuggling of subversive gold into Scotland and later a directing hand in the search for the missing gold.

As for the Gowrie mystery by itself and apart from the treasure story, we shall simplify matters for the critics by listing the claims of a new contribution. We have rejected the standing stories and theories that limited the solution: the Gowrie contrivance to kill the King, the King's contrivance to kill the Gowries or an accidental brawl. We have, as we said, thrown a new light on the mystery by linking Gowrie and Napier. We have put notary Sprott's Fast Castle testimony on a firm footing by exposing the conflict of prosecutors. We have strengthened the discredit of the King's account by exploring Inchaffray's appearance at Falkland stables along with Ruthven. We have introduced the casket letters or secret Stewart papers as a factor in the conflict between Gowrie and the King. We have brought in the Berwick governor, Lord Willoughby, with his mystery ship, and advanced the casket letters and a Bothwell invasion as the main subject matter of his dealing with Gowrie and Logan. We have looked into the mirrors of the English embassy in Paris and watched the ambassador intriguing with English Catholic rebels on the Scottish King's behalf, and followed through James's elaborate international intrigue for the Double Crown. On the other hand, we have explored the depths of the moves against James Stewart with which Gowrie became mixed up on his road home from Padua. It was the King's design and interest to make them seem a one-man plot since he could pretend to defend England only by being absolute master of Scotland; we have endeavoured to do more than has been done before to demolish the idea of a one-man plot.

All this is very large and fine. But how far does it take us on the road to discovery of the Fast Castle treasure? We think it has at least put our feet on the road of discovery. The material we have accumulated disinclines us to believe that the concealment was haphazard and hasty or that the searching involved only random divining. Because of Fast Castle's esoteric features and history, we are inclined to the idea that both the concealing and the searching conformed to some pattern. Napier, we suspect, was a distant heir to the megalithic sciences and arts of building, measurement and astronomy. The driving force which led him to the discovery of logarithms apparently derived from the need for better tools for his astrological studies, and he may have aimed to employ a kind of geometrical key from the past to locate a place of concealment that had been devised on the base of the old mysteries. It is curious that he undertook either to find the treasure or to determine that it had never been there, as far as his ability would allow. The best we can undertake is either to find it or remain benighted, but we think we must seek the key that Napier was to have employed.

We have had the kindness of a reply from Professor Alexander Thom, who has made recent discoveries of a remarkable kind in the field of megalithic science and measurement, and are a little chastened by his verdict that he does not see how his knowledge could help us or how Napier could have been equipped to apply his methods. We had explained ourselves poorly. Napier, we felt, might have been a inheritor and not a discoverer of some of the old secrets, allowing for the existence of the cults we have mentioned and considering his family tree and some of the strange blossoms that grew on it. A co-worker in the field in which the professor labours has patiently listened to our explanations and some instruction limited to the search in hand has resulted.

As for the Gowries and their techniques, here we are within the same bracket. In the posthumous trials of the Gowries the Crown made sorcery part of the case—against the Earl at least. His friend William Bogie, who was called as a witness, testified that he had never found any treasonable intent in Gowrie, but he recalled the incident of someone killing an adder during the hunting at Strathbran and Gowrie saying, 'Bogie, if the adder had not been slain I should have caused her to remain still by pronouncing a Hebrew word.' This had led to a discussion on the Cabala, in course of which the Earl explained it was not the word itself but the power of the spirit in the word that worked the miracle. He spoke of a very learned man he had met in Italy, a necromancer, with whom he had discussed the curiosities of nature; apparently one of the potential curiosities was bringing to perfection the seed of men and women otherwise than in the matrix of the mother. If Napier anticipated our refinements of the war game, Gowrie and his Italian friends were making an early approach to such modern scientific amusements as test tube babies.

Yet we are impressed most by the 'reckless toys of Padua' in the armoury of the Gowries. So was Logan. Ruthven's 'consety' attitude in relation to them, that is his conceit and cocksureness, rather scared the laird. There have been modern inquiries made at Padua about the cryptic story of the gentleman of that city who had apparently produced some sensational result by employing these dangerous toys; it was evidently the kind of thing you could laugh at afterwards, just because you were still alive to laugh. Unfortunately Professor Sambrin of Padua returned a negative report to enquiries made on behalf of Mr W. F. Arbuckle, who was preparing an article on the Gowries for the *Scottish Historical Review* which appeared in 1957. Our own esteemed publisher has carried inquiries to the point of suggesting that Padua was then an important centre for the manufacture of gunpowder. On balance, we would fall back on explosives as being a principal ingredient in Gowrie's projected search, although the use of astrological calculations or 'craft and ingyne' similar to Napier's may have been involved before reaching the gunpowder stage. Logan's fancy and fear about being 'eirdit quik', buried alive, suggests that the explosives were to be dangerously employed in subterranean places.

This is the material that helps us reconstruct the search as it involved the chief actors nearly four hundred years ago. There remains the Napier contract which in the original may convey more than the facsimile. Chemical ink is not to be discountenanced and the attempt to trace the original is continuing. The reason for drafting the document is something to be pondered; it was an unwitnessed document and, since it conspired against the Crown's rights of treasure trove, it could hardly have been drafted for the contingency of an appeal to law. But there was another contingency that had to be provided against: Logan could have been forfeited or even hanged. This was the fate of Bothwell's rebel brother and a year earlier Logan had been pronounced a rebel for not appearing before the Privy Council during Fintry's examination. A warrant was also out for two of his servants.

From Logan's later bafflement concealing the riddle that Fintry left behind, it is clear that he could not have answered the precise questions in the minds of the King and the Privy Council, nor could his servants have done so. Logan had gone to Huntly after the disgrace of his cousin the Master of Gray and had put himself in the hands of the Armada conspirators. They had obvious need of Fast Castle when they were planning to seize Eyemouth with Bothwell's 'waged' soldiers, just as on the occasion when his step-father, Lord Home, provisioned it and turned it over to Elizabeth's rebels. The castle was never a normal place of residence anyway; as Throgmorton said, it was more fit for prisoners than folk at liberty, and normally Logan lived at Restalrig or Gunsgreen and had some howf in the Canongate.

After Fintry's death Logan was saved by the tide turning soon in Bothwell's favour. Gowrie's mother and sister admitted the outlawed Earl to Holyrood Palace during the night, and Bothwell cornered the King and forced from him a pardon and the promise of a whitewashing trial to clear him of the charge of black magic. Soon after the trial young Gowrie joined Bothwell in arms, and all winter and into the next spring the King had his hands full. Our reading of the events is that during this time, that is in the twelve months following Fintry's execution, Logan, Bothwell and young Gowrie pursued Fintry's secret with what imperfect knowledge they had. In relation to Bothwell, the seventeen-year-old Gowrie was a sorcerer's apprentice. Then, in the summer of 1594 the 'blanks' conspirators stole back into the country; they included George Ker, Fintry's young comrade, and Father Tyrie, Fintry's longest and closest associate, who had been organising the 'blanks' conspiracy at the Spanish end, and they brought additional insight and also the specialist astrologer Napier, through Sir James Chisholm his brother-in-law.

By now the tide had turned back towards the King, chiefly, it may be said, with the support of the Homes who had been bribed into becoming Bothwell's enemies by receiving his estates. Exile was round the corner for the rebel Earl. Gowrie was on the point of departing for Padua. Logan might have had to make shift too, or be hanged, but in the event he was shielded by his half-brother, Lord Home. These precarious circumstances made future access to Fast Castle for the search quite uncertain, and the agreement between Napier and Logan seems to have been a provision to meet this contingency. If Logan had fled or been hanged this innocuous-looking private bargain to find treasure at the castle would have roused the cupidity and disarmed the fear of the successor to his estates, and would have enabled the search to go on. Naturally, the Chisholms and Father Tyrie would not have been over-fastidious about observing the contract with the new owner: their success, if it had come about, would never have been known. It is only this contingency confronting the searchers that can reasonably explain why such a curious document ever came into being. Of course Napier had to dissemble in his drafting and lay stress on 'old reports, motives and appearances'. It would have been a similar case if the present writer had been looking for a more modern and dangerous hoard. He would not have gone to the owner of the Dunglass estates and said:, 'look, a big part of the proceeds of the Great Train Robbery has been buried somewhere around Fast Castle and the man who hid it has been bumped off. May I please dig for it?'

It was providential that Fast Castle possessed old mysteries that could be invoked as a cover in the search for subversive gold. Our golden string, referred to in the Prologue, has led us by twists and turns towards the invasion gold of the Spanish plots. All of our characters drawn together by the golden string were connected in one way or another with the Spanish invasion plots or succession intrigues, and take in the Chisholms and their in-laws, Ker, Fintry, Bothwell, Logan and, ultimately, even the Gowries—all of them. We would be quite happy if we found the golden string terminated where Fintry's secret lies, and if we completed winding the ball there, but it would not be extraordinary if the string went trailing on into the shadows in a place like Fast Castle, towards a treasure behind a treasure. We said in our chapter on the prize for Fast Castle hunters that, if you did not find the pois you were looking for, you might find something better. Napier's invoking of the older mysteries raises just that possibiltiy.

There is a strange riddle connected with hidden treasure that raises a corner of the curtain a little on the whole background of the mysterious subject. This riddle arose out of the burning for witchery of William Stewart, Lord Lyon King of Arms in 1569 at St Andrews, during the power struggle that followed the dethronement of Mary Queen of Scots. Drury, who was on the spot in Scotland, informed Cecil in London of a plot to kill the Regent Moray which involved some mummery 'above Edinburgh' (presumably on top of Arthurs Seat). He referred to those who took part as 'conjurors' and said they devised their work with devilish skill; the painted plan of it, he mentioned, he had sent on before. Consequently, they had found some money and there was some business about the one judged to be the finder being the one who should be the regent. He named the Lord Lyon King of Arms as one of the 'conjurors'.

From this despatch to the English government we get a bare glimpse of a Scottish secret cult dabbling in high politics. Their 'work' of finding treasure was carried out on a ritualistic site (the volcanic cone 'above Edinburgh' had such associations). They operated according to a plan devised with 'devilish skill', which means that the concealment had been carried out in accordance with such a plan. This has a bearing on what we have just said about the probable scheme of concealment at Fast Castle which had the appearance of a secret treasury locked up at an earlier time. Only a few initiates who could penetrate the 'devilish skilfulness' of the plan would have a chance of access and the one of their number judged to have made the breakthrough would come under a sign of grace and be accepted as the leader, in this case accepted as ruler and virtual king. In this way leadership was raised above factional strife and invested with a mystical quality by the contrivance of an earlier age; this is what appeared to be implied in the curious election of a leader through the treasure hunt. It was also implied, of course, that the cult arrogated to itself the right of king-making and king-breaking and up to and including the time of Mary Stewart there had been plenty of exercise of the latter proclivity. William Stewart, the Lyon King of Arms, was eventually hastened to the stake at St Andrews after enjoying military protection for a time at Dumbarton Castle, by the party that still supported the imprisoned Queen of Scots; this identifies him with the camp of Lord Home and Logan of Fast Castle, both of whom were last ditchers for the Queen.

It may seem bold to say offhand that this was the same tradition that was expressed in the old mysteries of Fast Castle, more remote than our story of Armada gold, but Arthurs Seat, the venue of the cult, belonged to the Logans, as well as Fast Castle. Again, the Lyon King of Arms had an unnamed soothsayer friend whom he quoted for his remarkable prophecies; John Napier's father was one noted for remarkable prophecies, according to Mary Queen of Scots' secretary, Nau. Andrew Lang was, therefore, probably justified in his inference that Stewart's soothsayer friend was John Napier's father—it was a small world, that marvellous world of magic and conspiracy.

We will make an irrational leap from the strange Lyon King of Arms to the still more strange William Blake, poet and mystic of the eighteenth and nineteenth centuries. We brought Blake into our prologue and parted company with him outside Heaven's gate at Jerusalem's wall; we cannot possibly leave him standing alone there or leave standing the riddle that concerns the golden string. Are we in any sense, or in Blake's sense, qualified to enter by Heaven's gate into Jerusalem's wall when we have wound up the last foot of the golden string and stand armed with the golden ball? Perhaps. It depends, as we said, on what Blake meant. The few popular verses of his long poem of Jerusalem give imagery and colour to anyone's vision of a better land, the Christian's, the patriot's, the Conservative's or the Socialist's, but the rest of the long poem is unsingable and nearly unreadable. Southey thought it was a mad poem and blamed the Welsh Lexicographer, Will Owen, for the incomprehensible burden of Cymric mythology it seemed to carry. The eighteenth century revival of secret societies, however, dredged up a great deal of such mystic lore; Blake had friends in the revolutionary societies such as Tom Paine who, with his colleague Flaxman, was associated with the Swedenborg mystics who founded the New Jerusalem Church. Later on in Blake's life, the painter and astrologer, Varley, exploited him as a kind of spiritual computer. There is a long unpoetic catalogue of the counties of the British Isles in Blake's poem, grouped into trinities not linked by geography but by some affinity, each trinity representing a gate in the wall of Jerusalem. It seems patent that Blake's Jerusalem wall stands for the Templar order or its archetype and the gates are its units of organisation. The golden ball of string and Heaven's gate are subject to whatever interpretation we put on his Jerusalem wall and its gates in general. This is not vital to our conclusions, and it is not our mission to explore the strange store-house that was William Blake's mind or to tour the world of secret associations, but we choose to treat the golden string as Blake's version of the legend of secret treasure bequeathed by the Crusaders to advance their ideals down the centuries. As such it would tie up with the treasure hunt of the Lyon King of Arms and his fellow 'conjurors' 'above Edinburgh', and also perhaps with the older mysteries of Fast Castle or its enigma of the period when it first became 'False' Castle; that is the sole reason why we are interested in this legend or strange inheritance. After we have carried Fintry's invasion gold up the steep path from Wolf's Crag, we may have to wipe away the beads of sweat and return to follow the golden string deep into the Crusading past.

Fintry's hoard of invasion gold, and the search it provoked, is not contradicted but rather strengthened by these older legends and practices, and so is our assumption that concealments were devised with 'devilish skill', as Drury put it. The case of the Lyon King of Arms shows that this element of hidden gold became an institutionalised and even ritualised part of feudal conspiracy in Scotland. We have a blind guide into this deeper past or, more precisely, an eyeless one: there is the skull we found with the cross bones in the back court of the castle, above the great cave and the sea. We said we replaced our diviner's hunch about witch rites with a kindred idea, which is that the skull with its accompaniments served a ritualistic purpose for a meeting on Wolf's Crag similar to that of the Lyon King of Arms and his fellow 'conjurors' on Arthurs Seat. (The skull's age and the associated coins bring the two affairs within the same period). At the same time, Wolf's Crag and Arthurs Seat were linked with the Logans, and they both were also links in the bale-fire system of invasion warning that stretched from St Abb's Head to a hill near Linlithgow Palace.

The balefires that came to serve as a warning of invasion were originally the Baal-fires of pagan worship which continued to be lit in Christian times for the joy or the hell of it, despite the prohibitions of ecclesiastical authorities. The seven hills were surely linked in early tribal ritual long before they were ever linked in a defence system. The bad name that Berwick Law got for itself as a scene of sixteenth-century witchcraft strongly hints at its pagan pedigree. As for Arthurs Seat, the lure of pagan rites still draws the youth to its slopes every May 1st. Other common features are to be looked for on these charmed sites, as well as the lighting of sacred fires; probably votive offerings were brought to the fires and later secreted in nearby concealments by those who presided over the rites. This could have created a tradition of sacred banks on these cones, under divine protection and hedged by powerful curses against violators.

The collections of iron implements and weapons at the bottom of lakes which were once thought to be smithy's scrap are now considered to be votive offerings brought in to mark some thanksgiving occasions. It is as rational to speculate that the silver and precious metal hoards that turn up on hill sites are of the same character, especially when the items are mixed and drawn from many sources. The chief thing to bear in mind seems to be that the hill sites had ritual significance as well as the sacred lakes; the theory of priestly hoards fits these sites better than the theory of pirate hoards.

Two of our seven hills bear evidence of a sixteenth-century treasure search, the search of Drury's conjurors on Arthurs Seat and the Fast castle search under Dow Law. The Traprain treasure on a third of these hills, uncovered in 1919, relates to the fifth century; it perhaps emphasises the depth of the tradition of the sacred hill banks to which our 'conjurors' of the sixteenth century were anchored. Their cult indeed seems to have been very deeply embedded in the past since their quest for the hidden treasure was linked with the election of a regent or ruler, in a manner reminiscent of the legend of the Holy Grail—the replacement of the existing regent was conspired at in the Arthurs Seat treasure hunt involving the Lyon King of Arms and his friends. Just as evidently the replacement of James VI was aimed at in the treasure hunt at Fast Castle that involved the Earl of Gowrie. Small wonder, it may be thought, that James raced to Gowrie House on the merest whisper that a new treasure hunt was in hand. The knowledge that the mummery of the Holy Grail was about to be enacted again must have sent a cold shiver down his spine.

At this point we may recall, for further enlightenment, the curious overture made by Francis Bothwell to the English ambassador in Spain. His offer to find half a million a year from Scotland for King James, and that without burdening any of his subjects, could have been based on initiation into the secret of plural treasures and on a confidence or pretence that he would systematically uncover them all, year after year. His link with Fintry's secret specifically was perhaps not involved in the bargain after all.

Admittedly all this has the savour of an Arabian Nights tale, this Crusaders' cave bulging with wealth that is later distributed and buried to shape the fate of future generations. We have to picture men leading pack mules through the land at night and digging at hillsites under the moon not to lay greedy hands on silver and gold but to put it away from them for generations yet unborn. Perhaps the sea and lakes as well as the hillsides were the repositories. Can we be too sceptical as to this picture when we bear in mind Nazi money sunk at the bottom of Swiss lakes or the gold which Mussolini sought to convey through mountain paths for the future resurrection of his ideology; and its secret and unfathomable transfer by the partisan leaders who hanged him and were bent on hiding the funds to serve a rival ideology? There are confines of reality to accommodate the older legend of Crusader gold. At the one end of the time scale is the suppression of the Order of the Templars while in possession of vast wealth and at the other end Drury's report on the cult of the Scottish treasure hunt.

In his *History of Magic* Eliphas Levi affirms that after their suppression the surviving Templars went underground and transferred the centre of their western organisation from Paris to Edinburgh. We have explained that Scotland was their only safe place of refuge and Levi's account is quite credible. The organisational centre would not be transferred without the treasure being transferred too, if only on the princple that where your heart and home are there must your treasure be also. In the light of what we have written about the early enigma of Fast Castle and its Templar associations it may well seem that the castle was a secret treasury for the Templars long before their suppression. Especially in the last years of the Order was there need to place some of their great wealth beyond the clutches of the feudal monarchs. King Edward plundered the Temple in London even in its more halcyon days, and the repeated bankruptcies of King Philip of France were warning signs. This is probably what John Napier referred to when he used the word 'motives' in describing grounds for belief in an ancient Fast Castle treasure. The 'motives' turned to necessities as far as the Templars were concerned when the persecution began.

There would be one paramount purpose behind the concealment of the treasure near the Scottish centre of the Order: the preparation for a new Crusade and the re-opening of the gates of Jerusalem as a necessary condition for restoring the open power and leadership of the Templars within Christendom. Scottish diplomacy from the time of Bruce repeatedly bent its efforts in this direction. Bruce himself was mortified because disease overtook him and death approached while his dream of Jerusalem was still unfulfilled. Douglas, Sinclair and the Logans threw away their lives to keep the dream eternally alive. All this was some confirmation that the war chest for the new crusade was locked up and sealed somewhere in Scotland, where the inspiration for the new crusade resided along with the hidden centre of the old Templars organisation.

The existence of such treasure was manifest in Bruce's decision to draw on it for the mission that was to convey the casket containing his heart, and the gold plate brought out on the high ceremonial occasions marking their mission also gives a glint of it. There were pointers to the location of the main inheritance from Bruce and the Templars. The ruthless seizure of the old monk lands of Coldingham and Fast Castle by the Homes in the next century, leading to a conflict with James III which led to regicide, was suggestive—the King made a parade of Bruce's sword on the battlefield. But there were more precious legacies and the debated monks' lands of Coldingham appeared to enclose the most precious legacy of all, the Crusaders' treasure cave; Bruce's presence at Auldcambus and Fast Castle during his and the Templars' conflict with the Pope puts a seal on that thought.

Significantly James IV, who was the instrument of the Homes against his royal father, was, according to legend, eventually left by them to his fate at Flodden when they might have rescued him. Alternatively, there is a legend that he escaped his fate and survived for some time mysteriously in the custody of Lord Home; his widow, Queen Margaret, when she was seeking dissolution of her second marriage alleged that he was still alive three years after Flodden, and also testified that before Flodden he had confided in her concerning his hidden treasury. Flodden liquidated nearly an entire generation of the Scottish nobility and secrets of this sort might well have become lost or vague after the disaster. Whether or not this was so, Fast Castle continued to possess a special significance, as we have seen. When the Homes lost it for a time they were prompted to make a raid and level it to the ground, rebuilding it only when in secure possession. Then it passed to the Logans through marriage, because a Logan appeared to be the most favoured candidate to follow after the Sultan's friend, Cuthbert Home—the Logans were already the keepers of other secrets.

Our tavern door reflections and speculations may seem to have drifted far out to sea, but we insist that the key to the Gowrie and Napier treasure search at Fast Castle is a key similar to that designed to unlock older mysteries, and is of a pattern with the key employed by the 'conjurors' that Drury spied on at Arthurs Seat. To put it another way, there may be common denominators underlying the plan of treasure concealment at Arthurs Seat, at Traprain Law, at Norrie's Law in Fife (another hill treasure site) and at Dow Law or Fast Castle where the Napier and Gowrie search was focussed. A set of common features may be discovered which will serve as pointers to treasure concealment in all these cases, a combination of ancient origin. Once recognised or identified the telltale signs would assist discovery in each particular case.

Consequently, something may be gained by widening the survey to take in at least the seven linked hills from the Border to Holyrood and Linlithgow Palaces—to widen the survey may be to narrow it. It has become our ambition, therefore, to scan the seven charmed hilltops from the air with the modern survey instruments and cameras that have been specially perfected to penetrate the secrets of the earth. The other design on this scale is to rekindle the seven balefires simultaneously for any benefit or bonus of understanding that such a re-enactment of old rites might produce; considering that the ancient rites were probably not unconnected with the treasure cult, the reconstruction might deliver just such a bonus of understanding. A step has been taken by an approach to the authorities that could promote or sanction this temporary pagan revival. In the matter of the aerial survey, we are taking a sidelong look at the concerns that are rich enough to possess helicopters and such expensive cameras and equipment; before this a dummy run over the seven hill-tops is being contrived with some television friends.

In the meantime, the more down to earth work of digging continues at the castle. Eric, Keith and friends mop their brows over the new task of opening up the stone-lined well in front of the drawbridge and proceed also towards a nether region at the site of the spiral steps. Straightening their backs they find that the Dow Law balefire site on the top of the nearby precipice is exerting a steady hypnotic appeal, and protesting against neglect. At the same time there is something that poor Yorick is trying to say, but it is hard to make out; the skull found with the cross bones in the soil of the courtyard was, we feel sure, a participant or ingredient of the search of nearly four hundred years ago. At least, we are more certain that it had a ritual part in the search, than that it was employed in active witchery on the crag top. The meeting of the 'conjurors' at Arthurs Seat, which Drury got wind of, was probably repeated with all its mummery at Fast Castle and Dow Law and the skull and cross bones were a feature of such mummery. The age of our Yorick fits the period and there is every indication that our Fast Castle searchers belonged to the same cult. Both sites, also, were in the custody of the conspiratorial Logans, and both occasions—the Arthurs Seat search and the later search at Fast Castle—involved the fabulous Napiers, father then son.

We have not yet determined how deep the well is. It can never be so deep as the well of time that holds the secrets of Fast Castle in their entirety. We have captured a glimpse of it as a wrecker's castle, beheld it as the Faux castle associated with Anglo-Norman Templars, and seen it become in time the castle of conspiracy of the Homes and Logans in the fifteenth and sixteenth centuries. But all this was perhaps only the guttering candle of its life; the whole place has the air of a more ancient past. The little flower that we mentioned in our prologue is the same flower that grows or glows on Blake's mystic Primrose Hill; the dumb signs we spoke of are, by name, the great Black Mask rock on the shore and the guardian Wheat Stack near the castle hole or cave. On the next headland there is the marker in the path of the sun, a nameless monolith distinctive for its sentinel position in the picture of the sky, and beyond it lies Tun Law with its prehistoric cliff forts, thought by Dr Christison to be the most remarkable on the Scottish coast The crag and castle themselves, with the secret haven and cave below, are a complex that belong more to the half-lit realm of Arthurian legend than to this world. The complex compares eerily with the grail castle of the Fisher King, or it recalls the palace of King Arthur himself, where he rose at night and looking out to sea saw a ship's sail approaching like a dim candle in the dark. Then the ship came in under the castle and the questing Percival or Parsifal appeared.

There is one slight hint of reality in relation to the ancient, unwritten history of the place; it lies in the place name, if we may finally return to it. For Elizabeth's ambassador, Throgmorton, who spent an uncomfortable night there, it was still Faux Castle. But it was Fascastle for John Napier who was to have conducted the treasure hunt and for the castle owner Logan it was occasionally Fa'castle. Sometimes also, as in an early map, it appeared more broadly as Faws Castle. Maybe after all it was the Anglo-Normans who corrupted the original name, and called it Faux Castle in the light of their deceitful purposes, and perhaps Logan and Napier were nearer to etymological truth. The etymology of Faws Castle makes it the castle of the versi-coloured or painted people or the castle of the gypsies. In relation to a Border castle the meaning is as clear as the sun because on both sides of the Border *faws* was the traditional name for the race of Egyptians or gypsies. It was, however, a name covering two migrations and probably two different strains or races; there were the fourteenth- and fifteenth-century *faws* belonging to a migration that appeared then in Scotland as elsewhere and, strangely, received protection from the King and particular nobles and the judges, and there were the earlier *faws* who had some privileges under Bruce and gave their name anciently to Falkirk. (In case this seems like word play as far as Falkirk is concerned, which was and is natively Fa'kirk, the Gaels and the Romans also linked the versi-coloured people with Falkirk and each had their own word to express the connection.)

Our Fast Castle, then, was at the beginning Gypsy Castle perhaps, but gypsy in the sense of a people or leaders apart with a special heritage of secrets relating to metals in particular and the cosmos in general. Even the later faws were not mere menders of pots but were also the makers of dreams, as manifest by their annual season of plays in Roslin Glen under the distinguished patronage of the Sinclairs. The earlier faws who gave their name to Fa'kirk and presumably Fa'castle were doubtless an even greater cultural leaven in the community. It is significant that while the earlier Stewarts were gypsy protectors and patrons, even if the protection sometimes alternated with persecution, when we come to the Stewarts' Double Crown we enter fully the era of savage suppression of folk culture, when witches were burned and faws were hanged. James VI himself became the chief persecutor, striking not only at the witches themselves but also at patrons they had, such as Francis Bothwell, and simultaneously putting the fear of death into jurors with tender and tolerant hearts. It may be said that with the loss of the gypsies and witches the Kingdom was lost. At least the State went, leaving only a separate Kirk and College of Justice and that only to discipline the population to joyless toil and herd them cultureless and naked into a shivering future.

The ancient culture and the old mysteries had channels of propagation right through the Christian era to the Reformation and beyond, and the faws supplied one of these channels. The stubborn Celtic church and the resistant Culdees also harboured hidden cults as did also, eventually, the orders of chivalry, the Templars and St John. Finally the pre-

Reformation church in Scotland was dominated by temporal magnates and enclaves of temporal power and the political conspiracies thus served had little to do with either Pope or Christ. There is, in other words, no great mystery concerning how the old mysteries survived. Our Fast Castle appears to have been a unique vehicle in serving this end. It served all the cults of the ages, original pagans, shadowy faws, pirates and wreckers who had their secret lore too, the Templars and their successors and right up through the king-breaking and king-making Homes. including the Sultan's friend Cuthbert, to the circle of 'conjurors' and sorcerers round Robert Logan. Chief amongst the last lot were Francis Bothwell, the noble fortune teller, the astrologer Napier, the cabalist student of Padua, Gowrie, and the conspirators of Vaison.

Our end of the golden string which Napier wilfully left lying around has led us into all this company through heaven or heaven's gate in Jerusalem's wall. The later cults in the row which we have observed were cults of power with gold as one of their necessary inner secrets. Their inheritance if totally discovered, according to the oblique intimation of Francis Bothwell, was something that could yield half a million a year, a figure that must now be multiplied many times. In their quest Bothwell and Gowrie were frustrated by exile and death, and fear of death may have prompted Napier to pass the assignment to posterity. As the deserving representatives of posterity, the present searchers will probably receive a dark and disturbing sign when they come near to the great discovery. They will be seized, like Robert Logan, with the panic thought of being buried alive. Curiously, Logan suffered the opposite fate—instead of being buried alive he was dug up when he was dead. Nobody enjoys a good jest better than the Gremlins.